Sheffield Hallam University
Learning and IT Services
Adsetts Centre City Campus
Sheffield S1 1WS

102 095 942 8

KT-446-147

Introducing
Public Relations

SAGE has been part of the global academic community since 1965, supporting high quality research and learning that transforms society and our understanding of individuals, groups, and cultures. SAGE is the independent, innovative, natural home for authors, editors and societies who share our commitment and passion for the social sciences.

Find out more at: **www.sagepublications.com**

Introducing
Public Relations
Theory and Practice

Keith Butterick

SAGE

Los Angeles | London | New Delhi
Singapore | Washington DC

© Keith Butterick 2011

First published 2011

Apart from any fair dealing for the purposes of research or private study, or criticism or review, as permitted under the Copyright, Designs and Patents Act, 1988, this publication may be reproduced, stored or transmitted in any form, or by any means, only with the prior permission in writing of the publishers, or in the case of reprographic reproduction, in accordance with the terms of licences issued by the Copyright Licensing Agency. Enquiries concerning reproduction outside those terms should be sent to the publishers.

SAGE Publications Ltd
1 Oliver's Yard
55 City Road
London EC1Y 1SP

SAGE Publications Inc.
2455 Teller Road
Thousand Oaks, California 91320

SAGE Publications India Pvt Ltd
B 1/I 1 Mohan Cooperative Industrial Area
Mathura Road
New Delhi 110 044

SAGE Publications Asia-Pacific Pte Ltd
33 Pekin Street #02-01
Far East Square
Singapore 048763

Library of Congress Control Number: 2009928025

British Library Cataloguing in Publication data

A catalogue record for this book is available from the British Library

ISBN 978-1-4129-2114-5
ISBN 978-1-4129-2115-2 (pbk)

Typeset by C&M Digitals (P) Ltd, Chennai, India
Printed and bound in Great Britain by TJ International Ltd, Padstow, Cornwall
Printed on paper from sustainable resources

659.2
BU

Lorna, Chloe, Charlotte, Fiona, Ellie.

CONTENTS

ACKNOWLEDGEMENTS

As ever with a book of this nature many people and sources have contributed to it, some can be easily acknowledged whilst others will have to settle for a more general thanks. My wife and family had to endure many long hours of my absence as this book unfolded and developed from what was originally meant to be a relatively simple project into something more substantial. Thanks for their patience and understanding. My colleague at Huddersfield University, Eileen Jones, read an early draft and made useful comments. Many of my students on a number of modules have contributed in their own way and then gone on to work successfully in the PR industry. Some have contributed to this book. Many were not PR specialists and providing material for their projects was part of the genesis of this book, their collective comments and feedback on what became draft chapters have been very welcome. Thanks to them all for their co-operation. Special thanks also to all the PR practitioners that I have worked with over the years and those who were prepared to share their working day with me through their diaries and also contributed their thoughts and ideas on the PR industry. These have really made the book stand out. To all the contributors who gave their time during the various interviews, thank you, I hope I have represented your views and thoughts correctly.

The editorial and production staff at Sage have been brilliant and very patient throughout. Mila Steele deserves many thanks, rescuing the book on more than one occasion and making some useful contributions.

Thank you to Professor James Grunig for allowing me to quote from his book and also making some valuable contributions to the manuscript. Palgrave McMillan for the quotes from Argenti and Druckenmiller, the Chartered Institute of Public Relations for using material from a variety of sources. Cengage Learning Services for permission to use quotes from Kitchen's book, 'PR Principles and Practice'. Pearson Education for permission to use extracts from Brassington and Pettit's, 'Principles of Marketing'.

INTRODUCTION

There were a number of reasons why we believed a new public relations textbook was needed at this time. One of the main reasons was to address the needs of an increasing number of non-PR students taking a PR module as part of their degrees. Academically, public relations is no longer a new subject, there are now a number of excellent undergraduate and postgraduate courses and an increasing number of PhD projects. However, the increasing importance of professional communications is demonstrated by the number of degrees that now include public relations modules – advertising, events management, sports management, journalism, marketing to name a few. Experience of teaching such students highlighted the need for an easy to access introductory textbook explaining the basics of public relations in a simple, clear manner. That is what this is meant to be – an up to date study looking at the basics of the industry and where it came from but one that also looks at some of the problems it faces. Since the first introductory textbooks were produced for the new PR degree courses, the PR industry has grown and developed and it now has to confront a number of challenges which, many argue will alter the whole nature of the industry.

We also wanted to produce a book that actually explained what the PR industry in the UK is – who works in it and what is actually involved in PR work. We decided the best way to do this was by allowing PR practitioners to describe their working day. A number of practitioners also offered their thoughts on various aspects of the industry. The contributors range from the newest entrants to the industry (graduates from PR degrees) to senior directors with many years experience.

One of the purposes of the book is to demonstrate the wide variety of PR practice and while the PR industry attracts easy criticism it is also responsible for raising the profile of many good causes. However, much of the creative work highlighted by the activities of campaigning charities and pressure groups goes unnoticed. Hopefully, we have helped to shed a little bit of light in this area. There are many working in this sector who do not receive the attention their efforts deserve.

What this book is not is a definitive work that attempts to cover every angle and aspect of PR theory and practice. Its style is designed to be accessible to non-specialists and to this end language and issues have been simplified. In some cases I am aware that I may have gone too far.

One of the reasons why I felt able to write such a book was that my career has traversed both journalism and public relations. I have therefore, been able to watch the way they interact with each other on many different levels. As a former business journalist and editor I experienced the worst and the best examples of what the industry could offer. Working in PR, because of my background and interests, I have had an interesting and somewhat unusual career in that it has included spells in financial PR, business-to-business PR and public affairs and this experience again is reflected in the book.

There are many critics of the PR industry who attribute the decline of critical journalism to its growth. This is a simple and facile explanation and one that is made by those who only have a partial understanding about what public relations is. One of the issues that this book attempts to address is whether it is possible to speak of a single industry or whether it is becoming fragmented and specialised and what might be the implications in the future.

Keith Butterick
Director
Huddersfield Centre for Communication Research
University of Huddersfield

PUBLIC RELATIONS IN THEORY

INTRODUCING THE THEORY

PUBLIC RELATIONS IN THEORY

Part One does not provide an in-depth analysis of every public relations (PR) theory and different area of research, instead it is an overview of why theory matters in PR and provides a detailed analysis and critique of the dominant model or paradigm of excellence theory. PR theory is based on and related to practice which is why two of the most important aspects of current PR practice, reputation management and crisis management, are discussed in detail in chapters 4 and 5 respectively. For many reputation management is how PR should be defined, as it represents its future and has been embraced enthusiastically by many in the industry. However, there are those who would express caution believing that PR is not in a position to fulfil or meet such demands. Crisis management, according to some commentators, demonstrates the practice of PR at its best and most effective – at the centre stage of events, providing clear information and help at the most difficult times. Part One closes with a consideration of PR and ethics which is now a vitally important part of PR practice. This chapter also analyses some of the difficult ethical issues facing the individual PR practitioner as well as the whole industry.

The notion that PR has both a historical and a theoretical basis may appear strange to some but it does indeed possess this and that is important. PR theory is vital because its aim is to assist practitioners in the practice of PR, making them better and more effective. When looking at the history of PR it is worth noting that some pre-20th century events have been incorrectly described as PR events. PR starts in the 20th century and is linked to the growth of the media as it begins to influence actions, behaviour and policy. Attempting to get coverage in the media was for a long time the primary function of PR and the main qualification for working in the industry was the ability to write a news release that would be used in the media.

PR is a relatively new discipline which is epitomised by the debate surrounding its definition. Some subjects are easily defined, history or mathematics for example. PR, however, appears to have several definitions and this fact is used by critics to demonstrate its fundamental weakness. However, PR is essentially a practice based subject and as its practice changes and evolves then it could be argued that its definition will also evolve. In the early years of the 21st century we are currently going through a period of fundamental and radical change, with digital media transforming our channels of communication and the practice of journalism. This has, and will continue to have, a major effect on the way PR is undertaken.

Could this produce a new definition of PR? Quite possibly. This all suggests a dynamic, changing industry that is evolving, developing and challenging and that is also one of its attractions.

There is keen debate surrounding the relationship between advertising, marketing and PR. Students looking at PR for the first time sometimes struggle to distinguish between advertising and PR. It is not too long since the latter was seen as the poor relation of advertising but that is changing, for example, when it comes to brand reputation PR matters more than advertising. There is value in a brand's reputation – well-known brand names such as Heinz have a tradable value and when a brand's reputation suffers the company finances also suffer. Chapter 4 analyses reputation management and the direct financial link between a company's poor reputation and their finances in more detail.

According to research by Context Analytics (2009) PR is more important than advertising for maintaining a brand's value. The research states that on average 27% of brand value is tied to how often the brand name appears in the press, while in some sectors where more research is required before purchases are made PR can account for nearly half of the brand value. For example, with computers media prominence accounts for 47% of brand value.

Ethics in PR was rarely mentioned in early textbooks, however ethical considerations and questions are now playing a growing role in PR practice reflecting the growing significance and impact that PR has. PR theory has drawn heavily on the work of Grunig and others in order to develop what has become known as the excellence theory. The reason for this is not necessarily because we believe it represents the best or only model, indeed far from it, rather it is because it is still the most dominant theory in US and UK thinking. This will doubtless change and one of the more interesting aspects will be to see in what way PR's international growth will encourage the flowering of different theories.

Those coming to PR for the first time will find an incredibly dynamic, fast-moving industry that is full of challenges and opportunities and looking for new talented people to make their mark. That is one of the attractions for those who want to work in PR – the fact that they have the chance to make a splash – and who knows, it could be you!

THE ORIGINS OF PUBLIC RELATIONS

By the end of this chapter you will:

- appreciate why there are problems with defining PR
- have a clearer understanding of why the history and theory of PR matter
- understand the current dominant theory and the main theoretical origins of PR, as well as see how and why PR theory relates to PR practice

INTRODUCTION

This chapter looks at the relationship between the history and theory of PR and the way that PR history has influenced the development of PR theory. It is important for PR practitioners to have an understanding of theory because it can, among other things, help them to understand why some campaigns succeed and others do not.

PR theory is drawn from different but related strands of thought – firstly communication theory, and secondly the analysis of how PR has been practised in the past – and together they have produced a distinctive PR theory. Communication theory is the study of the transmission of information and the methods by which information is delivered: it is a huge subject in its own right, encompassing many different schools of thought. For the purposes of this book, we will look at those areas of communication theory that are most relevant to PR, for example, the study of the processes of communication from sender to receiver. From PR theory, we will go on to examine in detail the excellence theory, developed by American academic James Grunig. This theory is currently the most influential and although it has many critics it is still worthwhile to look at it and understand how it emerged, why it is significant, and why it is criticised.

PR: ONE OR MANY DEFINITIONS?

There are some books, mostly hostile to PR (and also the occasional first student essay on PR), that will start with almost gleeful opening lines: 'It's very difficult to define public relations' or 'There are many definitions of public relations and each one is as relevant as the other'. Critics of PR will then seize on this apparent lack of agreement about a definition as proof that PR is fundamentally flawed. They will argue that a definition cannot be provided because there is nothing of substance to PR: it is an illusion, all spin and floss. On the other hand, how can there be any confusion about what it stands for when we all know what PR is – namely getting publicity for your client or company in the media? One of the aims of this book is to demonstrate that PR has a lot more to it than this and that it now stands at the very centre of modern day communications.

The American academic Rex Harlow produced what he claimed to be the first all-inclusive definition of PR. His research identified 472 definitions that had been produced, from the early 1900s when modern PR emerged, to 1976 when he was working. He put together their common elements to produce the first global definition:

> *Public Relations is the distinctive management function which helps establish and maintain mutual lines of communication, understanding, acceptance and co-operation between an organisation and its publics; involves the management of problems and issues; helps management to keep informed on and responsive to public opinion; defines and emphasizes the responsibility of management to serve the public interest; helps management keep abreast of and effectively utilize change, serving as an early warning system to help anticipate trends; and uses research and sound and ethical communication as its principal tools.* (Harlow, 1976: 36)

Critics of Harlow have said that precisely because this definition tries to cover everything, it becomes too detailed and is therefore useless. There are also many who would argue that it is not possible to provide a definition for a profession that covers such diverse practices, ranging from the campaigning activities of Greenpeace to getting coverage for an out-of-favour actor in the tabloids.

In 1978, at its first meeting in Mexico, the World Assembly of Public Relations agreed upon a definition that became known as 'The Mexico Definition'. This was significant because it was the first time that various national organisations had agreed on one that they could all accept:

> *Public Relations is the art and social science of analysing trends, predicting their consequences, counselling organisation leaders and implementing planned programmes of action which will serve both the organisation's and the public interest.* (Warnaby & Moss, 2002: 7)

The key element in this was the attempt to enhance PR's credibility by linking it with social science and suggesting that there was a scientific, objective, and therefore factual basis for it. In contrast to these somewhat lengthy definitions theorists have also made their contributions to the definition game. James Grunig and Todd Hunt produced this more focused definition: PR is *'The management of communications between an organization and its publics* (Grunig and Hunt, 1984: 8).

Cutlip, Center and Broom (2000: 6), who produced one of the first books summarising PR theory and practice, defined PR as follows: *'Public Relations is the management function that identifies, establishes and maintains mutually beneficial relationships between an organisation and various publics on whom its success or failure depends'.* The key link between these two definitions is that it embeds PR as part of an organisation's management, which gives it clout and credibility and lifts it away from the mechanical process of merely supporting a company's sales (see below).

In the UK, the Chartered Institute of Public Relations (CIPR) offers a definition that introduces another new dimension:

> *Public relations is about reputation – the result of what you do, what you say and what others say about you. Public relations practice is the discipline, which looks after reputation – with the aim of earning understanding and support and influencing opinion and behaviour. It is the planned and sustained effort to establish and maintain goodwill and mutual understanding between an organisation and its publics.* (www.cipr.co.uk)

This new element equates PR with reputation management. While this might seem reasonable, as we shall see below, there are many who would criticise the idea that PR is 'about' reputation management (for a detailed exploration of this argument, see Chapter 4). Interestingly, the above CIPR definition evolved from an earlier one. These evolving definitions illustrate the dynamism of PR and show how the industry has had to adapt to changing circumstances.

Another definition with a different emphasis is offered by the Public Relations Society of America (PRSA):

> *Public Relations helps an organisation and its publics to adapt mutually to each other. Public Relations is an organisation's efforts to win the co-operation of groups of people. Public Relations helps organisations effectively interact and communicate with their key publics.* (www.prsa.org)

Where PR comes from and why history matters

When did PR start? Who was the first PR person? Does it matter if you don't know where PR came from? Will knowing its history make you better at your job or enhance your effectiveness as a PR practitioner? The history of PR matters because it has been used by theorists to explain how PR is practised and to produce theories. Practice develops theory and theory helps develop practice, so theory and practice are however linked thereby.

There are those together who want to give PR a very long history because in so doing they believe it enhances its credibility. For example, according to Cutlip et al. (2000: 102):

> *The communication of information to influence viewpoints or actions can be traced from the earliest civilisations. Archaeologists found a farm bulletin in Iraq that told the farmers of 1800 BC how to sow their crops, how to irrigate. Public relations was used many centuries ago in England, where King's maintained Lord Chancellors as 'Keepers of the King's Conscience.'*

The Boston Tea Party, which helped start the American War of Independence, is another example of a PR event that any modern PR company would be proud of because of the publicity it generated. We must remember that these 'PR-like' events (Grunig and Hunt, 1984) were not carried out with the intention of producing publicity. The motives of those who carried out these actions were totally different to those of a 21st century PR planner, and while it might appear to be a bit of harmless fun to describe the Boston Tea Party as a 'PR event' there is a serious element to such interpretations. *In viewing these events as early PR events* we are placing our values and viewpoints on the past when in fact they might have had a completely different meaning in that time and place. The past can only be understood by understanding historical events in their specific cultural context.

One of the problems with the study of PR history is that there is no single history of its development worldwide, instead there are a number of different and unrelated public relations histories (Pearson, 1992). The majority of the research about the history and development of PR has been conducted in the USA and this has been for a number of reasons. Firstly, the USA has the largest PR industry in the world and many of its consultancies have played a role in developing PR practice and 'exporting' it abroad. Secondly, the USA has a long established community of PR academics who have been able to carry out more research. However, there is a problem in simply relying on a history that is so focused on one country. This could lead to the belief that PR can only be practised in one way and with one set of values and ignore the contribution made to PR practice by other countries, cultures and traditions.

Academics are now beginning to look at the history of PR practice elsewhere. L'Etang and Pieczka (2006) include chapters on German and Swedish PR and L'Etang (2004) has also written a valuable history of PR in the UK, which highlights the different origins for PR there from those of the USA. Zerfass, van Ruler and Siramesh (2008) have produced an important book on European PR history and theory. Having said that we do need to know about how PR developed in the USA because the key PR academics James Grunig and Todd Hunt drew on that history in order to develop their influential four models of PR and also what has become known as the excellence theory.

The early years: Ivy Lee and Edward Bernays

PR, as we understand it today, began in the last years of the 19th and in the early years of the 20th century. Early practitioners were known as publicists. The most well-known of these was the circus owner Phineas T. Barnum (1810–1891) who became infamous in the 19th century for the often cynical way he promoted his shows. Barnum coined the phrase 'There's no such thing as bad publicity' and used a variety of dubious publicity stunts to attract crowds to his shows. In one example, Barnum toured with a blind and paralysed African-American slave called Joice Heth, claiming she was the former nurse of George Washington and was 160 years old. In fact when Heth died in 1836 she was no more than 80 years old. Barnum didn't mind if he was attacked in the press – it all added to the publicity for his shows (Grunig & Hunt, 1984).

As we shall see later on in the book publicists are still at work and some of them are using those selfsame and dubious publicity stunts to attract attention to their clients.

This link between theory and practice is nowhere better illustrated than in the career and work of two of PR's most influential figures – Ivy Ledbetter Lee (1877–1934) and Edward Bernays (1891–1955) – who made contributions to both the practice and theory of PR. Interestingly they also represent two different and opposite ways of practising PR: to Lee it was an 'art' in which creativity and innovation should be critical, while Edward Bernays, influenced by the psychological theories of his uncle, Sigmund Freud, thought PR could be a 'scientific' practice. Lee and Bernays were contemporaries who were practising PR in New York at the same time. Lee was in many ways the ultimate PR practitioner and unlike Bernays was not interested in developing a theoretical basis for PR or even in attempting to understand how it operated. He is supposed to have told Bernays that when they died PR as a profession would die with them. While that story may or may not be true, it usefully illustrates the difference between the two. For Lee, PR activities were no more than a series of short-term events to attract publicity and fulfil a specific purpose. Bernays, however was always looking for deeper theories and understanding about how to control and influence audiences.

Ivy Lee

In the USA in the early 20th century big industries – such as coal, iron and steel production, railways and banking – were run by companies that were owned by several powerful families. The Rockerfellers, the Vanderbilts, the Astors and the Carnegies were among the richest and most powerful businessmen in the world and their names have become synonymous with wealth and power. Collectively they were known as the 'robber barons', because the dominance of their respective industries was often based on anti-competitive and unfair business practices. Big business also virtually controlled federal and local government.

The communication practice they and their companies carried out is sometimes called 'the public be damned' phase of PR, as it summarises their lack of concern and interest in communicating with the general populace. The actual phrase was uttered by William Vanderbilt, and although it is often used to characterise the contempt that the robber barons had for ordinary people history might have been a little unfair to Vanderbilt in this instance. He was replying to a reporter who had asked him why he ran one of his railways at a loss and had then suggested he was doing so for public benefit (Toth and Heath, 1992: 121). Vanderbilt's reply was: 'The public be dammed. What does the public care about the railroads except to get as much out of them for as small consideration as possible. Of course we like to do everything possible for the benefit of humanity in general, but when we do we first see that we are benefiting ourselves'. According to Tedlow (quoted in Pearson, 1992), Vanderbilt's sentiments then were similar to those of any modern day chief executive of a modern public company – that the interests of the company's share-holders are paramount and that companies are not run as 'social enterprises'.

These companies used press agents or publicists to communicate for them and their role was to try to restrict and control the activities of the media. They banned the press from industrial activities because they believed that public disclosures about what they did would have been fatal to many operations. Press agents were often hired to serve as buffers between businesses and the public in order to prevent the truth from getting out (Hiebert, in Toth & Heath, 1992). As a consequence of businesses not communicating their side of the story, the media ran hostile stories which helped to create an anti-business climate. Anger at poor working conditions caused a series of major strikes, indeed some estimates suggest that half a million workers were either killed or injured during this period. There were a series of nationwide strikes such as in Pensacola, Florida and New York. Twelve people died when a strike in Mckees Rock, Pennsylvania, erupted into a bloody battle between striking steel work-ers, private security agents, and the Pennslyvania State Police. And at least 50 people died in what became known as the first mine war, in West Virginia in 1912–13. Incidents of this nature seriously damaged the reputation of busi-ness, which was made worse by a communications policy that not only refused to speak to the outside world but that also treated journalists as the enemy.

In 1902 the pressure on business increased after *McClure's Magazine* published a series of articles by Lincoln Steffers on corruption in municipal and city government, accusing big business of buying politicians and controlling the government. The Commissioner of the New York Police at the time, Theodore Roosevelt, described this type of ground-breaking journalism as 'muckraking'. This marked the lowest point in the relationship between business and the media and led to the emergence of a new mode of business communication. Ivy Lee (Pearson, 1992) was a journalist working in New York at the same time as the 'muckrakers', but unlike many of his fellow journalists, he sympathised and identified with the powerful businessmen he wrote about and thought they were good people, although misunderstood.

Lee spotted a business opportunity in representing the interests of big business and in 1904 he opened his own PR consultancy, Parker & Lee, with George Parker, another ex-journalist. He became an adviser to big business corporations who were under attack on a variety of fronts. He took a totally different approach from that of the press agents and publicists. He believed that rather than keep quiet and say nothing, the best policy was to be as open as possible and to communicate with the outside world.

Lee's first PR job for an industrial client was in 1906 when the 29 year old was retained by the Pennsylvania Railroad Company (Harrison and Moloney, 2004). It was a company that was typical of many at that time, refusing to communicate with journalists or to give any information about accidents in which it was involved, and believing that by doing so they would be admitting to weakness. Lee changed such practices by granting access to journalists and speaking to them. In October 1906, after a train crash that killed 50 people, Lee produced what historians of PR believe was the first clearly designated 'Press Release'. 'Statement from the Road', the public statement from the Pennsylvania Railroad, was printed verbatim by the *New York Times* and won the company praise for its openness and honesty. By systemising communications and encouraging companies to be more open Lee demonstrated the benefits that good communication could bring.

To make clear that his approach was a totally different way of communicating, he sent newspaper editors his famous 'Declaration of Principles' in which he made clear how he intended to work. The principles were to set new standards in relations between PR practitioners and the media (see Box 2.1).

Box 2.1   Extracts from Ivy Lee's 'Declaration of Principles'

'This is not a secret press bureau. All our work is done in the open. We aim to supply news.

'This is not an advertising agency. If you think any of our matter ought properly to go to your business office, do not use it.

'Our matter is accurate. Further details on any subject treated will be supplied promptly, and any editor will be assisted most carefully in verifying directly any statement of fact. ...

'In brief, our plan is frankly, and openly, on behalf of business concerns and public institutions, to supply the press and public of the United States prompt and accurate information concerning subjects which it is of value and interest to the public to know about.'

The important point about this Declaration of Principles is that it says that PR will be different and this marked a revolution in relations between business, the press, and the public. This was no longer the 'public be dammed' phase but now 'the public be informed' phase (Hiebert, 1966).

Edward Bernays

For all Lee's impact and influence on developing a new way to practise PR, it is Edward Bernays who is known as the 'father of public relations' for his attempts to introduce systems and science into PR. As the nephew of the psychologist Sigmund Freud he tried to use his uncle's insights to manipulate public opinion. In some ways Bernays illustrates the darker side of communication practice; he was an elitist and believed the manipulation of public opinion was necessary as society's tendency to follow the 'herd instinct' was irrational and dangerous. While his motives might have been well-meaning, history was to demonstrate what could happen when such theories where used for evil purposes.

Bernays was born in Vienna in 1891 and his family moved to the USA a year later. In 1913 he started his PR career by working as a press agent for a number of theatres, concerts and ballets. When America entered the First World War in 1917 Bernays began working for the Committee of Public Information. This committee was an American propaganda machine set up to package, advertise and sell the war as one that would 'make the world safe for democracy'. Its aim was to get the American people to support the war. Here, Bernays had an opportunity to put his interests in psychology, as applied to human behaviour, into operation.

In 1919 when the war ended he opened his own practice in New York, describing himself not as a PR practitioner but famously as PR counselor. In 1923 he wrote the first PR textbook, *Crystallizing Public Opinion*, and in the same year set up the first PR course at New York University. Bernays was a pioneer of modern propaganda techniques and applied theories of mass psychology and persuasion to the needs of corporate and political organisations. He believed these techniques could sell anything, from bacon to cigarettes to soap. In the 1920s, whilst working for the American Tobacco Company, Bernays pioneered the practice of linking corporate sales campaigns with popular social causes when he persuaded women's rights marchers in New York City to hold up Lucky Strike cigarettes as symbolic 'Torches of Freedom'. Women at the time did not smoke cigarettes in public, but by linking smoking to the freedom to vote – a right that women had just won – it made smoking look like the activity of the modern, emancipated woman and was a gesture demonstrating their equality with men. It was one of Bernays biggest publicity successes.

In 1929 he organised the first global media event when he dreamed up 'Light's Golden Jubilee' for General Electric, a world-wide celebration commemorating the fiftieth anniversary of the electric light bulb. This, Bernays said, was an example of what he called 'overt acts' (modern media events) that could awaken apparently subconscious feelings. Bernays openly described what he did as propaganda but was forced to apologise for using the term after Joseph Goebbels, the Minister for Public Enlightenment and Propaganda in Nazi Germany, adopted the term in 1933.

The different ways that Barnum, Lee and Bernays practised PR were used by the theorists Grunig and Hunt as the basis for three of their four models of PR practice. These are discussed later in this chapter in the section on PR theory.

International growth

The international growth of PR practice began with countries with strong links to the USA and US companies. In Brazil, for example, PR can trace its origins back to 1910, about the same time that PR began in the USA. In the UK, American PR companies began opening offices in London after the Second World War. In Japan the first PR society was founded in 1964. As political regimes changed even countries previously hostile to the USA began to embrace PR. In Russia, one of the most recent PR markets, the emergence of PR can be directly linked to a campaign for the opening of the first McDonald's restaurant in Moscow in 1990.

Significantly, the least developed PR markets are those which have had least exposure to US influence. China is the most recent PR market where the 2008 Olympic Games played an important role in helping the industry to develop. The development of Chinese businesses globally, and the inward movement of multi-national companies to China, have also been important factors in the growth of the industry. In 2006 it was estimated that turnover for the PR industry in China was US$1.1 billion: from 2006 to 2007 the annual growth rate was 33% (Zhao, 2008).

There is increasing interest in whether specific economic and social circum-stances will produce a particular type of PR practice. For the US/UK model of PR to thrive it has to have two essential requirements – a market economy to allow for the uncontrolled buying and selling of goods and a free press that will allow communication that is free of censorship of news. In China and Russia these conditions have been relatively recent – Russia has only enjoyed a free media since the mid-1980s, following the collapse of the Soviet Union – and as a result the PR industries in both countries are not robust but are nevertheless growing very quickly.

As the number of studies into how communication is practised in other non-English speaking culture increases a different picture might emerge of the US/UK type practice. Zerfass et al. (2008), for example, bring together contribu-tions from a number of largely German-speaking theorists and argue that PR has a longer history there than in the USA. Van Ruler and Vercic argue that PR in continental Europe is increasingly becoming known as Communication Management and encompassing a wider range of disciplines. It might be from this point that we shall see alternative forms of practice emerge.

The history of PR in the UK

The only complete history of PR in the UK was written in 2004 by Jacquie L'Etang. According to her research, the main driver of PR activity before the Second World War was central and local government: 'There was relatively little public rela-tions in the private sector prior to the Second World War. Activities in the private sector were generally confined to advertising, but are nevertheless significant in the story of public relations in terms of their relationship with propaganda, the self-image of practitioners, and the structures and terminology adopted in consultancies. Public relations was limited to a handful of press agencies, international companies, and national organisations' (L'Etang, 2004: 58).

During the Second World War the British government was engaged in communications activity across a wide range of fronts. On the Home Front it helped keep up morale during the war. In key neutral countries, such as the USA, it was used to counter German propaganda and build support for the Allied cause. Propaganda was also aimed at occupied countries and Germany itself. L'Etang argues that the wartime experience had an impact on how the UK population reacted to news, 'sensitising civilian and military populations to issues of propaganda, information and intelligence. Although Britain cultivated notions of media independence and truthful information, there was an extensive internal and external propaganda effort' (2004: 65).

According to L'Etang, those who practised propaganda during the Second World War took that experience into private practice when the war ended. She highlights the case of Colonel Maurice Buckmaster, who was head of the Special Operation Executive's 'F' section during the war. Before that he had worked for the Ford Motor Company and returned to it at the war's end as Director of Public Relations.

THEORY: WHY SOME CAMPAIGNS WORK AND SOME DON'T

The reaction of many people outside PR when confronted by the phrase 'public relations theory' might well be the type of baffled bemusement similar to that experienced by the comedian Peter Kay's father when first confronted with the delights of garlic bread: 'Garlic? Bread? Garlic and bread?' Public relations? Theory? How can PR have any theory? What theory do you need to construct a press release to publicise your company's product, service or charity? What is the theoretical basis for gaining publicity for your celebrity client by getting a story in the *News of the World*? Because at the end of the day, that is what PR is all about – generating as much coverage in as many newspapers, magazines, TV and radio stations as possible for your clients. Well, that might be the 'popular' image, but as we will continually demonstrate throughout this book, there is a lot more to PR than that.

Austin and Pinkleton (2006: 271) highlight the importance of theory to PR practice: 'Theories – essentially generalizations about how people think and behave – help determine appropriate goals and objectives for a communications programme. Scientifically tested theories also help communication programmes develop effective strategies to achieve those goals and objectives'. And according to Windahl, Signitzer and Olson (1992: 1): 'All communication planners use theories to guide their work. Often these are their own theories based on their own experiences and on common practice. Many are unaware that formal research, both academic and non-academic has generated a continuously growing body of theories applicable to planned communication'.

We shall see later how PR occupies a powerful and influential position between those who send out messages and those who receive them. As PR practitioners we are working with the way humans absorb messages and information. Some campaigns work, some do not; some messages will have a resonance and impact, and others will not. As a PR practitioner it is necessary to understand why one campaign has worked but others have not, to explore the language that we use and how and why it is important. This is where theory can help. To understand this and a great deal more – such as, for example, the role that culture plays in shaping the way we perceive and understand facts and information – we require a theoretical basis.

PR research emerged as a distinct activity in the 1950s and 1960s as an off-shoot of mass communication research (Botan and Hazleton, 2006). The research focus was on producing results that would help the daily work of PR practitioners, that is, it looked at how to make what they did in their practice more effective. Theories that have such a practical focus are known as 'normative' theories: 'Most public relations practitioners in the 1950s and 1960s saw public relations primarily as an activity to influence the all-powerful media – through day-to-day media relations and activities and planned public information campaigns. Public relations researchers, therefore, joined with mass communications scholars to document the effectiveness of public relations' (Grunig, Grunig and Dozier, in Botan and Hazleton, 2006: 22). Research started in the USA because of the size of the PR and advertising industries there and their relationship with the media.

COMMUNICATION THEORY

Communication theory is the study of the way that humans communicate with each other. It includes the analysis of interpersonal communication and also theories about how the brain functions. It encompasses both written and spoken language. The term *communication theory* can refer to one single theory, or it can be used as the summary, the 'collective wisdom' of all those single theories (Littlejohn, 2002). There is no one theory which we can say provides the fundamental explanation of communication. Instead, there are many different communication theories and each has a validity because they can help us to understand different aspects of reality or why some actions work and others do not. From among the many communication theories, we shall only look here at those that can help to explain how the process of communication works. These are the most relevant to PR as they can assist us in understanding why the transmission of information through certain channels of communication does or does not work.

The act of communication is arguably one of the most important activities, if not the most important, we undertake and it is central not only to our role in the world but also to our ability to make sense of the way we live and relate to others. Think of how much we communicate not only verbally but also non-verbally through our body language, which is said to betray our real emotions and feelings. Through body language we are communicating even when we believe we are not. As body language experts tell us when analysing the body language of politicians, we may say one thing but our body language may tell a different story (Littlejohn, 2002).

The study of communication has had a long history that goes back to Ancient Greece and Aristotle, but its academic study really only started in earnest after the First World War. This was stimulated by a number of factors, with possibly the most important being the rise and growth of the mass media and advances in communication technology. This growth of the mass media was accompanied by a rise in advertising. With the emergence of potentially new and influential media such as television and radio, advertisers wanted to know whether the adverts they were placing there were having an impact and the ways they could make them more effective (Littlejohn, 2002). After the Second World War sociology and social psychology also emerged as legitimate academic disciplines and began to contribute to communications theory from their perspectives.

At the end of the Second World War a difference developed in the way that researchers in the USA and Europe approached communication theory. Broadly speaking, US researchers followed research methods that were used in the physical sciences. In an attempt to try and find a fundamental explanation of communication they based their methods on objective and quantitative research and statistics. In Europe, however, research focussed on the analysis of cultural and historical factors and was broadly influenced by the Marxist philosophical tradition which argued that an individual cannot be separated from their economic and social context. Communication must therefore be understood within this setting.

McQuail and Windahl (1993: 6) offer the following explanation for the motivation of communication research, illustrating how it drew on a wide range of sources: 'Research into communication in general had its origins in the wish to test and increase the efficiency and effectiveness in the spheres of education, propaganda, telecommunications, advertising and public and human relations. Research activity began with practical concerns and was fed by developments in psychology and sociology and by general advances in methodology, especially the use of experiments, social surveys and statistics'.

Laswell's communication model

Two early, influential, and similar theories that emerged from the US scientific research tradition were Laswell's Model of Communication and the Linear Model developed by Claude Shannon and Warren Weaver.

Harold Laswell (1902–1978) was an American political scientist whose thinking was influenced by behavioural psychological theory. During the Second

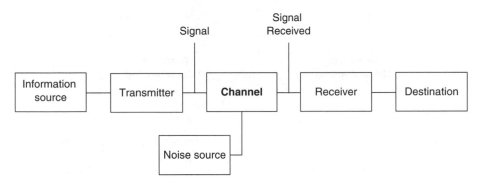

Figure 2.1   Linear Model of Communication – Shannon and Weaver, 1949

World War he was Chief of the Experimental Division for the Study of War Time Communications at the Library of Congress in Washington. One of his jobs was analysing Nazi propaganda and identifying how it was used to secure the acquiescence and support of the German population for Hitler and his regime's atrocities.

Laswell's 1948 model is based on a series of questions: Who? Says what? In which channel? To whom? With what effect?

Table 2.1   Laswell's Communication Model

Who?	Says what?	In what channel?	To whom?	With what effect?
Communicator	Message	Channel	Receiver	Effect

His answers offer an explanation as to how the mass media impacts upon an audience and explore the emerging 'mass media' – newspapers, radio, films and TV. Laswell's theory assumes, firstly, that the communicator intends to influence the receiver, and secondly, that the receiver is not only a passive receptor of what is sent from the source and that we all respond in exactly the same way. The theory does not allow for any feedback, interruption, or interference with the message.

Linear model

In 1949 telecommunication engineers Claude Shannon and Warren Weaver were working for Bell Telephone Laboratories and together they developed a similar model to Laswell's. This became one of the most influential of the earliest communications models. Shannon and Weaver's Linear Model is based on Information Theory which grew out of the boom in the telecommunications industry after the Second World War and involved the quantitative study of signals. In *The Mathematical Theory of Communication* (1949) they outlined their Linear Model of Communications. This prompted social scientists to look at communication

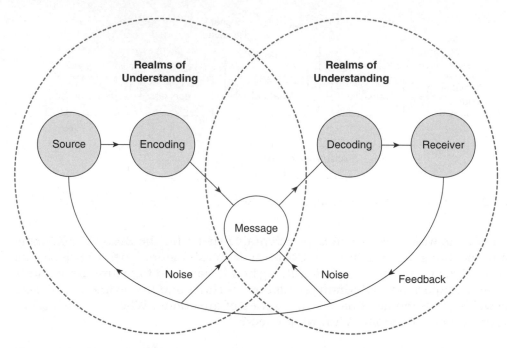

Figure 2.2   Linear Model of Communication – based on Schramm (1955) and Shannon and Weaver (1962)

within the framework of a model. According to McQuail and Windahl (1993) this use of models was initially appealing to communication scholars of the time primarily because they were developing a particular interest in effects and effectiveness. It was also consistent with the stimulus-response model of behaviour control, which was then becoming popular in psychology research. Mass communication scholars were also increasingly interested in ordering and codifying existing knowledge and enquiry in their research.

Laswell's and Shannon and Weaver's models are known as transmission models – where communication is reduced to transmitting information. However, the aim of PR is not just to transmit information in a passive way, but also to influence or persuade the receptor to a course of action. As with other transmission models, Shannon and Weaver were interested in looking at the channels of communication; theirs is a linear, one-way process from sender to receiver who apparently communicate in isolation with no social context.

According to Shannon and Weaver – *a source* selects and then transmits a *message* (consisting of the signs to be transmitted). The *transmitter* then translates the signs into signals that are sent over a *channel* to a *receiver*. The final element in the model is *noise*. Noise can be any outside distortion or distraction from outside that interferes with the transmission and receipt of the signal. For students in a lecture theatre, for example, noise can be any anything outside that disturbs or interferes with what's being heard – a car or conversation coming from other students, or someone moving their chair in the room, anything which disturbs how the lecture is received. Thoughts that are more interesting than the lecturer's words are also part of this noise (Fiske, 2002).

Noise is any outside interference that is not intended by the receiver (Fiske, 2002), for example the crackling of a telephone line, or 'snow' on television screens. 'Noise, whether it originates in the channel, the audience, the sender, or the message itself, always confuses the intention of the sender and thus limits the amount of desired information that can be sent in a given time' (Fiske, 2002: 8). 'The inability on the part of the communicators to realise that a sent and a received message are not always identical, is a common reason why communication fails' (McQuail & Windahl, 1993: 17).

The Linear Model has been heavily criticised for being too linear, i.e. one-way and mechanistic without offering a sufficient explanation of reality. This Model does seek to understand how communication takes place, but only for a limited range of situations, and it is certainly not a universal explanation for all forms of communication. It is helpful in explaining what happens in interpersonal communication – the speaker's brain is the source, the voice is the transmitter, and the air through which the voice travels is the channel. The listener's ear is the receiver while the listener's brain is the destination (Littlejohn, 2002).

The linear model, or bullet theory as it is sometimes called, was one of the most popular among PR practitioners. For many, it reflects actual PR activity such as the production of a press release and its distribution through the mass media. Austin and Pinkleton (2006) however point out its limitations – it might produce plenty of coverage and press cuttings but it does not show the quality of the coverage, that is, whether anyone took any notice of what they read or whether the right aspects of the campaign were covered in the newspaper articles.

Shannon and Weaver's model stimulated further research and this in turn produced other models which refined the basic theory, thereby producing a closer approximation to reality. This process of taking a theory and refining and adding to it is how scientific knowledge advances, through a public examination of theories, criticism refinement, and further development. Later theories also criticised process models. Wilbur Schramm, explaining the difference between the linear model and the one he developed with C.E.Osgood, said: 'It is misleading to think of the communication process as starting somewhere and ending somewhere. It really is endless' (McQuail & Windahl, 1993: 20). Osgood and Schram's circular model is the complete opposite of Shannon and Weaver's: it is not concerned with the communication channels but with the participants in the process.

What their model demonstrates is the way in which people will believe that news and information is disseminated through the mass media, undiluted and unadulterated by any other influences. Another criticism of the Linear Model is

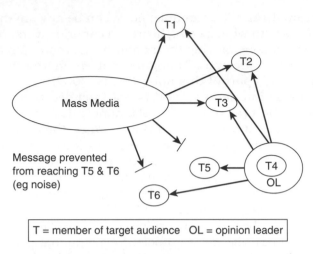

Figure 2.3 Two-step Model of Communication
Links to the importance of opinion leaders (Midgley & Dowling, 1993)

that it implies equality between the sender and receiver, which in practice is not the case as clearly the sender has more power than the receiver.

Two-step communication model

PR theorists are interested in theories that look at how information is transmitted and received. One of the most interesting communication models, from a PR perspective, was developed by Paul Lazarsfeld and his colleagues. Lazarsfeld analysed voting patterns in New York in 1940, and found that voters seemed more influenced by their friends during an election campaign than by the media – opinions were therefore created in many cases not directly but indirect (Littlejohn, 2002).

Messages distributed through the media are influenced not directly but by interpersonal communication (Littlejohn, 2002) and from this, Lazarsfeld developed his Two-step Communication Model which has had a significant influence on our understanding of the role of the mass media. According to this model, information flows from the mass media to opinion leaders/formers in the community and from them to people they know who are in effect receiving their information second and third hand. Many people's views of the world are, therefore, influenced by outsiders.

In their 1955 book, *Personal Influence,* Paul Lazarsfeld and Elihu Katz developed the two-step flow theory by identifying the role played in the dissemination of information by those individuals they had identified as opinion leaders who exist in all social and occupational groups. They receive their information from the media and then pass it to the rest of their peer group. (Littlejohn, 2002).

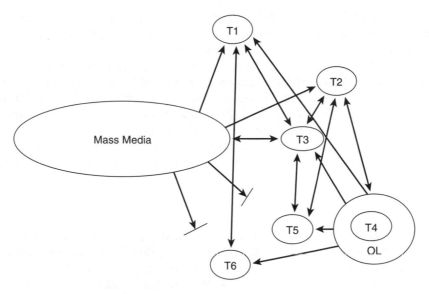

Figure 2.4   Multi-step Model of Communication

In practice we have all experienced how the Two-Step Model of Communication works when someone asks: 'Did you see that programme on TV last night?' If you didn't, they will proceed to tell you what happened. Your opinion and perception about the content and even the quality of the programme will be shaped by their opinion and what they have chosen to tell you. The internet has given inter-personal communication a new dimension, with users having access to a whole range of different sources of information through chat-rooms, message boards, Myspace, Youtube and blogs, and this growth leads to diversity and richness of opinion.

These are useful models to PR and illustrate how theory can help practical campaigns – simply using 'the mass media' in order to get a message across is no longer possible or appropriate. A sophisticated campaign will need to be targeted and based on a proper understanding of where key audiences receive their information from, and that may not be via any of the traditional outlets at all.

PR THEORY

Communication research and the PR theory that grew out of it look at the relationship between the senders of information and the receivers of it and in many ways this defines that most basic of PR activities – how to communicate effectively with a group. But how do we characterise the group to whom we are communicating?

Readers? Viewers? Listeners? While all of these are appropriate it is more common to use the term found in communication theory – the 'audience' or 'mass audience'. An analysis of this leads to one of PR's most basic theories – 'publics'.

In PR theory 'publics' has a precise and clear definition and whilst well established in academic literature it is not as widely used by PR practitioners who will often use similar terms as used in marketing and advertising. This can sometimes cause confusion. 'Publics' describes the recipients in the process of communication between the sender and receiver and according to the theory there are different categories of publics. The confusion occurs because other terms can also be used to describe these recipients, such as 'target audience' and 'stakeholders'.

Mass audience

In the 1950s and 1960s when most of the first 'mass communication' models emerged the process communication theories made it all seem relatively simple. A mass (large) audience was reached directly through a limited range of media – radio, television, newspapers and films. Newspapers still had large readerships: daily national newspapers were read by millions, so it was possible to speak of a 'mass media' that communicated with a 'mass audience', and the emerging public relations research was largely based around how to make PR messages work more effectively through mass media channels reaching mass audiences.

The term 'mass audience', however, suggests an audience that is largely passive and simply and uncritically consumes whatever they are watching, listening to, or reading, with little or no critical feedback from them reaching the media. There is also the implication that such audiences might be easily manipulated by media owners. However, even if that was the situation in the 1950s today this most certainly isn't the case. Modern audiences are far more aware of what it is adverts are attempting to do. They are more active and discriminating in their media consumption. Meanwhile the speed of technological change appears to be increasing and consumers have to work hard to keep up with the latest developments in mobile phones, TVs and satellite receivers, and internet and PC-based communications.

We live in a fragmented world where there is greater access to new ideas, trends and developments from across the globe and the technology has swung the balance of power away from the media owner towards the audience and the consumer. The new channels of communication, such as the internet and digital television, mean the audience is no longer in the hands of the TV programme makers. Audiences can now choose when to listen to the radio or watch TV programmes, and in effect create their own TV schedules, cutting across the traditional idea of a single channel.

Social network sites, blogs and an ability to download TV programmes onto computers all increase consumer power. In the face of such a fragmented market, it might appear impossible for advertisers or anyone wanting to communicate with an audience to decide where and how to deliver their message. In fact, the reverse is true as it provides them with more opportunities. It is now possible to identify channels of communication that will appeal to niche audiences who have consciously chosen a specific medium rather than simply watching something because it is on. It is also now possible to identify much more easily than before those key niche markets, or more appropriately, to target audiences, and this can command a higher advertising premium than one based simply on volume.

Target audience

In this fragmented, rapidly changing landscape what advertisers need are communication channels that will deliver targeted groups with precise socio-economic information about their make-up. They can answer such questions as who do we want to communicate with and why? And knowing who it is you are going to communicate with is an absolute prerequisite for any successful PR, marketing, or advertising campaign. Before the launch of any campaign, intensive research should be carried out into the nature of the target audience. For example, what is the social composition? The target age group? What newspapers do they read? What TV programmes do they watch? What radio stations do they listen to? Where do they shop? What are their spending patterns? What are their typical likes and dislikes? Only when there is a clear idea of all this can a proper campaign be planned. This campaign can then utilise a whole range of different communication channels, such as TV, radio, print, and now social networks in order to reach their target audience.

Publics

'Mass audience' and 'target audience' are terms used in advertising, marketing, and PR and mean roughly the same in each discipline. PR also uses 'publics' which whilst initially appearing to mean something similar to audiences in fact does not. 'Audiences' is used to describe a group of people who are to be communicated to, while 'publics' when used in PR describes people who are affected by an issue.

In a democracy, people have the freedom to choose a course of action, while those who are concerned about how an issue might impact on their lives have the freedom to join together to try and do something about it. The theory of publics helps PR practitioners understand why it is and under what circumstances people will come together to take action.

American philosopher John Dewey (1927) first introduced the concept of publics and using it to describe a group of people who will consciously choose to act and work together to confront a similar issue or problem. They recognise that it exists and then organise to do something about it. Elements of the definition were taken up by two American PR academics James Grunig and Todd Hunt (1984) and adapted for PR. They argued that there will be a range of responses from different people when confronted by a problem – some will ignore it and live with it, perhaps not even recognising it as a problem; or they will recognise it is a problem but choose not to do anything about it. Others will actively do what they can and campaign against it. What is interesting in this context is whether or not these different groups will always have similar socio-economic characteristics, or whether a problem will unite people from different backgrounds around the issue. As people take sides according to their interest in the issue, and join together with other like-minded individuals on the subject, they will collectively become a 'public' (Grunig and Hunt,1984). Individuals can be members of several different publics.

Grunig and Hunt defined four types of publics:

- *Non-public* – the organisation has no consequence on the group or the group has no consequence on the organisation.
- *Latent public* – a group faces a common threat from the organisation, but they do not detect a problem.
- *Aware public* – the group recognises a problem exists.
- *Active public* – having recognised that a problem exists, the group organises to do something about it and to establish what should be done to stop such problems emerging.

The role of PR practitioners working for the organisation is to identify which category their various publics fall into and then to organise their communication programme to deal with the most pressing problems. If, for example, the organisation has to deal with a non-public, then there is no PR problem and no need to do anything about it. However, Grunig and Hunt believe that a common mistake made by PR practitioners is to start organising a communication programme only when a public becomes active.

Active/activist publics can be difficult to communicate with because they have already made a decision and formed their views about both the issue and the company; they are not looking to be persuaded by the company's point of view. They will only have negative opinions about the company and will not believe either the company or any independent third parties. In these situations there appears to be a fundamental breakdown in trust. Later in this book we will explore further the importance of trust and the consequences for an organisation when it breaks down. PR practitioners, both in-house and as consultants, often forget that publics will and do change, that they are not static. It is therefore necessary to be constantly reviewing what the company is doing and how it responds to its publics. Most importantly, companies should attempt to be proactive by identifying issues in advance to attempt to prevent issues becoming a problem. PR has an important role to play here – not only should it be responsible for sending communication out, it should also listen to what is happening outside of the organisation. It can then feed what it learns back into the organisation and help to shape not just the presentation of information but also its actual content.

THE FOUR MODELS OF GRUNIG AND HUNT

Publics theory is an important tool for PR practitioners but Grunig and Hunt's most important theoretical contribution in 'Managing Public Relations' was to identify four types of practice based on the work of practitioners. Three of the four models were drawn from their analysis of PR history described above, and although based upon historical practice they nevertheless found it still described in the way many practitioners practise PR in the UK and USA.

The press agentry/publicity model

The first model is based on the work of the press agents and publicists who were active from the middle of the 19th century to the early years of the 20th century. Their role was straightforward – to try to get as much publicity as possible for whomever they were working for. Grunig and Hunt (1984) argued that in many ways their PR practice was similar to propaganda because the information disseminated by the practitioner was probably incomplete, selective, distorted, or partially true. The flow of information was one-way and one-sided from the organisation to the intended recipients and no feedback was expected from them. The sole purpose of the publicity was to persuade people to pursue a specific course of action. Press agents and publicists used whatever tactics were necessary to achieve their aim – from the conventional press release to a range of publicity stunts and events – to maximise media coverage. Some of them, as we saw with the circus owner Phineas T. Barnum, were downright dubious and deceitful.

Box 2.2   Propaganda, Publicity and Public Relations

Grunig and Hunt, when considering the relationship between propaganda and press agentry, linked some forms of PR activity to propaganda: 'Public Relations serves a propaganda function in the press agentry/publicity model. Practitioners spread the faith of the organisation involved, often through incomplete, distorted or half-true information' (1984: 21).

(Continued)

(Continued)

What is propaganda? Is PR propaganda? What is the relationship between PR and propaganda? The modern PR industry is understandably nervous of accusations that any of its activities are in any way propaganda. This has acquired sinister overtones that imply deliberately lying in an attempt to manipulate the minds of others, usually by using concealed or underhand means. Propaganda developed negative associations during the Second World War, when the Nazi regime used sophisticated techniques to promote their ideal of the supremacy of the Aryan race, which led to the demonisation of Jews and the horrors of the Holocaust. People realised that one-sided, unchecked, state-inspired propaganda could have devastating consequences.

The techniques of propaganda are well established. At their most benign they aim to deliberately persuade a group of people to adopt a particular point of view. Some critics argue that PR is propaganda used on behalf of the commercial sector.

With the growth in PR–originated content in much of the contemporary media, there are dangers that if not operated responsibly, the modern PR industry could be accused of attempts at manipulating public opinion. These issues are discussed in detail below.

Barnum was an infamous, historical example of a press agent but does the press agentry/publicity model have any relevance today? It does indeed describe the work of *some* PR practitioners. Look, for example, at the pages of tabloid newspapers and celebrity magazines, or television and radio chat shows when a new film or book is launched – the stars are all there plugging their latest project. Even the so-called 'exclusive' pictures of a semi-naked celebrity on a beach in a Sunday newspaper can sometimes be the result of a collusion between the star's publicist and a photographer. In the UK, the activities of Max Clifford, and others like him, are the modern equivalent of the 19th century publicist/press agent – although interestingly Clifford denies that he is a publicist (see Case Study, page 206). And although the phrase has sometimes acquired pejorative connotations, it also describes the way that many small and medium-sized PR practitioners operate by attempting to generate as much publicity as possible for their clients.

The public information model

Grunig and Hunt's second model is based on the way PR was practised by the big companies that dominated some sections of the US economy in the latter part of the 19th and the early 20th century. Their public information model is based upon the work of Ivy Lee and the 'public be informed' approach where information is sent out by an organisation. It is still a one-way process as in the press agentry model, with information flowing from an organisation to recipients. The intention is to persuade, but crucially – and here is the real difference from the press agentry mode – there is no attempt to deceive the recipients. The public information model is based on an honest approach to communications. The role of the in-house PR practitioner is to transmit information objectively, reporting on the company just as a journalist would (Grunig and Hunt, 1984). A modern example of such a campaign would a public information campaign such as the anti-smoking campaign launched by the UK government in 2009, which aimed to show parents who smoke how much their teenage children worried about their future health.

Writing in 1984, Grunig and Hunt argued that the Public Information Model was the way that most companies practised PR at the time. It was also characteristic of the way the public and voluntary sectors, education organisations, and non-profit organisations practised communication. These organisations communicate information about themselves using a variety of methods – not just news releases but also newspapers, guidebooks – and these would now include electronic communication such as websites.

The two-way asymmetric model

To Grunig and Hunt this model is characteristic of the type of PR practised from the mid 1920s through to the 1950s and is associated with the work of Edward Bernays, who attempted to provide a scientific basis for communication. Two-way asymmetric communication shares many features with the press agentry model, though the major difference between them is that the two-way asymmetric model attempts 'scientific persuasion' rather than the crude and sometimes manipulative techniques used by publicists. The communication, however, is still all one way (asymmetric) from the organisation to the target audience, and the attempt is to persuade those on the receiving end of PR campaigns to take a form of action, whether to buy a product or in the case of a charity to support its campaigns. The communication is aimed at changing one type of behaviour to another. There is no dialogue or communication with the audience, or if there is it is only in order to improve the sales message.

What makes it different from the previous two models is persuasion. This is the type of communication practised, for example, when a company wants to try to persuade consumers to buy its products. It is also, arguably, the most dominant model practised by PR consultancies working on behalf of their clients. In the two-way asymmetric model, the communicator gets feedback from the public and then applies it the latest communication and persuasion theories to persuade that audience to accept the organisation's point of view.

The two-way symmetric model

In terms of historical development the model of the modern era is the practice of two-way symmetrical communication. The key characteristic of this model is that the company engages in a real dialogue with stakeholders – not just to persuade, but also to listen, learn and, most importantly, to adapt organisational behaviour as a result of the communication process. In contrast to linear one-way communication models this is intended to be a circular two-way process, with the parties engaged in communication on equal terms.

Two-way symmetric public relations is supposed to rely on an honest two-way communication with give and take rather than one-way persuasion, focusing on mutual respect and efforts to achieve a mutual understanding between parties. Negotiation and a willingness to adapt and compromise are important elements in this process. It requires organisations engaging in public relations to be willing to make significant adjustments in how they operate in order to accommodate their publics or audiences. Significantly, it appears to be used more by non-profit organisations, government agencies and regulated bodies rather than by competitive, profit-driven companies. South Shropshire Council (2006) for example, in its statement of principles, stated it would operate in a two-way symmetrical manner as a matter of policy.

The Calderdale and Huddersfield NHS Trust, in its 2006/07 'Communications Strategy', states that its aim is: 'To protect and enhance the reputation of the Calderdale and Huddersfield NHS Trust'. The principles supporting this aim are:

- Good, honest and open two-way communication. This is the lifeblood of any successful operation.
- Strong communication with stakeholders. This is essential to how the organisation works and provides services.
- Clear communication. All written, spoken and electronic communications should be clear, easily understood, timely, and up to date.

Without it being openly stated, this is two-way symmetric communication in action.

While, with some credence, Grunig and Hunt could point to historical practice to substantiate the other models, the evidence for the symmetric model in 1984 was rather thin. Their research estimated that 15% of all in-house PR practitioners used two-way symmetric communication (15% of organisations practised press agentry/publicity, 50% public information and 20% two-way asymmetric communication). However PR practitioners working in consultancies were in 1984 only starting to practise it. So it remained more of an ideal, the way that many believed PR should be undertaken. It was only with the research that Grunig and others carried out for the excellence project (see below) that enough evidence was accumulated to suggest that the best way to successfully practise PR was symmetric communications.

In later work James Grunig (1992) had to accept that, in practice, the idea of 'the best' model was irrelevant because organisations used communications that were relevant to the environment in which they operated. Different circumstances demanded different solutions and organisations will use a combination of models depending on their specific circumstances. They may, for example, as an overall principle, say that they will operate in a two-way symmetric manner, but might find that on starting a campaign to support the launch of a new product they must then utilise asymmetric communications in order to boost sales.

The excellence project

The excellence project matters to PR because the depth of the research and the conclusions drawn from it have made a contribution to the way PR is practised and it has been a stimulus to academic research in the subject. 'Over 20 years, a leading body of work has developed around excellence theory, which has probably done more to develop public relations theory and scholarship than any other single school of thought. Its founder, James Grunig, is the most widely recognised public relations scholar' (Botan & Hazelton, 2006: 6). Magda Pieczka (L'Etang and Pieczka, 2006: 348) also agree with the influence that James Grunig has had, stating that his work: 'Provides a theoretical basis for public relations claiming for it the status as an academic discipline'.

The idea of building 'excellence' in a company was a popular management theory in the 1980s and was developed by the management theorist, Tom Peters.In his book, *In Search of Excellence* (1982), co-written with Robert H. Waterman, Peters profiled 43 different companies and identified the eight basic principles that made them successful. Becoming an 'excellent' company meant becoming a leader in its sector, a world-class company, respected and admired by others, and this could be achieved by any company provided they followed the practices identified by Peters and Waterman. In applying this to PR, what Grunig and his team looked for were those factors that would enable every company to practise excellent PR.

Grunig and a team of academics – Larissa Grunig, David Dozier, William Ehling, Jon White, and the only PR practitioner, Fred Repper – started their research in 1985 with a grant of £400,000 from the International Association of Business Communicators (IABC). The aim of their research was to identify how and why PR gives value to an organisation and they sought answers to the following questions:

1 When and why are the efforts of communications practitioners effective?
2 How do organisations benefit from effective public relations?
3 Why do organisations practise PR in different ways?

(L'Etang & Pieczka, 2006)

They undertook a huge research programme looking at the practice of PR in the USA and UK, with the aim of producing an action programme that companies could follow in order to practise excellent PR.

The research conclusions were published in an influential book, *Excellence in Public Relations and Communications Management* (1992), which was a practical guide for in-house and external PR practitioners that demonstrated how to achieve excellence in communication for their organisation. It analysed excellent PR on four different levels:

- Programme level: why, when, and how individual communication programmes were implemented.
- Departmental level: how PR departments operated and fitted in with other departments and the organisation as a whole.
- Organisational level: how an understanding of, and respect for communication processes and audience feedback could impact on the organisation.
- Economic level: how the tangible value to the organisation provided by excellent PR could produce happy internal and external audiences.

So how is excellence theory applied to PR? At its heart is the following proposition about the role of PR:

Public Relations contributes to organisational effectiveness when it helps to reconcile the organisation's goals with the expectations of its strategic constituencies. This contribution has monetary value to the organisation. Public Relations contributes to effectiveness by building quality long-term relationships with strategic constituencies. Public Relations is most likely to contribute to effectiveness when the senior PR manager is a member of the dominant coalition (that is the ruling group who actually run a company) where he or she is able to shape the organisation's goals and help determine which external publics are most strategic. (Grunig, 1992: 156)

To really provide value to an organisation and to achieve excellence in communications, PR practitioners must be working at the highest levels in the boardroom. The issue of the role PR plays in a company and whether it should have any influence or input into the strategic decision-making of a company is a crucially important one that we will return to in later chapters. Grunig's research also provided the practical evidence to support Grunig and Hunt's earlier argument that the practice of symmetrical communication was the most effective of the four models. They asserted that two-way symmetric communication was the foundation for excellent PR practice and that the value of PR comes from the relationships that organisations develop and maintain with their publics.

There have been criticisms of the excellence theory and Grunig continues to develop it in light of changing situations and circumstances. One major criticism is that it aligns the PR function in a company too closely with management and PR then becomes a management tool that might be used to justify appalling environmental or labour practices. For example, many of the companies that Ivy

Lee worked for were terrible employers and the fact that he improved their public image by telling their side of the story didn't make them better employers. This can sometimes place the PR practitioner in a difficult place ethically if they do not agree with the actions and activities of a company. The ethical dimension of PR will be explored in Chapter 6.

Magda Pieczka (2006) has questioned the basis upon which Grunig's research was carried out, arguing that the nature of the research determined the outcome and that the nature of the research questions limited the answers. The assumptions present in the questions meant the researchers were basically determining the outcome, which is to support the management role of PR.

Pieczka (2006: 355) criticises those who 'believe' in the excellence theory – they have, she argues, the characteristics of religious converts: 'One finds a somewhat proselytising approach emanating from the theory of excellent public relations: if public relations practitioners resist or do not understand the excellence ideas, it is because they do not know any better, even if through no fault of their own'. Quoting Grunig (1992), she claims that his comments are patronising: 'Practitioners often do not understand or accept theories like ours because they work from a pragmatic or conservative world-view. We argue that practitioners with a pragmatic worldview have symmetrical presuppositions even though they do not realise it. They take an asymmetrical view, usually a conservative one, because their clients hold that view'.

Excellence theory is not the only PR theory but it has achieved its dominant position partly because of the level of support for it amongst the powerful US PR academics and partly because it provides an acceptable theoretical justification for PR. The symmetrical company is an ideal. Pieczka (2006: 355) describes excellence theory as: 'The proselytizing of the rather heavenly "symmetrical" communication model which would allow young students (and teachers) to feel good about their occupation'. If it is practised it is likely to be in public sector organisations but there has been too little research into this field to identify how far the practice goes.

Why then should we still continue to study excellence theory if it only applies to a limited number of organisations? Its significance is the contribution that it has made to the development of PR theory: it was 'The first cohesive theoretical effort to make scientific sense of public relations work and tie it to essential research and evaluation. Excellence Theory focused on organisational relationships and the attainment of managerial power and influence for the PR role. A key assumption of the dominant paradigm seems to be that academic work should directly contribute to practice'. It raised the status of PR research by presenting PR 'As an outgrowth of management sciences, to democratic and functional. By linking the discipline to other scientific disciplines, public relations could gain a respectable academic status that could deliver "strategic" communicators worthy of boardroom status' (L'Etang & Pieczka, 2006: 252).

That so few organisations actually practise symmetrical communications led Grunig to adapt his theory, introducing elements of game theory to produce a model which effectively utilises and combines asymmetric and symmetric communication. This model is a continuum, with the company at one end and the public at the other. At the far end of each the public and company engage in asymmetric practices. In the middle of the continuum, the organisation and public meet and create opportunities that are beneficial to each of them. When this happens, it is a win-win situation for both the company and the public.

Theories rise and fall, change and develop. No theory is immutable, particularly in the social sciences, and this is so with the excellence theory. Alternative frameworks are emerging, although one problem with many of them is that they still share many of the fundamental assumptions of the dominant theory.

One alternative that has developed outside the dominant paradigm and is independent from it is the Critical Paradigm, but even this still has to use the excellence theory as a reference point (L'Etang & Pieczka, 2006). The Critical Paradigm: 'Points out the limitation of systems by asking hard questions about the possession and use of power, the nature of authority, morality and political economy. Critical academics explore questions about propaganda, corporate power, the public sphere culture and commodification' (2006: 256).

SUMMARY

This chapter has deliberately covered a lot of ground and should, among other things, illustrate what a complex subject this is. Communication theory can help PR practitioners understand why some campaigns work and others do not. However, PR is not solely based on communication theory: the history of PR has contributed to the growth of PR theory and in turn helped to develop its practice.

The current dominant paradigm in PR is the excellence theory which argues that the most effective form of both external and internal communication is symmetrical communication. This means that organisations must engage in a constructive two-way communication with stakeholders, but in addition should be prepared to change policy as a result of that dialogue. The most effective companies practising excellent PR have the PR function operating at the highest level in the company. For most businesses however PR practice tends to be pragmatic and to use a number of different PR models depending on the situation and circumstances.

What students should draw from this chapter is that PR is not a static subject – it is constantly developing, changing, and adapting to new circumstances and situations. For new entrants this opens up many exciting possibilities, and equipped with the right skills, the desire to succeed and a commitment to hard work, new PR practitioners will have the opportunity to make an impact.

MARKETING, ADVERTISING & PUBLIC RELATIONS: SIMILARITIES & DIFFERENCES EXPLORED AND EXPLAINED

By the end of this chapter you will:

- understand the characteristics and functions of marketing, advertising and PR
- appreciate the differences and similarities
- understand how and when marketing, advertising and PR work together

INTRODUCTION

Marketing, advertising and PR are, for many people, simply different ways of describing similar processes and this can cause confusion. Cutlip et al. (2000) state that PR 'Gets confused with its activities and parts. For example, many think that "publicity" is simply another way of saying "public relations"'. They offer the following definition of publicity: publicity is information from an outside source that is used by the media because the information has a news value. It is an *uncontrolled* method of placing messages in the media because the source does not pay for the media placement (2000: 23).

Although the distinction between advertising and PR may appear obscure to outsiders, in practice, practitioners of both disciplines understand the boundaries. One of my first jobs in PR was running the PR department of an advertising agency and the question over who was responsible for which type of activity was never an issue – anything to do with words was our job, while drawings, images, pictures in magazines and papers, and putting together the advertisement was all down to the other lot! Pity it is not so simple nowadays.

Why marketing matters

The UK Chartered Institute of Marketing states 'Marketing is the management process which identifies, anticipates and supplies customer requirements efficiently and profitably'. The American Marketing Association provides a slightly different definition: 'Marketing is the process of planning and executing the conception, pricing, promotion and distribution of ideas, goods and services to create exchange and satisfying individual organisational objectives'. Some (Cutlip et al., 2000) would argue that marketing helps to identify and then fulfil our most basic human wants and desires and organises resources in order to meet and satisfy these wants.

For Brassington and Pettitt (2000: 5), such definitions are useful because they illustrate two fundamental points about marketing. First, that marketing has an important role at the highest levels of a company as part of the management process; secondly, they demonstrate that at the heart of marketing is the need to listen and respond to an organisation's customers and then, having done so, to give them what they want: 'All marketing activities should be geared towards this. It implies a focus towards the customer or end consumer of the product or service. If "customer requirements" are not satisfactorily fulfilled, or if customers do not obtain what they want and need, then marketing has failed both the customer and organisation' (2000: 20).

According to this view of the modern company, marketing is – or should be – as much a part of a company's most senior management as, say, the human resources or the finance department. Why? Because without sales a company, any company – whether a service provider (i.e. bank, insurance firm, building society) or a manufacturing company (i.e. a machine tool manufacturer or boat builder) – will not survive.

The focus for marketing is delivering sales. PR however has a wider remit – to build and maintain a range of relationships with an organisation's stakeholders which will include not only its customers but also its employees, investors, and neighbours, as well as special interest groups and governments.

Marketing is the overall driver of an organisation's sales strategy. It says – 'this is how we will get the purchasers of our goods and services to buy and advertising and PR are among the tools we will use to attract and interest potential purchasers'. We can see the importance of marketing to a company by looking at two different types of business, a market-led and a product-led company.

Market-led companies

Market-led companies will put consumers at the heart of their business, constantly listening to them changing and adapting products and processes as a result. By attempting to anticipate market trends and changing consumer patterns such companies aim to satisfy future needs and hopefully produce the right products just as consumers are entering the market with the intention to buy. Market-led companies exist in every sector of business and will have dynamic reputations, capable of not just responding to different trends but also able to lead them. In these companies, the Marketing Director will occupy a senior position in the company hierarchy.

Product-led companies

Product-led companies will react differently: they will expect customers to go to them, often believing that their reputation alone is enough to attract them. The characteristic response of the product-led company is epitomised by a comment made by Henry Ford, founder of the Ford Motor Company. His Model T brought affordable, mass-produced cars to the working man, but had a limited colour choice: 'You can have any colour you like providing its black' was Ford's comment to customers – hardly the most customer friendly response. Product-led companies will have usually been around for some time, their products or services will be well regarded, and they will have probably been market leaders at one time. However, at some stage the company will have lost touch with its market and allowed newer, younger rivals to arrive in the marketplace to challenge its position. Business history is littered with examples of companies that failed to grasp the basic principle of listening to their customers and stopped providing them with what they wanted.

No business has a divine right to exist and no business can live on past glories alone. Continued success in business means always having to adapt to changing social, economic, and political conditions. Customers change and a company must change with them.

Marks & Spencer is one of the best examples of the way in which a company can change from being a product-led to a market-led company (see Box 3.1). Advertising and PR played a crucial role in changing the fortunes of M&S.

Box 3.1   Advertising and the Rebirth of Marks & Spencer

Ten years ago Marks & Spencer was regularly voted the most admired company in Britain: it was a by-word for quality, with loyal customers who appeared to continue shopping there almost irrespective of what was on sale. It had a reputation for producing quality products most of which were made in the UK. It was a fine, grand, British institution.

(Continued)

(Continued)

But then it all went wrong and within the space of a few years those previously loyal customers had turned their backs on the company, attracted by newer, cheaper more nimble competitors such as Matalan and Gap who produced fashionable clothes at a fraction of the price. Effectively Marks and Spencer had lost touch with its customers. In both its core markets of food and clothing it no longer seemed able to sell the goods customers wanted to buy. The clothes range appeared dowdy and expensive while their food products was regarded as too traditional and unappealing.

If we regard the product-led company as a state of mind, then Marks & Spencer had all the characteristics. Effectively, what the company was saying to its customers was: 'We are M&S, these are our goods. Take them or leave them' – a classic example of a product-led company.

The company had become complacent, with an inflexible, top-heavy, centralised management structure that was remote from its customer base. It was losing out to faster-moving, more innovative, cheaper and more fashionable clothing chains and in food it was being overtaken by the big supermarkets.

Marks & Spencer's problems peaked in July 2004 when, following months of declining sales and negative press coverage, the company fought off an audacious takeover bid by a rival firm, the Arcadia Group. The shareholders decided to back the recently appointed chief executive Stuart Rose, and to give his plan to turn Marks & Spencer around a chance. This was based on an aggressive and unprecedented advertising campaign. Up until this point, Marks and Spencer's had never advertised – it never had the need to. In August 2004 the ad campaign that has since become most associated with the rebirth of Marks & Spencer was launched – the 'This is Your M&S' and 'Not Just Food, M&S Food' campaign.

Focusing on food and women's wear, the adverts restored public confidence in Marks & Spencer and communicated its overhaul to include more stylish, affordable clothes, improved service, and store refurbishment. The food adverts were attractive and evocative, and quickly became 'water cooler' moments as well as a commercial success. Sales of hot chocolate puddings, for example, increased by 288%, while sales of panacotta increased by 1207% and roast potatoes by 454% (Livesey & Howard, 2006).

The clothing adverts, featuring, among others, the model Twiggy, had a similar impact on some of the women's clothes. A cream, three-quarter-sleeve blouse worn by Twiggy sold more in one week than any other product in the history of Marks & Spencer. A £119 travel bag had to be re-ordered to cope with demand.

Of course, no matter how good the advertising, if the products do not meet the required standards or consumer expectations they will not sell. The fact is that the adverts were advertising products that people wanted to buy. It was a traditional advertising campaign that delivered publicity by using TV, posters, billboards, and a range of print media newspapers and magazines.

It was estimated that the advertising 'generated' an additional £6 million worth of positive press coverage in 2005 (Livesey & Howard, 2006). Conventional media articles announcing the start of the campaign, and who was going to be featured in the ads, were actually only a small element of this coverage. What created the most interest was the success of the advertising campaign itself, as this created column inches and communicated the difference the campaign was having on sales. Thus the ad campaign itself became part of the turn-around. Whether it had intended to or not Marks & Spencer had entered the age of viral marketing.

Marketers like to be able to demonstrate success, as they have to justify their budget to the finance director. That an advertising campaign like this one can point to increased sales is one reason why, traditionally, marketing directors have preferred advertising over PR. From a marketing perspective, PR has various problems – it is sometimes seen as a hit or miss proposition with results that are hard to identify and its direct impact on sales can be hard to measure. PR practitioners (in the opinions of some marketers) are also concerned about 'vague' things like public opinion when they ought to be thinking more like business people and concerning themselves with improving product or service sales.

PR practitioners meanwhile have their own complaints about marketing: they believe that it carries out short-run actions designed to sell more products and that such actions can at times seriously undermine a company's image. PR practitioners can therefore 'resent' this 'intrusion' into what has been generally recognised as their area. There is also the common complaint from PR practitioners that marketing doesn't use PR to its full potential.

Marketing is the process by which a company organises itself to satisfy customer needs or, in the popular phrase, 'Give the customers what they want ...'

Nowadays, it is not simply about organising a campaign to inform or persuade potential buyers to buy the product or service offered by the company. The modern consumer is more demanding and has more choice in the marketplace. The arrival of new distribution channels, such as the internet, means that companies have to work harder to attract and retain customers. As we saw with the Marks & Spencer's example brand loyalty, which used to be important in customer retention, can no longer be counted on.

Companies used to be able to rely on brand loyalty, with customers always buying the same tin of baked beans, or breakfast cereal, or dog food, or even car. In the 21st century, loyalties to brands appear to be breaking down, and modern consumers are prepared to shop around and look for value for money. This applies whatever the sector may be, including services such as banking, finance and utility supplies (gas, electricity, water). Not so long ago, customers would tend to stay with the bank where they first opened an account or would stay for life with their first ever electricity supplier. Today's consumers think nothing of regularly switching bank accounts, mortgages and electricity suppliers in order to take advantage of the best deals on offer. In fact, those that remain with the same provider are regarded as oddities.

Competition is also fierce. Financial institutions, just like other product and service providers, have had to change and respond to such challenges by being more responsive to the needs of their customers.

The marketing mix

The 'marketing mix' is probably the best-known phrase in marketing and describes the basic, tactical elements of a marketing plan. The term was first by used in 1964 by Professor Neil Borden, a professor of advertising at Harvard Business School, and it was one of many major contributions he made to advertising and marketing theory. Also known as the Four P's, the marketing mix elements are product, price, place and promotion. Putting these together in the correct combination and at the right time delivers the required product to the consumer.

Product – This category encompasses all the processes involved from developing the product prototype to producing the finished item. It incorporates the management of product features and benefits, branding, packaging, and even after-sales service schemes such as product, part and service guarantees.

Price – Getting the price of any product or service right requires the following factors to be correctly combined: costs, profitability, value for money, competitiveness, and incentives. Price, according to economic theory, is a reflection of what the seller is prepared to sell at and what the purchaser is prepared to pay. This implies that both buyer and seller have the same amount of information about the cost of producing the product. However, this is a situation that exists only as theory as purchasers clearly do not have the same information as sellers. Furthermore, companies will regularly use price as a marketing tool. Promotions and special offers (e.g. 2 for 1 promotions, or buy one get one free), competitive discounts against similar products, and competitions are all examples of where marketing will use the price mechanism.

To consumers, price is also a reflection of the perceived value of a product. This does not mean that purchasers will always follow the rational economic path and buy the cheapest available product. High-value goods have a status symbol for some people because possessing an expensive car, watch or handbag can provide invaluable esteem in the eyes of peer groups. This is an intangible that cannot be measured by monetary value.

Place – This is the distribution channels through which products or services are made available to the purchaser. It is an area of the 4Ps that has seen the most significant and challenging changes in recent times. Place includes how the product is accessed by the target market and also the logistics of how products and services are delivered to the purchase point. There is no sense, as supermarket chain Sainsbury's found to their cost a few years ago, in having a successful advertising campaign that does its job of attracting customers to the supermarket shelves only for those shelves to be empty because the company's logistics has not been able to supply products to the stores quickly enough. And every Christmas there always seems to be the annual problem of manufacturers not being able to meet the demand for toys and games that they have stimulated through advertising. In 2007, for example, Nintendo suspended TV ads for its popular Wii console because demand was outstripping supply.

For the vast majority of consumer goods, the traditional distribution channels are retail outlets, ranging from the corner grocery shop to an out-of-town shopping centre. However, these distribution channels are changing. The internet now allows consumers to shop from home and has revolutionised the way people buy goods. Manufacturers and retailers have had to adapt to these changes to survive in a competitive marketplace and to then anticipate where the next developments will take place.

Promotion – This covers all the activities that a company carries out in order to get the product or service in front of the customer. Promotion will be part of a campaign and the combination of advertising, PR, and direct mail adopted will depend on the nature of the product and the target audience. Promotion is what you would normally expect marketing to be – using a variety of innovative techniques to get your message across to the end-user. The appropriate promotional mix for the product and its markets will probably include a combination of the big promotional guns – advertising, sales promotions (how the product is displayed in shops), sales management (how the sales force operates), PR and Direct Marketing. When a new product is launched the marketing campaign will combine most or all of these elements.

Social marketing

Marketing can be applied to a number of different sectors and social marketing (or cause related marketing) is marketing which aims to change social behaviour. Examples include the regular anti-smoking or anti-drink driving campaigns that appear in the press and on TV. Kotler and Zaltman (1971: 5) offered one of the first definitions of social marketing: 'It is the explicit use of marketing skills to help translate present social action efforts into more effectively designed and communicated programs that elicit desired audience response'.

Social marketing raises ethical issues – is it right that agencies of the state, such as the NHS, should engage in campaigns to change people's behaviour, even though changing that behaviour will probably improve people's lives? We might all agree that it is on balance a 'good thing' that we should try and stop people from drinking alcohol and then getting into a motor vehicle and driving it. If they crashed the vehicle it could cause injury and even death to innocent people. So we accept that it is right that we should prevent them from carrying out such actions. However, there is the possibility that the powerful and persuasive techniques used in these campaigns to change people's behaviour might also be used to promote more sinister causes. Social marketing will be discussed in more detail in Chapter 13.

New forms of marketing

There are those who would argue that the marketing mix is an old-fashioned theory that was relevant in a time when marketing could use and rely on the mass media to deliver campaigns to a largely receptive and passive audience (Levinson, 1984). Times have changed however and new delivery channels and more active audiences need new marketing techniques.

The internet as well as electronic means of communicating are shifting the balance between consumer and producer. Environmental and ethical awareness and the desire to buy eco-friendly products are also influencing purchasing behaviour. In such a competitive environment, where demands and tastes change so frequently, marketing has to work even harder to attract potential purchasers. The companies that survive, prosper and grow are those which can adapt and listen to changing customer demands and produce an appropriate marketing strategy: 'The organisation that develops and performs its marketing activities with the needs of the buyer driving it all and with the satisfaction of that buyer as the main aim is marketing orientated. The motivation is to "find wants and fill them" rather than "create products and sell them"' (Brassington and Pettitt, 2000: 14).

Perhaps the best modern example of a company that appears to have gotten it in right in this respect is Google. Jeff Jarvis (2008) argues that more companies should adapt the Google approach because it is based on listening and responding to the customer. What, Jarvis asks, would a Google car be like? It would be safe and green because these are the features that customers now want from their cars. While many of his arguments are overstated, the basic point is still valid – Google does listen and benefits commercially from doing so, standing as an example of what other companies should be doing.

Guerrilla and viral marketing are perhaps the best known examples of these new forms of marketing. Guerrilla marketing was first developed by Jay Conrad Levinson in his 1984 book, *Guerrilla Marketing*. Although originally intended as a marketing technique for small businesses with limited marketing budgets, guerrilla marketing has been embraced by large companies who have seen just how effective these campaigns can be. Guerrilla marketing attempts to get maximum results from minimal resources by using unconventional promotion methods. According to its advocates, these campaigns use energy, imagination and the unexpected, targeting consumers in unexpected places and with unusual tactics such as street give-aways of products. The object of the campaign is to create a 'buzz' or get the product talked about rather than to try and 'sell' the product directly. PR stunts are an important part of this and because PR consultancies are experienced in organising such activities they will often take the lead on such campaigns.

Viral marketing and advertising campaigns will also use social networks to produce an increase in brand awareness through a self-replicating process which spreads like a computer virus. Such a campaign might involve getting an advert replayed on YouTube over and over again so that awareness of the advert or product spreads by word of mouth. One of the most successful examples of a viral advertising campaign was the Cadbury 'Something in the Air' advert featuring the drumming gorilla. The advert doesn't mention chocolate and you would not even aware that it was an advert for a product – what it did was to get people talking and from that product awareness grew. It was viewed more than 10 million times on YouTube and it is said to have played a major part in transforming the company's fortunes.

Box 3.2   Cadbury's drumming gorilla

The £6.2m, drumming gorilla advertising campaign was launched in 2007 to promote Cadbury Dairy Milk and was produced by the Fallon Advertising agency. At the time Cadbury Schweppes used traditional advertising schemes such as sponsoring ITV's *Coronation Street*. Fallon Advertising wanted to move the company away from pushing products and produce 'entertainment pieces' that would appeal to a broader range of consumers. Awareness of the product would then spread through a word-of-mouth viral marketing campaign.

Significantly, just before the launch in 2006 and 2007, Cadbury's reputation was at an all-time low, having suffered from a series of PR errors. In the middle of 2006 it was found that some Cadbury products had contained traces of salmonella, caused by a leaking pipe at the company's Marlbrook factory in the Midlands. Forty people became ill and the subsequent product recall cost the company £20m. However, Cadbury's didn't tell the Food Standards Agency for five months after the problem was discovered and although it was fined £1m, the real damage was to the company's reputation and its brands.

Other problems included Easter eggs containing traces of nuts being distributed without any nut warning. A £5m advertising campaign for Trident chewing gum was cancelled after complaints that it was offensive. In mid-2007, Cadbury's announced that it was cutting 7,500 jobs in the UK, and then a leaked internal memo revealed that many of the jobs were to be moved to Poland.

Against this background the first gorilla advert appeared on 31 August 2007, during the final of *Big Brother 8*, and in addition to the TV ad campaign there were posters and print adverts during September and October 2007.

It was, however, the viral aspect that maintained the campaign beyond this initial period. In its first week it was viewed over 500,000 times and in one year it had been viewed by over six million internet users: Facebook groups were even set up.

The effect was that sales of Dairy Milk increased by 9% over a similar period in 2006, while possibly more significant was the research by YouGov that showed that the advert was responsible for an improvement in the company's reputation – 20% more people looked favourably on the brand in the period after the advert's general release than in the same period the year before, reversing the impact of the earlier disasters (*Media Week*, 25/10/07).

Advertising: good or evil?

The Institute of Practitioners in Advertising (IPA) define advertising as follows: 'Advertising presents the most persuasive argument possible selling message to the right prospects for the product or service at the lowest possible cost'.

Advertising in the 21st century has become such an integral part of our life and so ingrained in our consciousness that there are many people who believe that our economy could not function without it (Jefkins, 2000). Advertising has power, but with such power also comes the potential for abuse. The alternative argument is that in the current economic circumstances, the power of advertising is such that it now poses a major threat to social cohesion and its power needs to be curtailed.

Remember the discussion about propaganda and persuasion in Chapter 2? Advertising is a one-sided way to communicate – it attempts to persuade those viewing an advert to take a specific course of action.

Popular advertisements can be memorable. They become the object of discussion and can remain with us long after the original campaign has finished, for example, the Guinness white horses ads, the 'Wassup' Budweiser ads, or the Coke advert with 'We'd Like to Teach the World to Sing'. Jingles and strap-lines can retain their power for years – i.e., 'For Mash get Smash', 'Beanz Meanz Heinz'. We now accept and understand advertising and the role it is trying to play, in whatever form it comes; we know it is attempting to persuade us to take a certain course of action. We can also appreciate that, in an increasingly sophisticated age, advertising comes in many different forms – from the two-minute ads that appear on television and display adverts in magazines and newspapers to firms sponsoring sporting events such as the FA Cup Final. We play the game with the advertiser because we believe that as we understand it we can also discriminate and not be seduced.

According to its defenders advertising is never static because it reflects society and the popular values and mores of the day and life without advertising would be very dull. There would be a lack of essential and desirable information, less entertainment, less street colour, and less to talk about with our family and people at work (ASA, 2002).

These are some of the arguments used by the Advertising Standards Authority (ASA) to explain why we need advertising. However, ASA is not objective because while it is the organisation that oversees the advertising industry it is also paid for by a levy from that industry: therefore it is a self-regulatory organisation (SRO). The Advertising Standards Authority deals with complaints about adverts and can ban them if it feels they make claims that cannot be substantiated. Research by ASA into what people understand by the term 'advertising' provided confirmation that adverts have become ingrained into our consciousness. The research illustrated that, for consumers, advertising encompassed every piece of 'brand, product or service communication' and included not only what we recognise as the media conventionally associated with advertising – such as TV, posters, press, cinema and radio – but also new and developing areas – such as direct mail, door drops, the internet, branding in store, commercial text messages and telephone sales. According to the survey, advertising has three main roles:

- It is a source of information for new products/services and for prices and promotions.
- It is a significant source of entertainment.
- It plays a role in our everyday culture: 'Advertising is part of everyday culture in the same way that television programmes are part of culture. Advertising is recognised as being a source of entertainment as well as information' (ASA, 2002: 7).

This defence attempts to portray advertising as an essentially benign source of information. Advertising, so the argument goes, has no influence on the initial purchasing decision: what it does is help the purchaser choose one brand from the many different available brands that are on offer. This was in fact the defence used by the advertising industry when fighting the ban on cigarette advertising and has also been used in the debate over the relationship between advertising and obesity. The argument is that as the smoker wants to smoke, he has already made the decision to buy cigarettes when he goes into a shop. Adverts for cigarettes do not make people smoke – what the adverts do is help the individual decide which brand to choose from the many brands available on the shelf. Cigarette advertising is therefore little more than an education process.

Is it good that we accept advertising so easily? And is it so apparently harmless and neutral? It is true that advertising attracts strong opinions either for or against, as is illustrated by these two conflicting views:

> *The modern world depends on advertising. Without it, producers and distributors would be unable to sell, buyers would not know about and continue to remember products or services and the modern industrial world would collapse.* (Jefkins and Yasdin, 2000: 2)

> Advertising is: *A manipulative tool, controlling the markets by creating false needs in consumers, and by extolling a general ethos of consumption whereby all needs come to be fulfilled through the purchase of goods in the marketplace* (Leiss et al., 1997: 18).

The argument that advertising attempts to persuade us to perform actions that we would not otherwise do is not a new one. As we saw in Chapter 2, theorists have long believed that the 'mass media' could, and did, influence perceptions and that it has more properties akin to propaganda than persuasion.

Children in the UK will see around 10,000 TV adverts (Piachaud, 2007) per year, leading to concerns that there are links between advertising and behaviour. The issue of childhood obesity and the link with 'junk food' advertising on TV is just one example here. A 2009 report commissioned by the Department for Children, Schools and Families highlighted the scale of the impact of advertising aimed specifically at children, with an estimated £100bn spent each year on advertising to children. The report's author, Professor David Buckingham, argued that children as young as five needed lessons in how to deal with the advertising campaigns aimed at them. Companies are increasingly using schools and playgrounds to conduct their market research, distribute free samples, and advertise their products using a variety of creative means. Nestle and Kellogg sponsor school awards, Tesco and Cadbury run promotions offering vouchers for computers for schools. Outside school, the report found that children were spending increasing amounts of time in 'branded leisure centres'.

Critics of advertising often talk about the way in which it stimulates and creates artificial wants and desires, that we are driven to consume – to buy a new car, for example – because of the power of advertising. But far from being the passive victims of advertising, as this argument might suggest, we are aware of what advertising is attempting to do and we are still prepared to play along with it because as consumers we feel in control of the process: 'It is recognised by consumers that advertising does create aspirations, something that has both positive and negatives attached to it. Advertising is seen to increase social pressures and to make people want ever more items. While this might mean that some people try to buy what they cannot really afford – it is also believed by a few more sophisticated consumers that this encourages economic growth in society' (Brassington and Pettitt, 2000: 593).

However, there are those who now argue that the power of advertising has become too great and that this benign view is no longer tenable and its power needs to be curtailed and controlled. According to the pressure group Compass (Gannon and Lawson, 2009), advertising has made a decisive contribution to our wasteful society because it aims to create dissatisfaction and an insatiable desire for more. In order to satisfy such desires we have been encouraged into higher and higher levels of debt and have helped create a society of waste, with almost half of the clothes in British wardrobes unworn and 900 million items of clothing sent to landfill, along with an estimated 13 million toys and 1 million tonnes of discarded electronic goods. If as a society we are serious about taking action on global warming then such waste needs to be stopped, and advertising – which helps create the desire – needs to be controlled.

How is PR different to advertising?

Brassington and Pettitt (2000: 783) explain the relationship between advertising and PR like this:

> *Advertising is usually about talking to customers or potential customers. Public relations defines a much broader range of target audiences, some of*

*whom have no direct trading relationship with the organisation, and thus
PR encompasses a wide variety of communication needs and objectives
not necessarily geared towards an eventual sale.*

Look again at the definition of PR provided by the Chartered Institute of
Public Relations that we used in the previous chapter: 'Public relations is about
reputation – the result of what you do, what you say and what others say about
you … ' By linking PR to an organisation's reputation, we immediately have a
wider definition that is associated with the relationships a company has with its
stakeholders who may or may not contribute to its sales.

Despite this it has certainly been the case that most marketing theorists believe
that PR is subordinate to marketing while marketing professional and academics
(Kitchen, 2002) see PR as a subsidiary of marketing and used simply to support
marketing goals. This role, however, according to PR academics ignores its wider
potential. Kitchen (2002), for example, argues that the role of PR is to look after
the nature and quality of the relationship between an organisation and its various
publics. In order to fulfil that objective, PR has to engage in a number of activities.

Advertising aims to persuade people to take a desired action, while PR aims to
create mutual understanding between an organisation and its publics.

PR and advertising occupy entirely different parts of the business world and
neither is more important than the other. While we have looked at the differences between PR, advertising and marketing, in practice of course they do
work together and few product launches would use one to the exclusion of the
other. Indeed, as we shall see below, for many in-house PR practitioners, and
practitioners working in consumer PR consultancies, the majority of their work
is aimed at supporting the organisation's marketing campaign.

Advertising agents and PR consultants

One of the most important differences between advertising and PR is that an
advertiser pays the media owner for the space to advertise a product so there
is a clear financial link between the advertiser and media owner. Furthermore,
the media owner offers financial commitments and inducements to advertisers
by discounting their rates as an incentive to attract them. By contrast, PR has
no, or should not have any, financial link with a media owner.

When a PR practitioner sends out a press release to the media in the hope
that it will get used, there is no control over its final destination. Assuming the
PR practitioner has carried out all the correct procedures – addressed the media
release to the right person, made sure it is relevant, and that all the information
is correct and in the right place – there is still no guarantee that the release will
be used or that it will be quoted in the correct context by the media.

There has been friction between advertising and PR because some short-
sighted PR practitioners have tried to sell PR as a cheaper alternative to

advertising. Traditional advertising costs such as those for TV, display advertising in newspapers, and magazines have increased dramatically over the past 20 years. In response to this some PR companies have attempted to sell themselves as a cheaper and more effective alternative and this has created problems for some publications. For example, when I was editor of a business magazine I heard of some PR companies saying to potential clients 'We can save you money by cutting your advertising budget and transferring the money to spending on PR.' Firms that had once advertised in the magazine said they would be prepared to contribute editorially but would no longer advertise. This meant the magazine would suffer financially. Such a strategy, however, is very short-sighted as most specialist magazines and newspapers will depend on their advertising revenue. If the magazine advertising revenue falls and it has to go out of business the PR company has then lost an editorial outlet.

Marketing public relations

The PR that specifically supports sales activity is marketing public relations (MPR). Its purpose, as defined by one of its key theorists (Kitchen, 2002), is to gain awareness and build sales through relationships between consumers and brands. In effect this means using PR as an essential part of marketing activity.

Marketing public relations is sometimes interchangeable with the term 'integrated marketing communications', and is indicative of a wider trend where once the separate disciplines not only work together but have increasingly lost the boundaries between them. The theory of 'integrated marketing' was originally developed in 1993 by the American author Don Schutz, who claimed that integrated marketing was the marketing theory that reflected a new age, where the balance of power had shifted from the producer to the consumer. Integrated marketing communications is a 'holistic' approach to marketing communications and will use any element that might be appropriate – advertising, PR, sponsorship, or brand management, in one integrated campaign. One practical outcome of this was the trend by PR and advertising agencies to combine and offer an integrated or 'one-stop shop' where all the required services can be found by clients under one roof.

Research in 2006 by the Chartered Institute of Public Relations identified that traditional display advertising in magazines, newspapers, and on television accounted for 40% of the UK's marketing budgets. The remaining 60% comprised 'below-the-line' activity such as sales promotion, direct marketing, PR, and sponsorship. And in this subgroup, areas such as brand PR and sponsorship were growing fastest. Revenues have grown by 6.8% since 2001 and their combined markets are currently worth around £3.6billion (CIPR, 2006). What these figures demonstrate is that overall PR is growing faster than traditional advertising and this may then lead to a realignment in marketing budgets. The report's author, Professor Philip Kitchen, is a long-term proponent about the benefits of marketing PR and argues that if it is adopted then its share of the marketing budget will increase and become the more important part of the marketing activity. Kitchen (2002) believes that MPR adds value to advertising campaigns. While it cannot substitute for advertising, it can make it work harder.

SUMMARY

Modern marketing is more than just organising a campaign to sell products or services. Marketing needs to be at the very heart of what a company or organisation does. In traditional marketing theory, marketing is the overall directing pilot, with advertising and PR as subdivisions.

This chapter has explored the similarities and differences between marketing, advertising and public relations. In some of the literature (not all of it academic), PR has sometimes been seen as the 'poor' relation, dominated by its better known and more effective elder siblings, advertising and marketing. Marketing provides the overall direction for the sales function while advertising and PR are tactical tools used as part of the campaign. PR advocates argue that it has more to offer a company or organisation than simply supporting the sales function, important as that is. PR can play a role in helping to shape the strategic direction of the company or organisation and should therefore be as close to the centre of power and influence as possible.

In practice, PR can and does support the marketing and sales function and a specific discipline, marketing public relations, has evolved to do just this. In many ways, this activity is at the cutting-edge of marketing and sales initiatives. Its proponents believe that PR will then be better placed to take advantage of new forms of communications such as guerrilla marketing.

REPUTATION MANAGEMENT

By the end of this chapter you will:

- see why an organisation's reputation matters
- understand why some people believe reputation management is the most important function of PR
- appreciate how a poor reputation can impact on the financial performance of a company
- understand the argument that PR only has a limited impact on reputation

INTRODUCTION

Although the definition currently used by the CIPR firmly associates PR with reputation management, it is in fact a relatively recent association and not one that has met with universal agreement among PR theorists. In this chapter we explore the debate for and against the argument that PR is, or should be, about reputation management.

This debate is not, however, an obscure one carried out between academics in the pages of academic journals. It goes right to the heart of what PR is. The protagonists in the debate are impressive: on one side there are the executives running companies who believe that maintaining and enhancing their company's corporate reputation should be the priority of the company's PR. On the other side are PR theorists who believe that simply associating PR with reputation management limits its role and does little to enhance its effectiveness.

WHAT IS A CORPORATE REPUTATION?

Dowling (1994: 18) defines corporate reputation as 'The evaluation (respect, esteem, estimation) in which an organisation's image is held by people'. Argenti and Druckenmiller (2004: 369) state that reputation is 'The collective representation of multiple constituencies' images of a company built up over time and based on a company's identity programs, its performance and how constituencies have perceived its behaviour' (1994: 18).

A corporate reputation is the 'collective representation' of a series of images and perceptions generated from many different opinions about the company. Building and maintaining a good corporate reputation involves dealing with a number of stakeholders who might all have a different opinion or view about the company but collectively contribute to the overall reputation.

According to L'Etang 'The emergence of corporate reputation as a concept and practice signifies the complex structures, instant communications and symbolic sophistication of contemporary developed worlds' (2006: 48). Those specialising in corporate reputation aim to help organisational insiders and outsiders make sense of organisational behaviour and media interpretations and to answer such questions as:

- What is this organisation all about?
- Why does it do what it does?
- Why has it done what it's done?

Reputation is created outside of the organisation on the basis of numerous subjective impressions. L'Etang says *'Reputation is a constant dynamic process of evolution, subject to review and re-evaluation we may make judgements about a company's reputation without having had any direct experience ourselves of that organisation. While reputation may be seen as some sort of generalised "public opinion", it is also the case that there may be varying or several reputations of an individual or organisation'* (2006: 50). For example, the investors in a company, who derive large dividends when the company makes a profit, might view a company differently from the workforce, who may believe their pay is too low.

Companies with good reputations are held in high regard – they produce good quality products we like and use, provide good customer service, and give customers what they want by listening and responding to their concerns. A good corporate reputation is not just limited to customer service; modern consumers are also concerned with a company's environmental and ethical practices. For example, the Co-operative Bank has an ethical investment policy, promising not to finance any organisations that contribute to global warming, use child labour, or manufacture weapons. In another example, in 2009 Cadbury Dairy Milk was certified as Fair Trade, meaning that Cadbury would pay their suppliers in the developing world a fair wage. For 21st century companies, a good reputation is reliant on more than just customer service.

Companies with a poor reputation will often deliver poor customer service and little value for money; they may also produce poor quality goods. A company may produce a good quality product but as we saw in the case of Marks & Spencer (see Box 3.1, page 35), if that product is seen as being out of date and is not what consumers want then that company's reputation and finances will suffer. Corporate reputation is vitally important because a direct link has been found between company reputation, good or bad, and financial performance.

Box 4.1 Reputation and finance

The Hill and Knowlton study, *Return on Reputation* (Corporate Reputation Watch, 2006) focuses on the significant role that corporate reputation plays in investment analysts' decisions when assessing company performance. The results are striking – reputation is a critical deciding factor on a global scale. The results of the study showed that:

- Setting financial performance aside, for 53% of respondents 'quality of management' is by far the single most important factor that drives a company's reputation.
- A strong leadership team, keeping promises, and corporate strategy are just as valuable as financial performance.
- Nearly half of those surveyed, 46%, say that the CEO's reputation is an extremely important factor when determining whether to recommend a certain company as an investment.
- 85% of participants argue that the CEO should be let go if their behaviour negatively impacts on the company's reputation.
- Nearly all analysts surveyed, 93%, say that clear communication with key stakeholders factors into their financial assessment of a company.
- 79% say that poor communication would contribute to a negative rating.

The financial implications and effects of good corporate reputation were explored by Dowling (1994), who argued that a good corporate reputation works against competitors by inhibiting their mobility and effectively acting as a barrier to market entry. It also acts as a signal of the quality of a firm's products to customers and consumers. A good reputation can attract better applicants for jobs as well and make it easier to raise finance from banks and investors.

Conversely a poor reputation can harm a company in a number of ways. It has a direct impact on a company's financial performance and can lead to poor staff morale, which then contributes to a further decline in services (see Box 4.2).

Box 4.2   British Airways and the Reputation Nightmare

In April 2008, British Airways opened its new terminal at London's Heathrow Airport. Terminal 5 (T5) had taken 15 years to plan and was built at a cost of £4.3 billion. Its opening was meant to herald a new era of hassle-free flying for passengers and was hugely important to the future of BA, the sole operator for T5. On its first day of operation catastrophe struck as flights had to be cancelled because of a series of relatively simple problems,which, when combined, created huge difficulties. There was a shortage of baggage handlers, some of whom could not get into the staff car park, whilst others had not been security cleared in time for the opening. Those who did turn up had had insufficient training and did not know how to work the new computer system.

These problems mounted and their scale grew. Flights were unable to leave or land due to unclaimed luggage. A BA spokeswoman said on the first day 'We have had a few minor problems in our first day of operation in T5. It is not unexpected following one of the most complex and largest airport moves in history … '

That, however, was not the end of the fiasco. After a day that the Chief Executive of BA, Willie Walsh, declared was 'not our finest hour', the situation got worse because of the build-up of problems.

With the world's media watching and blogs circulating, recounting the many hours of suffering by unhappy passengers who were eager to share their experiences, there was no shortage of allocating blame. Disgruntled BA baggage handlers were unhappy at being blamed for the situation and were keen to tell their side of the story. They used social network sites to air their grievances. One blogger said that the opening 'turned into a shambles the moment the doors opened … '.

While BA claimed that a lack of 'staff familiarisation' was to blame, the staff pointed to insufficient training and support. A staff member said that, 'During the inadequate training days prior to the opening, any staff questions were bounced back with "I don't know" and "It will be clear on the day". Staff signage is non-existent and, quite frankly, how are we expected to help customers if we are not helped first?'

Facebook comments by unhappy staff undoubtedly contributed to BA's problems and harmed its reputation, making it, from every angle, a PR disaster.

THE RELATIONSHIP BETWEEN PR AND REPUTATION

The debate about organisational reputation and its association with PR is based around the following questions:

- How is reputation defined?
- How is a good or bad reputation measured? What criteria are used?

- Can PR influence or have an impact on reputation?
- What influence does PR have on the factors that determine reputation?

BOX 4.3   Cadbury and the disclosure problem

Those who believe that it is hard for corporate communications/PR professionals to manage a company's reputation would argue that so much of what constitutes a company's reputation – its products, the way staff interact with customers, etc.– is not directly controlled by the PR function.

As discussed in Chapter 3 (see Box 3.2, page 41), in 2006 chocolate giant Cadbury recalled a range of products because a batch had been contaminated with salmonella. While no cases of illness were directly attributed to the contaminated product, the general consensus was that the incident hurt Cadbury because its reputation suffered.

For quite understandable and non-sinister reasons, Cadbury decided not to publicise the issue when it first emerged, but when the story did break it looked as if Cadbury had been hiding something. As the story unfolded the corporate PR team appeared to be reacting to media stories rather than taking control of the situation. The message sent out attempted to reassure the public – that in its long history Cadbury products had never harmed anyone and the company could therefore be trusted.

One of Cadbury's problems was that it had taken too long to inform the Food Standards Agency (FSA) that there had been contamination. Cadbury discovered the contamination in January 2006 but did not inform the FSA until May. The FSA then forced Cadbury to tell the public. The Cadbury salmonella scare illustrates the commercial impact of a crisis. Its investment broker, JP Morgan, estimated the cost of product withdrawals at £5 million and another £20 million was lost in sales because of a lack of consumer confidence in the brand.

The issue from a PR perspective is whether the company made the correct decision in not saying anything in January. Being forced to come clean by the FSA made Cadbury appear guilty and as a result the company's reputation was damaged.

Advocating reputation management

Those who view PR as reputation management have an almost messianic belief in its role and the impact this can have on PR. They argue that it offers a clear, new direction, enabling PR to overcome some of the problems of definition discussed in Chapter 2. They regard reputation management as something that will enhance PR's stature, perceived value, and central role within organisations.

Acquiring a good reputation

How do companies gain a good reputation? Some advocates of reputation management would say that a company's reputation can be developed in a planned manner.

According to (2006) research conducted by Weber Shandwick and the Reputation Institute, there are six core elements that together form the building blocks of corporate reputation:

- *Responsibility*: supporting worthy causes, demonstrating environmental responsibility and community/societal responsibility.
- *Communications*: marked by transparency, full disclosure and openness to dialogue.
- *Products and services*: offering high quality and innovation, as well as customer satisfaction.
- *Talent*: rewarding employees fairly, promoting diversity, and demonstrating an ability to attract and retain staff.
- *Financial metrics*: outpacing competitors and demonstrating financial soundness and long-term investment value.
- *Leadership*: established by the CEO and senior team and showing good governance and ethical conduct.

The company that is aware of its external environment and responds to it by just doing the right thing will see its reputation grow and improve.

> *Better regarded companies build their reputations by developing practices which integrate social and economic considerations into their competitive strategies. They not only do things right – they do the right things. In doing so they act like good citizens. They initiate policies that reflect their core values, that consider the joint welfare of investors, customers and employees, that invoke concern for the development of local communities; and that ensure the quality and environmental soundness of the technologies, products and services.* (Fombrun, 1996: 87)

Fombrun's definition of how to build a good reputation requires companies to take the right environmental action and involve stakeholders, such as local communities, in the decision-making process. Fombrun's article was written in 1996, but it is only relatively recently that this theory has moved into mainstream business practice. In Chapter 6 we will look in more detail at how companies are not just taking such actions because they believe it will make them look good to the outside world, and therefore enhance their reputation, but also because they genuinely believe these are *the* right actions to take.

A 2009 IPSOS Mori survey – *Perceptions of Business Transparency* – highlights the reputation problems that business in general had following the 'credit crunch' of 2008/09. According to the survey, carried out on behalf of the Institute of Business Ethics, half of the British adults surveyed said that the conduct of banks during the financial crisis had damaged their trust in all businesses. The reputation of companies and brands has suffered and companies would have to work hard in order to rebuild them. Significantly, the survey also stated that one of the ways in which trust could be rebuilt was through greater transparency in the way in which companies reported their actions and conducted their business.

A more traditional understanding of a 'good' reputation is measured by what other businesses think about each others. In 2000, Gardberg and Fombrun (2002: 385) investigated companies in the USA and Europe with both good and bad reputations and found that:

> *Positive nominations by other companies (of companies deemed to have a good reputation) are given to companies with strong corporate brands that have identifiable subsidiary brands often of the same name. The gaining of favourable top-of-mind visibility speaks to the historical associations created in the minds of the public through strategic communications ... Negative associations with some equally strong mega-brands whose names have become synonymous with 'crisis' speaks to the inability these companies have in adjusting public perception.*

Box 4.4   Measures of Corporate Reputation

There are now a number of different indexes which measure corporate reputation. These include:

The Worlds Most Reputable Companies – companies throughout the world rated by consumers in their own country (www.reputationinstitute.com)
Fortune Magazine's Global Most Admired Companies – the 50 most admired companies voted for by business people (www.fortune.com)
Management Today, Britain's Most Admired Companies – awards based on peer reviews of corporate reputation (www.bmac.managementtoday.com)
FTSE 4 Good Index – measures company performance against globally recognised corporate responsibility standards (www.ftse4good.com)
Financial TimesWorld's Most Respected Companies – companies rated by chief executives and business leaders (www.ft.com)

In their (2006) research paper 'Contradictions in 'reputation management'', Campbell et al. suggest that one of the reasons the PR industry likes the idea of the term 'reputation management' is because PR has such a poor reputation: 'The term "public relations" has negative connotations, which lead many practitioners to use alternatives such as "corporate communications". Part of the difficulty in defining Public Relations appears to lie in a reluctance by practitioners and academics to acknowledge that it is linked to propaganda, manipulation and "spin"' (Campbell et al., 2006: 193).

Box 4.5   Shell and the Attempt to Change a Reputation

The energy and petrochemical company Shell is a good example of a company that has seen its reputation damaged by a series of high-profile international events. In 1995, Shell became embroiled in a public dispute with Greenpeace over its plans to decommission the floating oil storage station, Brent Spar. Shell had planned to send Brent Spar to the bottom of the North Atlantic but Greenpeace objected on environmental grounds and campaigners occupied the station for three months until Shell announced it would not sink Brent Spar. During the protest thousands of people in Britain and Europe boycotted Shell products, thereby costing the company millions of dollars.

In 1996 a civil suit was filed against Shell alleging complicity in the deaths of nine men in the Niger Delta. The Ogoni people of the Niger Delta also alleged that Shell's extraction policies in the 1970s and 1980s had caused major damage to Ogoni land. In 2009 Shell agreed an out of court settlement of $15.5 million.

In both cases Shell had lost the PR argument and stood accused of putting profits before principles.

Over a period of time the communications function at Shell attempted to counter negative perceptions about the company through a number of corporate communications measures such as Shell's Sustainability Report, launched in 1997. On their website Shell say, 'We began reporting voluntarily on our social and environmental performance with the first Shell Report that covered 1997. We do it to be open and honest, and to show how we are contributing to sustainable development'. Shell has produced environmental reports to counter the perception that it does not care about the environment and also participated in the UN Global Compact, a policy initiative for businesses committed to aligning their operations to principles in the areas of human rights, labour, the environment, and anti-corruption. It has also adopted International Financial Reporting Standards and participated in the Dow Jones Sustainability index in an effort to demonstrate its openness and transparency.

However, there will always be questions about why the company carried out these actions – did they do so because they were right and worthwhile, or were they forced into this by a critical audience?

Factors involved in developing a good reputation

These are some the factors that can assist companies/organisations in developing a good reputation:

- Quality of products and services – this is absolutely critical, if the quality of what is produced is not good enough then no amount of PR activity can disguise it.
- Customer relationship and listening to customers' opinions – if companies do not treat their customers well they will simply go elsewhere.
- Strong corporate governance and the organisational culture and structure – all of these matter not only with external customers, but also internally with staff.
- Contract fulfilment – not delivering on time and when promised matters.
- Chief Executive Officer's reputation, vision and leadership – research from a number of sources including research carried out by Burson-Marsteller, their report 'Building CEO Capital', highlights the influence that the reputation of a Chief Executive Officer can have on the share price of a public company.
- Developing a media profile – media management requires good, diligent management of the media and is central to reputation management. Companies should identify which media are the most influential within its target group and supply the press with information that is accurate and useful. They must build relationships with journalists and look for triggers within issues, as well monitor the media and other user groups in order to keep ahead of the issues.
- Community relations – successful companies can create problems for themselves by not paying attention to the community in which they operate. Bad news travels quickly so maintaining good community relations is vital.

Online reputation management

Electronic communication has brought a whole new dimension to communication. Conversations and opinions that were once shared face to face between people are now, within some age groups, conducted in public and between a number of people. Entire online communities have developed around shared topics, issues, and locations.

The proliferation of online content encompassing news sites, blogs, forums, social networks, user-generated content and videos now requires companies to understand what is being said about their brand, product or service on these electronic forums. As we have seen with British Airways and the opening of Terminal 5 (see Box 4.2), blogs and forums have the potential to damage a company's reputation. One of the problems companies face when dealing with online communication is the speed at which poor or damaging information can spread, sometimes causing an almost unmanageable whirlwind of publicity. In October 2008 a CNN-sponsored, citizen-journalism site published an article stating, falsely, that Apple CEO Steve Jobs had been rushed to hospital after suffering a suspected heart-attack. As a result company shares fell by 5%. In another example involving Apple, stock suffered a $4.50 per share drop in price and a $4billion loss in market capitalisation in just six minutes when a popular blog, Engadget, published a leaked but fake internal email from Apple Inc. that claimed the release of the iphone and the company's Leopard server project would be delayed.

Such situations are nightmares for CEOs as highlighted by Weber Shandwick's survey, which states that 7 out 10 CEOs are worried about the potential threat electronic communications pose to their company.

The PR industry is now active in monitoring electronic media and firms are developing an array of tools which can monitor what is being said about a company, track the demographics of those saying it, and devise an array of strategies to manage the situation.

AGAINST REPUTATION MANAGEMENT

PR academics who are attempting to build an independent reputation for the discipline are critical of the idea that reputation management offers a new direction for PR and that it will free it from its associations with spin. They believe that PR can play an important role in helping to shape the strategic direction of a company and that simply equating it with reputation management limits its capacity to play such a central role.

In fact, they believe that far from leading PR into new areas it would cause damage to PR's reputation: 'Reputation management will lead public relations even further towards a superficial role of spin doctoring and image-making' (Hutton, 2000). Hutton states that the advocates of reputation management see reputation management as 'A guiding new force or paradigm for the entire field' and that 'Concepts such as "reputation" and "image" are not something that can be managed directly, but are omnipresent and the global result of a firm's or individual's behaviour. Attempting to manage one's reputation might be likened to trying to manage one's own popularity: a rather awkward, superficial and potentially self-defeating endeavour (Hutton, 2000: 201).

The specific criticism of reputation management is that in practice, PR only has a limited influence on the main factors that influence reputation because they are not under the direct control of the PR/communications function. If the product or the service is not good enough then the reputation of the company will fall no matter how good the PR might be.

The critics of defining PR as reputation management argue that it will not lead it away from accusations of spin, rather the reverse will be the case: 'The rise of ... "reputation management", "perception management", and "image management" appears to be an ominous trend for the field, partly because they have come into favor for most of the wrong reasons: the tendency of managers who lack training in public relations to think in superficial terms like "image" and "perception"' (Hutton, 2000: 2006).

Perhaps the limited role that PR has in the area of reputation management can be illustrated by the way one author, Grahame Dowling (1994: 85), plays down the role of PR in creating reputation: 'It is a mistake to entrust to a spin doctor the task of trying to build a better reputation'. The job, he states, is so important to a company that it should be taken on board by the whole senior management of that company.

While PR and reputation management are intricately linked they are still different functions in practice:

> *PR is more specific and handles areas such as: media relations, public affairs, crisis management, event management and branding.*
>
> *Reputation management is more holistic in its approach and involves all employees.*

Traditional PR can be seen as less strategic, non-integrated (not involving the whole organisation), and focused on the short-term. It aims to present the best possible image of an organisation, is largely media-relations focused, and focuses its communications on transactional stakeholders. In contrast the supporters of reputation management would argue that their programmes are more strategic and integrated (involving the whole organisation) and because they have to look at the whole company and the impact that it makes on the entire organisation, their approach is holistic and long-term. Reputation management involves all employees, aims to deliver an image and brand promise, uses all forms and opportunities to communicate policy and values, and places greater emphasis on multiple stakeholder relationships.

BOX 4.6   What Can PR Affect?

To illustrate how difficult it is to manage a good corporate reputation consider the factors listed below. Each is important for establishing a good corporate reputation but not all of these can be controlled or influenced by the PR function in an organisation:

- Good corporate governance – the policies, processes and customs by which a company is governed.
- Increased share value – rises in the company share price.
- A reputation for innovation – because innovation is associated with listening to customers.
- Corporate Social Responsibility (CSR) –an important consideration for many people when assessing good corporate reputation.

- Role and leadership of CEO – the choice of Chief Executive can influence the reputation of a company.
- Satisfied employees – the reverse is also true. Dissatisfied employees can create problems, as British Airways found to their cost at the opening of Terminal 5 (see Box 4.2).

An organisation's PR function cannot possibly control all of these factors, but if this function is part of company's structure at the highest level it can help to shape issues around corporate governance and corporate social responsibility. A good PR function may even be able to help with employee relations.

A 'WRONG' INDUSTRY: HOW AN INDUSTRY'S REPUTATION AFFECTS BUSINESSES

Some companies operate in industrial and commercial sectors with a poor reputation. The companies themselves may possess all the requirements of a good reputation – good corporate, governance, CSR and innovation, and excellent customer service – but if they are unfortunate enough to work in an industry with a bad reputation they will face an uphill PR battle. An industry may have acquired a bad reputation because of its past business practices or because what it produces is now viewed differently by the public. Below are some examples of industries that have such a reputation:

- Fast food – blamed for obesity, environmental damage, and the homogenisation of the high street.
- Tobacco – now that we know that nicotine is addictive and that smoking is harmful to health, the sale and promotion of tobacco are viewed by many as a dubious business.
- Alcohol – the sales of cheap alcohol have been blamed for the rise in binge-drinking and subsequent anti-social behaviour.
- Oil – environmental disasters, suspicions of corruption, and unfair working practices in the developing world have all contributed to the negative image of the oil industry.
- Pharmaceuticals – animal testing and the high price of drugs are issues that have damaged the reputation of the drug industry.

A PR practitioner working in any of these industries will have a much harder job than practitioners working in industries with good reputations. Companies in a 'wrong' industry will often find that their actions are more closely scrutinised by the media and pressure groups than those in other industries. However, it is still possible to run a successful and profitable business in an industry with a bad reputation. Consumers may like a product even though they know excessive consumption is bad for them, or they may need to use a product regardless of what they think of the industry.

SUMMARY

Reputation management is a divisive issue in PR theory and practice. Some would argue that PR is all about reputation management – that because a poor reputation affects a company financially, protecting and enhancing reputations should be the main concerns of the in-house PR function. Advocates of reputation management also believe that it can enhance the PR industry's own image. If PR has a clear and understandable definition then critics will no longer be able to claim that PR has no substance. This, then, is the promise of reputation management by its proponents and it has had a powerful impact on thinking within the industry. It is the 'Big Idea' and a seductive promise. Yet there are those who would warn that the reality is very different because what constitutes reputation, namely the factors that determine it, are, generally speaking, outside the control of the communications/PR function. That does not mean to say that reputation management does not matter, it clearly does, and those companies and organisations that are unfortunate enough to have had a bad reputation will often suffer financially. However, an over-emphasis on reputation might come at the expense of other aspects of the communications process. Companies must adopt pluralistic approaches to managing risk and reputation management's emphasis must be one within many pro-active approaches. Reputation management must be strategic in nature and involve everyone, not just managers. In fact reputation management should not stop with senior management and staff who deal with customers: all employees should be involved.

CRISIS MANAGEMENT: PUBLIC RELATIONS CENTRE STAGE

By the end of this chapter you will:

- understand the nature of crisis communications
- appreciate the importance of the crisis communications plan
- recognise why a crisis handled badly can have a negative impact on a company's financial performance

INTRODUCTION

Crisis communications and issues management are popular prospective career choices for many PR graduates and it's not hard to see why. A big crisis grabs media attention and in the middle of it, there you are, responsible for all the communications. You are right at the forefront of the media action, dealing with a thousand and one different demands – calls from the media, clarifications, and requests for interviews. Within the crisis you are thinking on your feet: it is a fast-moving, challenging, stimulating environment and you are often functioning on adrenalin and nerves. To be able to respond effectively in a crisis, to take control of events and not be overwhelmed by them, requires planning in order to ensure that every eventuality is covered.

This chapter looks at two separate but related fields, firstly, the management of communications during the crisis, and secondly, the field of issues management. Issues management is the attempt to prevent a situation becoming a crisis through the systematic identification of and action on public policy matters (whether national or local) that might be of concern to an organisation.

WHAT IS A CRISIS?

A crisis is are indiscriminate and can happen to any organisation or company, large or small, and is no respecter of geography or reputation. There are the big, instantly identifiable, national and international crises such as an an airplane crash, or natural disasters such as floods and storms and accidents which (depending on their size) will also attract headlines (the miners trapped underground in Chile would be an example). Crises are relative – to a business a crisis can be a fall in sales or a drop in profits, a crisis to a school might be a poor Ofsted report, for a health authority a budget overspend or a case of MRSA in a hospital. To a police authority, the crisis might be a death in custody of a prisoner. Crises can also often attract unwarranted outside attention. These situations are all very different and may appear to those outside the organisation to be either trivial or irrelevant in the big scheme of things, but to those involved they can be stressful and cause major problems.

A single day's newspaper headlines can illustrate the different nature of these crises – a retail giant under fire for falling sales; an industry being criticised by MPs for its failure to change fast enough; another company being referred to the Office of Fair Trading; a female executive being passed over for promotion; one company has a problem with executive pay while another is imposing pay restraints on the workforce.

The common element in all these stories is that the companies involved have moved away from the business pages where they are generally happy to be and where, to some extent, they can control the agenda and ended up on the front page. This exposes them to a more critical, less sympathetic, less understanding audience who will often judge them by different standards. What suffers most in this context will be the company's reputation and that, as we have seen in Chapter 4, will have a financial impact on the company.

Is there a definition of a crisis that will satisfactorily cover all these different situations both large and small? From a communications perspective, Steven Fink offers the following: 'A crisis occurs when an event increases in intensity, falls under close scrutiny of the news, media or government, interferes with normal business opportunities, devalues a positive public image, and has an adverse effect on a business's bottom line' (Fink in Penrose, 2000: 159)

The common situation that all companies and institutions in the above example face is that the degree of media scrutiny has reached a crisis level.

Regester and Larkin (2005) highlight some of the consequences of a crisis: 'Failure to manage stakeholder perceptions around reputation risk issues will *always* impact on the financial bottom line, usually in a combination of the following':

- Products/services boycotted/abandoned.
- Share price collapse: 'Institution managers lose confidence in management – not because of the crisis event, but perceptions of management's ability to deal with it'.

- Loss of competitive advantage.
- Imposition of new, restrictive regulations – because actions of one company could lead to new restrictions on a whole industry.

The degree of media scrutiny has also been used by other commentators. In 1984, Lagadec defined a crisis as,

> *a situation in which numerous organizations are faced with critical problems, experience both sharp external pressure and bitter internal tensions, and are then brutally and for an extended period thrust to the centre stage and hurled one against the other ... all in a society of mass communication, in other words in direct contact, with the certainty of being at the top of the news on radio and television and in the press for some time.* (Ogrizek and Guillery, 1999)

A crisis tends to create doubt and suspicion about the reality and the dangers that could follow.

By nature a crisis is unpredictable and can occur quickly and with no warning, and although the initial problem might be short-term it may have long-term consequences. For example, it took Bristish Airway's reputation six months to recover from the first day debacle at its new Heathrow terminal. That is why all organisations should be prepared for a crisis and plan their response suitably.

Crisis communications is not the same as crisis management. Crisis management looks to the future, attempting to anticipate and prepare for possible events which might disrupt important relationships, either with customers or suppliers. Potential crises include natural disaster damage from floods, fires and break-ins, and as businesses have become more dependent on electronic communication their vulnerability has increased through a reliance on computer systems and telecommunications. When internet and email systems fail businesses are often cut off from customers, suppliers and other stakeholders – an indication of our dependence on such forms of communication.

Another sad reflection of modern-day life is the way that commercial interests are regarded as a legitimate target for terrorist activity. Incidents such as the London Bishopgate and the Manchester city centre bombings graphically illustrate this. The modern business, often at the insistence of their insurance company, now has to consider and plan for all the different types of crises that might affect it and produce a contingency plan about the way they would respond. Crisis management planning attempts to anticipate how a crisis might impact on a business and prepare contingency plans to enable them to get back functioning as quickly as possible after the incident.

Crisis management, then, is an organisation's planned response to a crisis and this has to be done in an effective, timely manner. It involves planning and coordinating actions to prevent a crisis from escalating: it also provides decision makers with the required information and arrangements to use in a crisis.

An important part of the crisis plan is the Communication Plan because if a company is faced with a crisis, then how it responds, how it communicates, how quickly it responds, and the messages it sends out can affect the company and its reputation more seriously than the incident itself. The importance of communications in a crisis cannot be underestimated. In an age of 24-hour rolling news coverage and a media hungry and desperate to fill time, space and pages, not responding promptly and correctly can send out the wrong message and create further unintended problems. In April 2010 the explosion on the BP oil rig, the Deepwater Horizon, in the Gulf of Mexico, became a full-blown PR disaster for the company following a series of ill-advised comments and actions by the then chief executive, Tony Hayward. Comments such as he 'wanted his life back' and going on a sailing holiday made him appear uncaring and unconcerned, and detracted from the clean-up efforts the company were carrying out.

Experience shows that companies will react in one of two ways to a crisis – they will either stick their head in the sand, say nothing, and wait until the media siege goes away, or they will respond as effectively and as quickly as possible to the crisis and, by doing so, attempt to control the media agenda. The first response used to be the traditional way that businesses would communicate. Times have since changed and, whether rightly or wrongly, poor communication or poor communication skills can have a significant impact on how people perceive a company – Tony Hayward from BP rapidly became known as the 'most hated man in America' and this eventually led to him losing his position. In a crisis situation a company is on trial and in some cases it might be for their very existence. Although larger companies may survive a crisis because of their reputation, research suggests that 80% of smaller, lesser-known companies, without a comprehensive plan, vanish within two years of suffering a major disaster (Brown, 1993).

THE CRISIS COMMUNICATION PLAN

A crisis communication plan will contain the following common elements:

- The plan.
- The management team.
- The communication process.
- The post-crisis evaluation.

In the course of preparing the plan the following issues must be addressed:

- Tough questions need to be raised: What is the worst thing that could happen to the organisation? How likely is this? Is there anything that could be done to minimise the risk of it happening?
- Different scenarios should be graded. For example, a power or telecoms failure would mean a building being cordoned off or employees unable to

get to work. How prepared is the company to deal with each scenario? A basic grading system should be used to illustrate the readiness – level one for the least prepared and level five for most prepared.

- What impact? Once the major risks are established, the impact on customers, suppliers, staff and neighbours should be analysed. The financial systems that would be affected should also be looked at. Can the company pay and be paid? How long could the business continue to function at a reduced capacity and what level would that be at?

The plan

The job of the plan is quite literally to keep the business alive in order to protect staff, save jobs, preserve reputation, and keep the company's capacity to operate. It will have been prepared by either the company's in-house communications team or specialist external consultants. Although there is a world of difference between the impact of a bomb, storm or commercial problem on a company, it is likely that the communication response will follow broadly similar lines whatever the crisis. The plan will outline the procedures that will give effective communication during the crisis, clearly identifying all areas of responsibility. It will also include a timetable of action showing when actions need to be completed by.

The management team

During the crisis the company's senior management must be its public face, as this is what the public wants and expects – answers and explanations from the top people. They have come to epitomise their businesses and as we have seen in Chapter 4, there is a close correlation between the CEO's reputation and that of the company. The public do not want to see the 'official spokesperson' because, whether or not it is the case, this only gives the impression that they are not treating the issue seriously enough. For the duration of the crisis it must be a senior management priority. If the senior management is not seen as the public face, this suggests that the company does not care or is insensitive, especially in situations where it has been involved in an accident.

Some executives, Sir Richard Branson for example, are comfortable with high profile media exposure and actually seem to relish it. Branson's businesses developed out of his entrepreneurial skills and it makes sense, therefore, that he should be the public face of the company. Branson's media skills have played an important part in the growth of his business and he recognises that to maintain its ongoing reputation he has to maintain that profile. The CEOs of most large public companies, however, are usually professional managers employed for their managerial skills rather than whether or not they can speak effectively in front of the TV cameras. Nowadays though they have to be prepared to learn media skills whether they want to or not. Senior management designated as the company's official spokespeople will undergo rigorous media training by specialist companies usually run by ex-journalists, who will coach them on how to respond under the most difficult and trying circumstances.

The spokespeople must be available 24 hours a day, seven days a week – a requirement that is made easier by mobile phones and laptops. One example of getting it wrong would be Tony Hayward of BP, who never seemed comfortable in the media spotlight and paid the price for this.

The communication process

This section covers how the plan will be put into operation once the crisis actually starts. A clearly mapped programme will list which actions need to be taken and when; a series of post-event milestones will be listed stating what action should be taken and at what time. The plan will vary according to the specific nature of each industry and every incident. If, for example, there have been casualties the priority will be to communicate with the immediate family to inform them and also to establish a telephone hotline to allow relatives to find out the latest news. Delays in doing this, even if they occur for perfectly rational reasons, will not reflect well on the company. The strategy should be pro-active and should aim to put the company in control of events rather than reacting to them.

> *We train people in the skills required to take telephone calls and how to answer them correctly in a crisis because you need a team of at least 10–12 people taking the calls 24 hours a day. You would have one team for the day and the other for the night. But the absolute key to it is that if you want the story to be reasonably balanced you have to be as accessible as possible to the media because if you are not accessible and you are not telling your story, other people tell it for you and you've lost it, so it is an absolute key that companies in industries which are the most vulnerable have the team set-up like that and teams also to take calls from the local community and from local families because they suddenly heard X has blown up and my husband works there.* (Regester, 2007)

This is an excellent example of pro-active planning in the event of a disaster. While the focus for most communication plans is understandably on how to communicate to external audiences, the organisation's own staff should not be ignored. As we have seen from the British Airways T5 example (see Box 4.2), unguarded critical comments by staff on social networking sites can exacerbate a crisis and have a major affect on a company's reputation. The crisis communications plan should consider how any situation will impact on the staff as they can be both the worst and best ambassadors for a company in a time of crisis. Ideally employees should hear news about a situation before it appears in the media and should also know who to call in a time of crisis. Customer-focused staff should have specific literature available on how to respond in such a situation.

Box 5.1 Crisis Rules

Commentators and experienced practitioners in this field believe that there are basic rules that companies should follow when confronted with a crisis.

Michael Regester, co-founder of Regester Larkin, one of the UK's specialist crisis consultancies, explains 'The worst thing is to lie. The second thing is to say nothing. The key is tell it all, tell it fast and tell it truthfully' (Regester Larkin, 2000).

- Tell it all: Try and tell as much as you know as soon as you know it. If the company doesn't have any answers to questions or issues it should honestly say so, get the correct information and then return with the answer.
- Tell it fast: Do so as soon as possible, as delaying bad news can send out the wrong signals and suggest there is something to hide.
- Tell it truthfully: Lying or any form of cover-up will only create a worse situation – there is nothing the media like better than dragging out the truth and watching the twists and turns of those attempting a cover-up.

The post-crisis evaluation

The communication plan should also include a truthful and critical analysis of what happened during the crisis – it will look at how the communications team responded during the crisis, what worked and what didn't, and any lessons that can be learned. The aim should be to learn from the experience.

Box 5.2 New technology and controlling the news agenda

Before the advent of the internet, most people's access to news was limited to traditional sources such as newspapers, radio and TV. The internet and developments such as Twitter have opened up a whole range of information sources and means of communicating which

(Continued)

(Continued)

have added another dimension to news management. An indication of the size of the problem is that there are an estimated 23,000 new blog sites created every day. Nowadays, if someone is unhappy about a company or its products, they can tell not only their friends but the whole world as well. It is the function of PR practitioners to try and control comment and opinions about a company/organisation, responding when negative comments appear. So how can they control what flows in and through the internet? Blogging has never been under anyone's control, which is why it is so disruptive. The disgruntled employee or dissatisfied customer can ignite a full-blown crisis, quickly and on a broad scale.

In the previous chapter we saw how British Airway's problems on the opening of T5 and comments on blogs by staff unhappy at being blamed for the situation added to the company's problems. This was added to by the derogatory comments staff posted on Facebook: one staff member commented that travellers were 'smelly' and that the situation at T5 was shambolic. This is another illustration of the problems that social networks can create for PR practitioners – while BA communications staff appeared to be in control of events their efforts were being undermined by comments on blogs. This also highlights the need to keep staff fully on side during a crisis.

HANDLING A CRISIS
The 2005 London bombings

The London bombings of 7 July 2005, were the type of crisis that organisations hope they will never have to deal with. Sadly nowadays the public sector and emergency services must always be prepared for them. The experience provided two contrasting examples of how to handle communications during a crisis. On the one hand the Transport for London (TfL) press office, which was at the heart of the response to the world's media, won the Crisis Communications category in the 2006 CIPR Excellence Awards for the way it handled the situation. In contrast, aspects of the way the Metropolitan Police dealt with the communication were heavily criticised.

On hearing of the bombings the TfL press office implemented a well-rehearsed crisis communication plan, and within 20 minutes of first hearing about the disaster six TfL press officers arrived in pairs at three Tube stations affected by the bombs to manage the media on site. By 11am the press office had responded to more than 200 interview requests from the world's media and in just one day the press team received at least 2,000 telephone calls.

The Metropolitan Police however were criticised for the way they handled the media following the attacks. According to a critical report, produced by the London Assembly, the response of the Met's communications team – which takes the lead on communication issues in a major incident – was too slow and ineffective. Richard Barnes who was in charge of the review committee on the bombings said: 'During a major incident, people need quick advice and information, yet in 7/7 the first press conference wasn't held (by the police) until 11:15am. Even then, the wrong information was given out in terms of how many explosions there had been'. One criticism by the committee was that the police did not take account of the speed at which the modern media works and that cumulative and sometimes small frustrations built into major problems. This can led to the perception that the organisation was not in control – even though it could well have been.

The Buncefield fire

At 6:02 am on Sunday, 11 December 2005, the Buncefield oil depot in Hertfordshire exploded, an explosion which was heard as far away as Holland. It soon became the UK's largest fire since World War Two. As a case study it is interesting because of the way in which a number of different parties – the police, the local authority and the company owning the depot – responded to different aspects of the crisis.

At 6:04am Hertfordshire police were called and by 6:08 press officers from Hertfordshire Constabulary had been alerted: at 6:50 the first press release from the police was issued. The first briefing was at 8:00am, the first police press conference at 9:00am.

The Hertfordshire police followed its crisis communication plan having learnt from other tragedies. For example, the Chief Constable was moved from management duties to concentrate on dealing exclusively with the media. According to Colin Connolly, head of corporate communications at Hertfordshire Constabulary, one of the problems at the start of the day was dealing with some media reports and speculation that the fire was the result of terrorist activity, so handling that issue and allaying people's fears became a priority: 'We mobilised the media in our canteen and the 9:00am briefing diffused the terror rumour. This meant that we could focus on other messages – not to call 999 and not to panic-buy petrol. On the day messages were that no deaths had been reported and that we were keeping an open mind as to the cause of the fire'.

When the fire started on Sunday morning crisis communications expert Michael Regester was called by the site owner at 6:20.

> *Over the first 24 hours we took 2,000 telephone calls just from the media, we gave 25 live radio and television interviews over the first 24 hours. The only way you could deal with the constant request from all the different kinds of media was to prioritise them, because to be honest if a newspaper from Wales calls up wanting an interview, we would probably not agree to it, but if it's CNN, Sky or the BBC then of course we would. That's the only way you can deal with a fragmented media.* (Regester, 2007)

Case Study: Interview with a Reputation Management Account Director

Andrew Fairburn is an Account Director with Regester Larkin, a specialist reputation strategy and management consultancy. He joined the company in early 2008 and has over 13 years' experience of working in political, crisis and issues management for a number of different consultancies. He advises senior figures from the corporate, charitable and public sectors on how best to handle challenging political or reputation related issues. He also advises overseas governments and international trade related bodies.

What do you like about your job?
Working in issues and crisis management, we get to be involved in a lot of very interesting situations. These might vary from 'traditional' bangs, crashes and spills to fraud, product recalls and corporate restructuring. We also spend a lot of time on helping clients manage ongoing 'issues', many of which have a political component to them. The novelty still hasn't worn off.

What are the most important skills?
I think an understanding of people and how they behave is essential. To communicate with people, you need to be able to understand them. On top of this you need additional attributes, such as being able to write clearly, understand the media and other important stakeholders – political, business, NGOs (Non Governmental Organisations) – and have the ability to prioritise.

Does PR meet your expectations in terms of a career?
Issues and crises management certainly does. It's interesting, policy rich and rarely boring.

Diary: The Reputation Management Account Director
Here is an extract from Andrew's diary

Monday
A colleague and I are in the Gulf working with a couple of major clients in the oil and gas industry. A big part of crisis management is preparing clients for potential crises so that they are able to respond effectively should the worse happen. We're coming to the end of nearly a week in the Gulf in which we have been (a) holding workshops on crisis management best practice, (b) helping clients test crisis management plans and (c) media training key staff.

Tuesday
To make best use of our visit, my colleague and I have bolted on a number of meetings with prospective clients to try to gain new business, a hugely

important part of life in a consultancy. The key is to meet the 'right' people, something which can vary a lot from company to company. On this trip, we met the head of PR for a major state owned oil company, the director of security (who is also responsible for crisis preparation) for another company, as well as a couple of government officials, one of whom offered to put us in touch with the director of communications of a large airline.

Wednesday
After an overnight flight back to London, a busy day in the office awaits. The priority is to catch up with what's been going on with my key clients whilst I was away. This involves a mixture of update meetings with colleagues and calling some clients to check that things are OK. There is also a lot of mundane 'admin' to plough through – sorting out invoices, planning workloads, and arranging the date of a major crisis exercise we're organising for a client.

ISSUES MANAGEMENT

Issues management is the process of trying to stop an issue emerging that might well develop into a crisis. As with a crisis, what defines an issue depends on the company. Chase and Jones (1979, in Regester and Larkin, 2005) define an issue as 'an unsettled matter which is ready for a decision.' Regester and Larkin (2005) say it is the 'gap between corporate practice and stakeholder expectation'. They believe that organisations should aim to eliminate any potential for stakeholder outrage by anticipating any trends, changes and events that may occur and by influencing the corporation's operations. An issue is an idea that has a potential impact on an organisation or public and may result in an action that brings about increased awareness and a reaction from the organisation or publics (Regester & Larkin, 2005).

There are two key factors in effectively carrying out an issues management response: an early identification of the potential problem and an organised response to the public policy process (Regester & Larkin, 2005). When an issue emerges, Regester and Larkin suggest that it is essential to understand the dynamics of public emotion and the practices of special interest groups and the media. The organisation needs to familiarise itself with the development of the issue by monitoring relevant information and organising an appropriate response. Any communications should be in a language that eases public anxiety.

If an issue is identified at an early enough stage then something can be done about it; the organisation can then change its plans or re-direct its communication efforts accordingly. The functioning or performance of the organisation and its future interests can be greatly affected if an issue is left unnoticed. This is why it is important for companies to establish an issues management system so they can monitor emerging issues and organise their actions into a response.

SUMMARY

Managing communications in a crisis is now an important function for many PR practitioners and those responsible are learning it has its own disciplines and demands. Crises by their nature can occur at any time and when one hits an organisation, how it responds in the immediate aftermath is crucial. Carefully planning how to respond to a crisis and implementing a pre-arranged crisis communications plan are both vital to the successful handling of a crisis. PR practitioners responding to a crisis today have to be especially vigilant to ensure that the modern media, with its reliance on rolling news as well as the blogosphere and social networking sites, don't make the situation worse.

CORPORATE SOCIAL RESPONSIBILITY AND ETHICS

By the end of this chapter you will:

- have an appreciation of why corporate and individual ethics and ethical behaviour matter in and to PR
- understand why businesses should always try to operate ethically
- understand the arguments that lie behind the issue of ethical PR practice
- know what Corporate Social Responsibility (CSR) is and what it means to PR

INTRODUCTION

The issues of ethics and ethical behaviour are relevant to PR in three main ways. Firstly, in questions surrounding the reputation of the PR industry and whether its practice is or is not ethical; secondly, in ethics and the ethical behaviour of the individual practitioner; and thirdly, in the relationship between PR and Corporate Social Responsibility (CSR).

Critics of PR will question its ethics because of its influence on the media – they believe it is unethical because it presents a one-sided, distorted, and biased reality.

This is not a new debate and is unlikely to be resolved because it goes right to the heart of the argument surrounding the definition of PR and PR practice.

What is it about the work of a PR practitioners that is, some would argue, unethical? There are two answers to this: firstly, the relationship between the media and the PR industry is often seen as 'corrupt', exemplified at its simplest level by the giving away of free tickets or trips to members of the news media. Secondly is the way that PR always seems to be used by those in power to protect and enhance their position.

In the course of this chapter we will consider the arguments advanced by those critics who associate the practice of PR with the worst aspects of corporate and government wrongdoing. While they are right to point out the nature of the relationship between PR and the media there are other issues here. Critics ignore a lot of positive PR work done; for example, activist, pressure groups and charities will use exactly the same techniques as corporate PR departments in their campaigns, yet little or no complaint will be made about the ethics of their tactics.

Whether the critics of PR like it or not, as Andrew Currah of Oxford University (2009) stated: 'We view the PR industry as an integral component of the media landscape, and as a pivotal agent in the gathering, packaging and dissemination of news to consumers'. However, the important position that PR holds should mean that PR practitioners exercise care and responsibility in their actions. They are in a powerful position and capable of influencing opinion for good or bad and that action needs to be exercised ethically and responsibly.

WHY ETHICS IS BECOMING MORE IMPORTANT TO PR

One reason why the PR industry attracts criticism is that whenever a politician, company or a celebrity is in trouble, one of their first actions always appears to be the appointment of a PR adviser. The former head of the Royal Bank of Scotland, Sir Fred Goodwin, appointed PR consultants Phil Hall Associates to handle the media interest in him during the 2008 banking crisis. However, when PR companies accept work on behalf of publically vilified clients or unpopular causes it impacts on the image of the whole industry.

And yet, in many situations, the appointment of a PR practitioner will often bring clarity and order to a chaotic situation which then benefits everyone, including the media. What this suggests is that it is not the *practice* of PR that is inherently unethical, rather that, like accountancy, it is broadly neutral and that is why similar techniques can be used by parties and causes from opposite ends of the political spectrum.

We live in a democracy and part of the richness of our lives is that many different views are able to flourish, so views that might be an anathema to someone with left-wing views would probably be perfectly acceptable to someone from the opposite political persuasion. PR companies and consultancies have been accused of immoral/unethical behaviour because they have acted for causes, issues, countries or products that some people do not like. But that does not make the whole PR industry unethical or immoral, because there will be people who work on these accounts who will believe in what is being said and it is their right to be able to do so.

Where problems do arise however, is in the disparity of resources available to opposite sides – companies/countries are able to deploy greater resources for their campaigns and to use dubious tactics, such as front organisations, to further their aims (see below).

Lawyers, accountants, bankers, actuaries – a whole range of professional and financial services can manage to work for the same clients without attracting the same degree of opprobrium as PR. The fact that PR does attract such attention might be an indication of the power and influence the industry has.

Some of the world's largest and best known PR consultancies have indeed worked for what some might call 'dubious' causes, but if their responsibility is to their own shareholders and employees to produce an income then should they turn such clients down? There are some PR practitioners who will work quite happily for so-called 'dubious' causes simply because they share the same views.

Burson-Marsteller is one of the largest PR companies in the world: established in 1953, it has a network of 94 offices in 57 countries across six continents. It has worked for numerous clients whose practices have attracted attention because many believe they are unethical. Some of their less popular clients include the Malaysian Timber Development Council, who were accused of cutting down tropical rainforests in Malaysia, Monsanto and Eli Lilly who produce growth hormones to increase milk production in cattle, and the Indonesian government who have one of the worst human rights record in the world and were condemned for committing genocide in East Timor.

When Burson-Marsteller began working with American International Group (AIG) after the financial crisis in 2008, the American talk show host Rachel Maddow said, 'when evil needs public relations, evil has Burson-Marsteller on speed dial' (www.prwatch.org). The issue here is that while some organisations may be 'unsavoury' is it right that the PR companies they hire are also held responsible for their employer's actions? Is it possible that even 'evil' companies might have a legitimate point of view that they want to get across?

Front organisations

One of the most controversial tactics used by PR consultancies is to create what is known as a front organisation. The website Sourcewatch (www.sourcewatch.org), which maintains a critical watch on the PR industry in the USA, defines a front group as 'An organisation what purports to represent one agenda while in reality it serves some other party or interest whose sponsorship is hidden or rarely mentioned'. It provides the example of the Center for Consumer Freedom (CCF) which 'Claims that its mission is to defend the rights of consumers to choose to eat, drink and smoke as they please. In reality, CCF is a front group for the tobacco, restaurant and alcoholic beverages industries, which provides all or most of its funding'.

A charity called TOAST (The Obesity Awareness and Solutions Trust) used a PR consultancy to recruit parliamentary 'patrons' to raise awareness of obesity in Parliament. TOAST admitted on its website that it was engaged in lobbying, noting that it had been 'extremely successful', however, the charity also claimed to be 'completely independent' and to 'derive its income from individual donations and membership fees'. An investigation by Spinwatch (www.spinwatch.org) revealed that almost all of its funding came from a diet company called LighterLife. In addition, two of LighterLife's directors were also directors of TOAST. This charity was, in other words, a kind of 'front group'. No fewer than 9 of the 21 parliamentary patrons went on record stating that they were not told of the links between TOAST and Lighterlife. Dr Ian Gibson stated 'I was absolutely not aware of this connection and my initial reaction is to be pretty cheesed off' (Spinwatch, 2006).

The question for the PR industry is, is this an example of an ethically unsound practice or is it good PR practice? The use of front organisations could be seen as one of a range of tactics that PR companies use in order to get their client's message across and that by doing so they are fulfilling their obligations to their client and its shareholders. The individuals who work for the PR consultancies may have no moral, ethical or legal objections to supporting causes that other people may regard as ethically unsound. While that position might be defendable, surely from an ethical perspective tactics that deliberately mislead people are wrong whatever the cause. Clearly, the MPs involved in lobbying for TOAST were not aware of the true intentions or background of the front organisation and were therefore being mislead. Actions like that are not justifiable under any circumstances.

ADVOCACY AND THE ADVISER–CLIENT RELATIONSHIP

PR advisers have a different relationship with their clients than other marketing professionals. The role of the PR practitioner is to act as an advocate for their clients and when speaking on behalf of the company or cause they have to take on its actual guise to do it effectively. Advertising agencies do not need as close a relationship with their clients as PR consultancy does. Visuals for an advertising campaign, for example, can be presented to the client who will either approve or reject them. There is thus a distance between the client and the company. With PR, however, there has to be a much closer relationship between the PR practitioner and company; they have, in effect, to become the company.

Acting in such a manner carries ethical problems with it: whether acting on behalf of bank, a hospital, a government agency or a tobacco company, in the public's eyes the PR practitioner is their advocate and in the public's eyes are inextricably linked with that organisation or cause (Parsons, 2004).

DOES PR CORRUPT THE MEDIA?

There has been a long-held view that PR corrupts the media because it always presents a one-sided version of events and a distorted view of reality. PR practitioners are often seen as no more than manipulators of the truth. This critical view of PR is however rather one-sided in assuming the journalists always tell the truth, always interpret reality properly, and never distort facts for their own reasons.

The practice by PR companies of inviting journalists to a free lunches, arranging press trips, and giving gifts is also viewed as corrupt. It can be argued though that as the journalist and the PR practitioner are aware of the game being played, and as all parties understand and are prepared to accept that the PR practitioner is trying to build a relationship with a journalist in order to try and get favourable coverage for a product, that this is acceptable. Journalists are aware of the motives behind free gifts and trips and are still prepared to go along with it because they will get what they want: it also does not compromise their editorial independence.

There is no guarantee that a journalist will write an uncritical report about the company or product simply because they have been taken out to lunch by a PR practitioner.

The issue of the 'corruption' of the media through press visits while important is not, however, the most serious issue in respect of the relationship between PR and the media. Currently, the balance appears to have swung away from journalists towards the PR industry. There is a legitimate concern that media owners will cut costs by reducing the number of journalists and will use instead the free editorial being sent to them from PR companies, and then critical and editorial standards will fall. The worry that everyone should have, both in the PR industry and the media, is that growth in the number of uncritical press releases appearing in the media will devalue the whole process for everyone.

This situation should place an extra responsibility on the PR practitioner, for while some might see this as a heaven sent opportunity to maximise editorial coverage, the more discerning and critical will recognise that if the situation is abused, it could devalue the quality of the media and reflect badly on the PR industry. That would be to no-one's benefit.

THE ETHICS OF INDIVIDUALS

According to Baker and Martinson (2002), there are five principles which an individual should adhere to and apply to their work. These are truthfulness, authenticity, respect, equity and social responsibility. PR practices, particularly around truthfulness, are under close scrutiny especially from journalists, some of whom regard PR practitioners as 'enemies'.

One reason for this distrust is that PR is often in the position of attempting to defend the indefensible. In such cases, what should the responsibility of the individual PR practitioner be? If they know a company is doing wrong, should they continue with their defence of it and its actions, or should they refuse to carry out the instructions and effectively work against that company?

Where should the PR practitioner's loyalty lie? In such situations, PR consultants who are called on to defend a company will argue that their loyalty lies with their management and those who pay their wages.

Grunig and Hunt (1984) suggested that what PR practitioners need is a general definition of what it is to be ethical which could then be applied to individual situations as they arose. Their two principles of ethics are simple. Firstly, that ethical practitioners must have the 'will to be ethical'. Ethical practitioners must not do what they can get away with, they should intend to be honest and trustworthy and not willingly injure others. Secondly, the actions of ethical practitioners should not have consequences for others whenever possible.

But what should a PR company or practitioner do if they are unhappy about the ethics of the organisation they work for? Grunig and Hunt's solution to this dilemma is that:

> Ethical practitioners should stay on the job and argue for ethical organizational behavior, even if they are not always successful. If an ethical practitioner quits, an unethical practitioner probably will replace him or her. In that case, no one will be left to advocate ethical behavior. Only when practitioners have no chance to change an organization, or when they are forced into unethical behavior themselves, in our view, should they resign. (1984: 73)

The website Spinwatch hopes that anyone unhappy with the actions of the PR company they work for will make use of their 'whistleblower' hotline.

Codes and conducts

Professional Codes of Conduct are used by industries to safeguard against unethical behaviour. The Chartered Institute of Public Relations' (CIPR) Code of Conduct was last reviewed in 2000. Any member found to have breached the code may have their membership terminated. Being a member of the CIPR promotes the fact that a person is aware of ethical issues within the business environment and follows the Codes of Conduct in every possible aspect.

However, unlike say the Codes of the British Medical Association (BMA), you do not *need* to be a member of the CIPR in order to practise PR. While being a member may provide you with more credibility as a professional this is not mandatory. If you are thrown out of the CIPR, this would not prevent you from practising PR.

For all their fine words do these Codes of Conducts mean anything in practice? According to Parsons (2004: 70) 'Codes of ethics, as set down by professional associations such as the CIPR, are really nothing more than conventions for behaviour in applying moral standards to practical dilemmas'. Are they minimum standards or wishful thinking? Do we really need these codes at all or are they simply window-dressing?

THE ETHICS OF BUSINESS

Business ethics can be defined as the principles or standards that guide behaviour in the business world (Ferrell et al., 2005). Whether an action is ethical or unethical can be determined by a range of stakeholders who are involved with a company's investors, employees, customers, interest groups, the legal system and the community. Although these groups are not necessarily 'right', their judgements influence society's acceptance or rejection of business and its activities.

This then raises issues that will enable us to explore two very different arguments about who business should be responsible to. This goes right to the heart of what a business is and who it should be run for. These are:

- Are all stakeholders equal in value and importance to the company?
- If not, who are the most important stakeholders and why?
- Are the owners of the company (the shareholders and wider financial community) the most important?
- Is the wider community/society in which the company exists the most important?
- Can all stakeholders be satisfied or are they incompatible?

In 2009 when the economy went into recession, these questions moved from the realm of theoretical debate into being practical questions. If a company makes its workers redundant and closes factories, how real is the equality of the stakeholders? Is it right that company directors take large salaries when the workforce are having to suffer reduced pay or factory closures?

To put some of these issues in context we need to understand first the philosophical foundation for business ethics.

Four traditions

Business ethics is broadly based on four philosophical traditions:

Aristotelianism
This defines virtues that can and should be followed and stresses one's personal responsibility for developing correct behaviour.

Kantian morality (The Deontological approach)

According to Immanuel Kant, (1772–1804) there are universally recognised virtues which it is the individual's duty to uphold; we have a 'categorical imperative' to do the right thing and must pursue the correct moral course because it is the right thing to do.

Utilitarianism (The Teleological approach)

Developed by Jeremy Bentham (1748–1832) this evaluates actions in terms of goals and is described as the pragmatic approach to decision-making. Parsons (2004) states: 'The rightness or wrongness of any action is dependent entirely on the outcomes that derive from it. In other words, neither the intent behind the action nor the fundamental rightness or wrongness of the action is at issue, only the consequences'. Utilitarianism has become associated with maxims such as any action taken should be from those that please the maximum number of people and the ends justify the means. This has had an impact on business ethics by enabling businesses to justify an apparently unpopular decision with the argument that the majority (or greatest number) will benefit from it. Parsons (2004) states that utilitarianism can be used in PR to justify actions: for example, a PR consultancy choosing to work on behalf of a country which has a dubious human rights reputation. However, a weakness in the Utilitarian argument is that it is difficult to establish what exactly will result in the greatest number of people benefiting. In addition it cannot always solve large ethical problems.

Contractarianism 契约主义

This emphasises individual rights and obligations and is based on the philosophy of Jean Jacques Rousseau (1712–1778) and on the theory that all people have the right to have freedom, yet should act ethically within the boundaries of a social contract. Although obligations, morals and goals are important, rights and duties also exist in society and these must be adhered to.

Of these traditions Kantian morality and Utilitarianism are the most useful when looking at PR and ethics.

Moral evaluations

Kantian morality and utilitarianism provide two useful means of evaluating not only the reasons for why a particular course of action should be followed, but also the motives of those who have taken a course of action. These can be used to assess why for example a company carried out a particular course of action.

Teleological: The results based approach. This defines ethical behaviour on the basis of either good or bad consequences and that the ends justify means.

Apply this then to the situation of the journalist being offered a free press trip by a company's PR – if the journalist accepts, his actions might be justified on utilitarian grounds that would argue the ends justify the means, if the result is that the journalist can write a story that they might otherwise not have been able to had they not gone on the trip.

Deontological: The act-orientated approach. This emphasises the intrinsic worth or value of the action itself. Ends do not justify means because there are certain fundamental truths that we must follow regardless of their outcomes. It looks to the actual *purpose* of the action rather than the *consequences.* Deontologists believe that there are certain actions which must not be taken even if utility results; some actions are morally acceptable while others are not, and the ultimate decision on what action to take is down to the individual person and not society as a whole. This is a rule-based ethics (Parsons, 2004) where being ethical is a matter of accepting that as individual human beings we have a duty to do certain things. If, for example, we accept that journalistic independence and integrity are absolute virtues, to be maintained at all costs, then under no circumstance would gifts be either offered or accepted as both parties would accept this fundamental truth of journalism.

In contrast to this is an argument based on post-modern philosophy, that there are no absolute rights or wrongs and morality is largely culturally based. So using our example in some parts of the world it might be acceptable to offer trips to journalists, while in other parts of the world this would be morally unacceptable and would undermine the credibility of the journalist and those who had made such an offer.

Ethics and the multinational company

In our global economy, where companies manufacture goods in one part of the world and sell them in another, multinationals in the developed world are expected to have high ethical standards when working in developing countries. We no longer believe it is acceptable to pay workers in the developing world unfair wages. In 2007, pictures of a 10-year-old boy in New Delhi making clothes for a company that supplied Gap had immediate repercussions for that company including an impact on sales. Four days after the story broke, there were thousands of posts on US sites mentioning Gap and child labour, with some 68% of the messages being negative (PR Week, 23/11/07).

Multinational companies face big ethical dilemmas when working in regions with differing standards and practices on such issues as health and safety. Many have moved production away from high-wage economies such as the UK and USA to low-cost economies such as China and India in order to lower the cost of production: as a result consumers have benefitted by having cheaper goods and companies improved profit margins. However, it now seems that consumers want more than just low prices, we expect businesses to treat employees fairly and we do not want to see child labour used in the production of fashion garments, for example. There has been a huge growth in Fair Trade initiatives, where local producers in the developing world are paid fair wages. Consumers today expect companies to conduct their business ethically and fairly and large multinational companies are having to respond.

Business is business: is CSR welcome at all?

There are some economists who would say that considerations such as ethics and CSR have absolutely no role in business. The American economist Milton Friedman epitomised this position. He argued that the company's main stakeholders were the shareholders and that 'The social responsibility of business is to increase its profits' (Friedman, 1970). In line with free market ideology, the only purpose of a business is to make as much money as possible for its owners, the shareholders. According to this argument, the only reason people go into business in the first place is to make as much money as possible. The business may grow away from a single owner, take on more employees, and move into bigger premises, eventually employing hundreds or perhaps thousands, but the fundamentals will still be the same – to make as much money as possible for the owners/shareholders.

For public companies (those whose shares are traded in public through exchanges such as the London Stock Exchange or the Paris Bourse or the New York Stock Exchange) the rationale is the same and enshrined in the phrase 'to enhance shareholder value'. Namely, to increase the profits and dividends paid by the company to their shareholders.

Proponents of this philosophy argue that maximising profits brings social benefits and is therefore socially responsible. If companies make a profit society benefits because they will employ more people who in turn will pay tax. Profitable companies must also pay corporation tax which pays for schools, roads, hospitals, doctors and nurses, and so on. Furthermore, the largest owners of shares in our public companies are the pension funds and insurance companies – when the equity markets perform well, (i.e. companies make profits) they are then able to meet their obligations and payments.

The credibility of this argument has perhaps now been undermined, possibly fatally, as it was this intellectual power-house that justified the climate of corporate greed that was responsible for the banking collapse in 2008.

The role of PR in this model is to help increase sales of the company's products/services and so enhance shareholder value, as well as to maintain communication with the shareholders and the wider financial community.

A number of factors have contributed to public disillusionment and dissatisfaction with the way businesses and governments operate: these have included excessive bonuses for bankers, huge payouts for sacked executives of failing companies and the BP oil spill in the Gulf of Mexico. The so-called 'dodgy dossier' that lead the UK into the Iraq War and MPs' expenses scandals are just two incidents that have seen the public lose trust in politicians.

Business is business: is it worth the hype?

One of the ways in which business has been attempting to improve its reputation has been by introducing CSR programmes. These programmes are not carried out just for the sake of improving a company's reputation: they benefit not only the communities they serve but also individuals in the company who participate in them and are therefore important in human resource terms.

For many of its proponents, CSR is not just about supporting worthwhile community projects but also represents a different and exciting model of how business should operate. In contrast to the 'Friedmanite' views outlined above, CSR recognises that businesses have to consider their impact on society and take responsibility for the impact of their activities on customers, suppliers, employees, shareholders and the wider community. CSR also means following policies that look at how a company impacts on the environment. In practice this will cover a range of activities, such as reducing the environmental impact on their products and establishing sustainable development principles across the supply chain.

There is a huge amount of interest in CSR and there is also a growing CSR industry of specialist advisors with plenty of advice for companies about how to implement a CSR programme. CSR helps companies feel good about themselves and also allow them to do something that is worthwhile and beneficial. But is CSR no more than a PR veneer?

There are two broad ways of looking at the growth of CSR. Firstly that it is a positive development where companies actually engage in active and meaningful relationships, and also an example of symmetrical communication where companies can engage in communication with stakeholders, and listen and change their actions as a result of the interaction. Secondly, that it is no more than a PR inspired activity – another example of a PR tactic to present an acceptable face to the outside world. Broadly speaking, however, in practice CSR can be broken into two separate types of activity, namely social and environmental.

Social corporate responsibility

CSR social programmes encompass activities in which a company may interact with the community and include, for example, staff participating in school-reading schemes and garden clean-up projects or making charitable donations. No-one would deny that these are worthwhile causes and projects which provide benefit to the community and also offer a sense of meaning and self-fulfilment to those people who participate in them. There is also some evidence that these types of grammes are often driven by Human Resource (HR) departments because y are good for staff morale.

Environmental corporate responsibility

Most CSR programmes are concerned with environmental issues. The UK government is keen to encourage CSR, stating that 'The Government sees CSR as the business contribution to our sustainable development goals. Essentially it is about how business takes account of its economic, social and environmental impacts in the way it operates' (www.csr.gov.uk).

At the heart of the government's understanding of CSR is sustainable development:

> Sustainable development is a key business issue that can improve both a company's reputation and their competitiveness.

Sustainable objectives

> *Sustainable development is a dynamic process which enables all people to realise their potential and to improve their quality of life, in ways which simultaneously protect and enhance the earth's life support systems.* (Forum for the Future Annual Report, 2000)

The aim of sustainable development is to ensure a fair society, operate in a way that does not damage the environment, and improve quality of life. If all businesses followed the practice of sustainable development, it is argued that society would benefit from increased prosperity and a clean and safe environment. Sustainable development can also help in tackling social exclusion and reducing the harm to health caused by poverty, poor housing, unemployment, and pollution.

The business benefits of adopting and signing into a CSR programme include:

- Improved reputation.
- Increased shareholder value.
- Happy, motivated employees.

CSR then can be regarded as the business community's contribution to helping society meet its environmental challenges. Many companies are no longer engaging in good environmental practice for cosmetic reasons or because it makes good financial sense, but because they believe it is the right thing to do. However, a true test of this commitment to CSR is whether such programmes can be sustained as the recession deepens or whether they are dispensed with. If the latter, then this would suggest that businesses do not regard them as an essential core activity but as an 'add-on', to be disposed of when the going gets tough.

Is CSR just PR in disguise?

Many companies will operate their CSR programmes through their PR or communications department, thereby allowing critics of CSR to argue that if the programmes are run by the PR department then they are being done for utilitarian terms and purposes – that is, to present the company in the best light possible.

Fauset believes CSR

> *Helps to greenwash the company's image, to cover up negative impacts by saturating the media with positive images of the company's CSR credentials.[CSR enables business to claim progress despite the lack of evidence of verifiable change]* Since *much of the business case for CSR depends on corporations being seen to be socially responsible, CSR will continue to be little more than PR for as long as it is easier and cheaper to spin than change.* (Fauset, 2006)

However Cutlip et al. (2000) believe that CSR can be good for PR, stating that 'Much good can be credited to ethical public relations practice, and opportunities for serving the public interest abound'.

CSR attracts critics from both ends of the political spectrum; there are those on the left, who distrust everything that business, particularly big business, does, and those on the right who believe that business should not be involved in CSR activities at all. Whatever the motivation behind them, many good CSR schemes have produced benefits to society and individuals and the move towards more CSR seems set to continue.

Delivering CSR

According to the CIPR, PR practitioners responsible for CSR programmes should be able to:

- understand society
- build relationships
- question (their own) business
- handle stakeholder relations
- contribute to the creation of a strategic vision for their company.

If a company is serious about its CSR and is doing it for the right (Kantian) reasons, and if it is operated through the PR function, PR will be able to provide the type of strategic advice that, some would claim, should be its proper role. In this scenario PR will provide information and feedback to the centre from the external publics influencing and shaping how the centre responds to the outside world. In this way PR can act as the conscience of the company, not just on behalf of the centre, but in the interests of the whole community.

SUMMARY

The PR industry cannot avoid the question of ethics, as it is central to its operation at both an individual and industry level. There are many critics who regard all PR activity as unethical because it necessarily presents a one-sided case and often uses tactics which could be regarded as corrupting the media. Because of its powerful position in relation to the media it is incumbent upon the PR industry to act in an ethical and professional manner and there are industry guidelines to advise individuals and corporations about ethical behaviour.

The relationship between industry and the public is changing and the growing interest in CSR is one aspect of this change. The PR practitioner could have an important role to play in this new relationship – acting as both a link to the community and as an advocate for it at the centre of the company.

Part Two

PUBLIC RELATIONS IN PRACTICE

INTRODUCING THE PRACTICE

INTRODUCTION

Part One explored the philosophical and historical roots of PR and the main debates and issues surrounding the industry. Part Two will look at how PR works in practice. It is not intended to be a comprehensive description of how PR is practised in every sector of business and government but an overview of the main trends in PR across both. It attempts to answer a number of questions, such as, what are the driving factors behind the growth of PR? Are all types of PR practice the same? Is the work done by a publicist on behalf of a film star similar to say the work done by an in-house PR consultant working for a large company or a small local authority? These are not just academic questions, they also but have implications for the career choices of those wanting to enter the industry and also its future direction. If PR is still a 'generalist' profession as the professional bodies argue then it should be possible for PR practitioners to move easily between different industry sectors. The current trend, however, appears to be moving away from this towards an industry where PR practitioners can specialise in specific niche sectors almost from the day they start work. Under such circumstances, is it still possible to use an all-encompassing definition of PR such as those we looked at in Chapter 2? Are they relevant for say both the financial and celebrity PR practitioner even though they move and operate in such different circles?

PR is a vibrant, growing industry and even during the recession of 2009, when other areas of the media such as advertising and journalism were suffering, the PR industry proved to be remarkably resilient. The 2009 Chartered Institute of Public Relations (CIPR) members' survey demonstrated this resilience, finding that whilst the recession was having an impact on some areas of PR such as sponsorship, overall the impact was limited and some areas, online digital PR for example, were even growing. The industry's strength suggests that for most public and private organisations communications is no longer a marginal service, but an essential part of the modern company. According to economic measures such as numbers employed, turnover and profitability the industry is an outstanding success story, making a significant economic contribution to the national economy. All this has been achieved in a relatively short period of time.

The PR industry's current strength stands in marked contrast with the continuing decline of traditional printed media such as newspapers and magazines. Indeed some commentators (Davies, 2008; Lewis et al., 2008) attempt make a direct connection between the rise of PR and the decline of the print media by arguing that PR has contributed to it. This is a serious issue and one that will also be explored in detail in Part Two.

These critics are only the latest in a series (Miller & Dinan, 1996; Dinan & Miller, 2007) who would argue that one consequence of the growth in professional communications has been a decline of critical journalism. A study by Lewis et al. (2008) looked at the rise of PR-sourced material in broadcast and print news pages, and while it might appear to confirm the argument that we live in a society where the supply of our information is controlled and we are receiving a sanitised version of the world, the actual situation is more complicated. Society demands more from companies and organisations and we want and expect them to operate in an open and ethical fashion. This demand for transparency can only be met by an increase in the communications function. Far from restricting the flow of information, corporate communications is being forced to increase this and evidence to support this comes from a number of practising journalists.

An illustration of this demand for information is that every organisation now appears to need a professional communications function – from oil companies to the Brownies, from fast food chains to churches, they all need PR. Although whether that makes these organisations more effective or not is another question altogether.

The argument about the growth of professional communication can be crystallised into two opposing positions:

- The growth is evidence that companies/organisations have responded to society's demands for more openness and transparency by introducing a communications function that facilitates this.
- The growth of PR is indicative of a widespread desire to try and control and restrict the flow of information from businesses and organisations to ensure we only hear and read what they want us to consume.

Regular critics of the PR industry find a willing audience for their arguments in a media which still remains largely hostile to and suspicious of PR. This is despite the fact that many journalists – even the critical ones – often find it a convenient career move. Alistair Campbell, the former director of communications and Strategy for Tony Blair's Labour government, began his career as a journalist, as did Andy Coulson, former editor of the *News of the World* and now David Cameron's chief media adviser.The generally critical press that PR receives fuels public suspicion of the industry and is cited as one reason why many young PR practitioners leave it (*PR Week,* 10/8/07).

Much criticism of the PR industry is, however, largely unfair as most PR practice is benign and uncontroversial and largely concerned with providing information about services and products that businesses and people generally find useful. Any criticism of the whole industry must include the work carried out by charities, including those campaigning to alleviate serious problems or change harmful patterns of behaviour. In fact, some of the most innovative and imaginative PR campaigns are run by small campaigning charities with limited resources. Chapter 14 looks at examples of these in more detail.

In Part Two we will discuss what makes a successful PR campaign, looking at the basics from planning and research through to devising a structured campaign that follows a clear strategy and uses tactics that are appropriate to a target audience. We will also look at how PR operates across a variety of sectors, including charity, sport, celebrity, government and the public sector, with a focus on the overall structure of campaigns rather than a detailed sector analysis. Communication by central government is looked at in greater detail than other sectors because over the last ten years it has been involved in some of the most important issues – those surrounding trust and 'spin' – which affect the PR industry as a whole.

PUBLIC RELATIONS PRACTICE IN THE UK

The UK PR industry is the most developed in Europe. There are two reasons for this: firstly, the strength and nature of the UK media has stimulated its growth; secondly, the UK was the launch pad for US PR companies looking to expand into Europe.

Although it was produced before the economic problems of 2008/09 had made an impact, the most comprehensive analysis of PR's economic impact was provided by the Centre for Economics and Business Research (CEBR). *The Economic Significance of Public Relations* not only analysed the economic contribution PR made to the UK economy it also provided many useful and fascinating insights into the industry. It looked, for the first time, at how both in-house and consultancy PR practitioners actually worked in practice.

The business of PR

The 2005 CEBR survey produced a wealth of information about the industry. Listed below are some of the main findings.

- Annual industry turnover in 2005 was £6.5 billion and contributed £3.4 billion to the UK economy and made £1.1 billion of corporate profits.
- In the UK, consultancy turnover grew by 5.9% annually between 2000 and 2005 and between 2005 and 2010, while annual growth is expected to be 11.6%.
- The UK PR industry employs 48,000 professionals, working either in-house or for consultancies. It is smaller than the advertising industry (80,000 people and an estimated £231,000 billion sales) but larger than the market research and public opinion polling industries combined.
- Spending on PR rose by a third from 2000 to 2005 to an annual average of £1.2 million per organisation. However, in-house PR respondents predicted the 6.2% annual rise in spend would slow to 2.6% by 2010. (Source: CEBR, 2005)

One of the surprises here was the break-down of the areas in which practitioners work. It had always been assumed that the majority of PR practitioners worked in PR consultancies of one kind or another. According to the survey, however, of the 47,800 practitioners, 8,600 worked for a PR consultancy and 39,200 (82% of all PR practitioners) were in-house. In-house PR grew by 20% in a ten year period, while consultancies grew by 14% in the same period. This growth of in-house PR has been driven by the need for better communication not only in the private sector but also by rapid growth across the whole of the public sector (i.e. central and local government, health authorities, etc.).

The People in PR

Every year the Chartered Institute of Public Relations (CIPR) surveys around 2000 of their members for their annual *State of the Profession Survey*. The 2009 CIPR survey showed that of the people working in PR:

- 34% were aged between 25 and 34.
- 31% were aged between 35 and 41.
- 35% were aged 42 and over.
- The greatest percentage of in-house and not for profit CIPR members were aged between 25 and 34.
- 51% of freelance PR practitioners were between 45 and 60.
- 6.5% were from an ethnic background compared with the UK workforce average of 8%, while 11% of in-house PR practitioners described themselves as non-white.
- Nearly half of all PR practitioners worked in London.

(*Source*: CIPR State of the Profession Survey, 2009)

The 2005 CEBR survey showed that 62% of PR practitioners were women, against 46% of the workforce as a whole. The CIPR survey revealed that this number had increased slightly in 2009 with 65% of PR practitioners women. The gender imbalance appears to operate in some sectors of PR and not others, with men, for example, better represented in financial, investor relations and public affairs. More men are also more likely to work as freelancers or self-employed consultants than as in-house practitioners. In addition there appears to be a disproportionate number of female employees at junior levels and a correspondingly disproportionate number of men at higher levels of the industry. A Public Relations Consultants Association (PRCA) survey in 2007 found that 77% of account executives and account managers (i.e. at the junior levels of the industry) were female.

75% of PR practitioners were graduates and most had a social science, arts or management studies background though only a relatively small number have communication or PR degrees. The 2009 CIPR survey confirmed this, finding that 76% of PR practitioners had a university degree. The most qualified sector in PR was the public sector where 81% of PR practitioners held a degree, whilst the lowest was the freelance/self-employed where 'only' 61% had gained a degree.

The average annual basic salary of in-house PR practitioners in the corporate sector was £46,200, consultancy staff earned an average of £51,000, and those in the Third and public sectors earned an average of £31,900 and £32,500 respectively.

Recruiting and keeping staff

The PR industry regularly complains of a shortage of quality senior staff, and difficulty in retaining existing staff and keeping them motivated.

The industry however continues to be a popular career choice for young people, even if it does appear to have problems keeping them.

According to the *Guardian* in 2006 (*'The Guardian Grad Facts*, 2006) graduate survey of more than 2,000 final year students, 16% said they would like to work in PR/marketing, making it the third most popular career choice overall.

However, the 2007 PRCA survey of young people working in the industry revealed that 15% said they would leave the industry after only one or two years, while 32% actually left after working in the industry for between two and five years, and 27% after staying five to ten years.

The rate at which people leave and join an industry is referred to as the 'churn' rate. According to a 2007 survey by *PR Week*, UK PR consultancies lost 1 in 4 of their employees over a year, while at larger consultancies the annual staff churn rate was 36% and at smaller consultancies 24%. The overall average was 27% (*PR Week*, 14/2/07).

The reasons people gave for leaving the industry were:

- a lack of training opportunities
- a long hours
- a dislike of working for an industry that has had a bad press

Another a survey in 2008, by Aurum Data Systems, on working practices in the PR industry revealed an industry under pressure, with staff dissatisfied and working long hours. The survey found that on average senior managers were working 59 hours per week, middle management 52, and executives 43 hours.

When asked what the main causes of job dissatisfaction 47% cited repetition of tasks, 44% were unhappy with the long working hours, 31% with the volume of administration, and 26% with unreasonable client demands (*PR Week*, 18/4/08).

Some of these problems are undoubtedly to be found in a growing industry which is still learning and adapting to changing circumstances. By its nature it is bound to be fast-moving and stress-inducing so it is not surprising that some people are unhappy in this type of environment. The challenge for the industry is how to respond to and encompass new ways of working and the demands of a workforce together with changing priorities. Employees are looking for flexibility in their working practices, such as the option to work from home or to work part-time. Employers within the industry who are flexible and who help their staff maintain a work-life balance will have greater success in recruiting and retaining the best people.

PUBLIC RELATIONS IN-HOUSE

By the end of this chapter you will understand:

- what an in-house PR practitioner is
- who they work for and what they do
- the reasons why in-house communications have grown

INTRODUCTION

In-house PR practitioners work for only one company or organisation. Their status, role and importance within organisations have developed dramatically over the last ten years. Many senior in-house practitioners now work at the highest level of their organisation, providing strategic advice to shape and influence the organisation's direction. This is the fulfilment perhaps of the arguments put forward by the PR theorists we looked at in Part One, who believed that public relations could play a decisive role in helping to shape strategy.

At one time in-house PR communication had a fairly limited role: the typical practitioner would usually be an ex-journalist who did a bit of PR and media work and produced the staff newspaper or magazine. The modern in-house PR practitioner, however, will operate as part of a team with a clear separation of functions between those responsible for external communications and those handling in-house communications.

Mark Douglas, executive director of corporate affairs and communications at General Dynamics, describes how the role has changed:

Today's in-house corporate communications bears little resemblance to that of 10 years ago. In retrospect, things were pretty amateur – the writing of the press releases based on the strategic decisions that others had made. Pay was pretty poor. And when the economic bad times came knocking, we were all too often the accountants' sacrifice. The corporate communications function just wasn't respected. (CIPR/DTI Survey, 2006: 10)

According to Douglas the most important change has been around job roles and expectations. While the tactical role – which includes, for example, producing press releases – is still being carried out,

Increasingly we are called upon to offer strategic advice too. In-house corporate communications professionals are breaking into the Boardroom. As companies have come to realise that reputation is their greatest asset, it is now realised that corporate communication managers have a central rather than a peripheral role.

One reason why in-house PR practitioners are now working at strategic levels has been the increased awareness at the most senior levels in company board rooms, council chambers and government departments that communication matters. A poor reputation, as we have seen, can cost a company dearly financially, and in an age of 24/7 communications responding regularly and quickly to media demands and requests this can make a significant difference to how an organisation is perceived.

Generally speaking the work of in-house PR practitioners covers two main areas, external and internal communications. External communications, or corporate communications as it is also known, covers all those activities involving and relating to communicating with anyone outside the organisation. All companies and organisations (whether they want to or not) will engage in some form of communication with external audiences. The big difference is that whereas twenty years ago companies could remain aloof and uninvolved from their community that has now changed. In the 'stakeholder' society businesses are 'allowed' to operate by the community providing they meet some basic obligations to it. External communications will be covered in detail in Chapter 11. Internal communications (see below) encompasses all the communication carried out inside the company/organisation to internal audiences, that is, the people who actually work there whether that is in the office next door or a factory on the other side of the world.

WHO DOES WHAT?

In-house PR practitioners stated in the 2005 DTI/CIPR Survey that their two most important job functions were, firstly, dealing with issues affecting corporate reputation, and secondly, internal communications. The high priority given to corporate reputation is to be expected, as discussed in Chapter 4, as corporate reputation is directly linked to a company's financial success. Sally Sykes is 'heartened' that communication directors ranked issues such as trust and reputation so highly:

> *These are much more strategic issues than, say, "media fragmentation" which is a tactical challenge. In the pharmaceutical industry, reputation is the most important challenge and there is a clear recognition that reputation isn't a quick fix. It's about building long-term confidence. The average CEO already spends a lot of time talking to shareholders or customers so we are seeing heads of comms move out of this handholding role to embrace a more rounded, modern approach to PR – where it's not all about the media or media relations. The world in which most of us operate is one where we're seeking to deliver a consistent message across a range of stakeholders. I believe that PR is going to continue to go that direction.* (Sykes, 2007)

According to Jonathan Walsh, corporate marketing and communication director at Nestle UK, in-house PR practitioners,

> *Must be more accountable to the rest of their organisation, while corporate affairs and marketing teams should ally themselves with the PR department. ... More and more of my assignments have marketing objectives built in because the corporate and consumer agendas are now the same. PROs should be the ones defining the corporate agenda because in theory, it is we who have the most skills to do so.* (PR Week, 1/6/06)

BOX 8.1   Strategic Adviser or PR Manager

Research by Broom and Smith (1979) identified four PR functions within organisations:

- Expert prescriber: In this role the PR practitioner researches and defines the communication problem, devises an appropriate programme, and assumes major responsibility for its implementation. They are in full control of the PR programme.
- Communications facilitator: Their main concern is the provision of information. The communications facilitator is concerned with the process of communication – of how to get the information out there rather than wider operational or policy issues.

(Continued)

(Continued)

- Problem–solving process facilitator: This role involves planning and co-ordinating public relations activities with senior management. The senior management are involved in the decision-making on PR activities.
- Communication technician: PR practitioners are involved in production work but not policy or programme making. They implement the PR programmes by using such skills as writing, editing, and conference organising.

A major issue at the time of this research was that too many in-house PR roles were at the communication technician level i.e. simply producing press releases, thereby illustrating the point made above by Mark Douglas. However important the role of communication technician might be it is a tactical role and if PR as a discipline is to grow and contribute to policy-making on the strategic direction of an organisation then there needs to be more practitioners employed as 'expert prescribers'.

> If public relations is to be recognised alongside other organisational functions such as human resources and marketing and practitioners are to be accepted as having a legitimate place at the 'top table' in an organisation then practitioners need to demonstrate their capability not only to counsel and advise but also to plan and manage budgets, supervise others, evaluate research etc. (Broom & Smith, 1979)

And this is what appears to have happened, as in-house PR organisations have grown in scope and size and those managing communication departments (expert prescribers) now carry out these functions.

Moss and Green (2001) synthesised research on job roles to produce a summary of key activities identified with the PR manager's role:

- Planning public relations programmes
- Making communications policy decisions
- Diagnosing public relations problems
- Counselling management
- Acting as a catalyst for management decisions
- Supervising the work of others
- Planning and managing budgets
- Meeting with clients executives

THE PR PRACTITIONER AS GATEKEEPER

Not everyone is convinced that the growth in the numbers of in-house PR practitioners is a welcome indication of a more open and transparent society. Critics suggest (Harcup, 2003) that the role of the in-house PR practitioner, whether intended to or not, effectively restricts a journalist from producing their own news story. When a story relies on PR contributions it becomes heavily mediated – that is to say, it expresses the views of the company. This must necessarily be a partial view because it portrays the company/organisation in the best way possible: 'PR is not just about *releasing* information, it is also about *controlling* information. Although many press officers have good working relationships with journalists, based on trust and even grudging respect, the fact remains that they are working to different agendas' (Harcup, 2003: 16).

In such situations, the in-house PR practitioner in effect acts as gatekeeper, a theory that was first applied to news media when developed by Galtung and Ruge in 1965 to describe the role of a news editor on a newspaper. The gatekeeper's role is to act as an interpreter, selecting and filtering from all the possible and potential news stories those that will actually appear in the news pages.

Despite all the progress in getting PR higher up the managerial ladder there is still a great deal to do, and how much is indicated by the fact that only 8% of FTSE 350 companies (that is public companies and the largest businesses) have a PR/communications director on the board of their companies.

One reason, and there are others, for this lack of board level representation in public companies is that there has been a general trend among public companies to reduce the size of their boards. However, in those companies where PR does not operate at main board level, it is usually situated one level below, that is, on an executive/operational board or management committee. The CIPR Survey 2006 included both public and private companies and overall only 20% of the in-house PR respondents had board–level positions. Companies with the largest turnovers are less likely to have a PR practitioner on the board, with 16% of respondents on the board at companies where the turnover was over £10m. There are those who would say that the issue of whether the PR/communications director sits on the board or not is irrelevant and what really matters is their closeness to the chief executive. If they are operationally close then, it is argued, they have the opportunity to influence and shape decisions by working with or through the chief executive. Encouragingly, there appears to be a widespread appreciation of PR among CEOs, with 46% of the communications directors surveyed stating their chief execs 'completely' understood the importance of PR; 45% saying that their chief executive 'partially understood', and only 7% having chief executives who understood 'a little' or 'not at all'.

Box 8.2 Views on the Job

Senior Public Relations practitioners offered the following thoughts on their work and roles. Sally Sykes, communication director of the Health and Safety Executive, says that the best part of her job is the,

(Continued)

> Challenging and interesting work, a great team, and the opportunity to occasionally be part of amazing events and experiences.

Whilst the worst aspects are,

> Long hours, conflicting demands and pressures, and being brought into the loop too late and expected to deliver to a tight deadline. (Sykes, 2007)

Peter Morgan, group director of communications at BT, said,

> I have a word of advice for any would-be comms directors. If you have trouble sleeping, think about a career change. This is a job where you never win ten-nil. On the day when there are great headlines in very nearly every paper there will always be a single rogue headline to spoil it. The internal comms plan that you had thought had reached every corner of the empire missed one critical group. The parliamentary reception that went so well ends with an MP cornering you with a humiliating tale of woe from one of his constituents. To do this job and enjoy it you have got to believe the story you are telling. You have got to have a board that's convinced about the power of communications. And you have got to engage your audiences. Being the director of communications in a company whose story I did not buy, or in which the board had a bunker mentality – now that would keep me awake at night. (*PR Week*, 24/6/05)

Julian Mears, corporate affairs manager, at Britvic, says that,

> For me, my job is how to turn consumer knowledge into corporate action. On average, everyone in the UK is exposed to 1,500 media messages every day and I worry about breaking through the noises in such a fragmented environment. PR must also be accountable. We're facing competition from advertising and marketing and I need to convince the board of my worth – and not just by showing press cuttings. (*PR Week*, 24/6/05)

COMPARING IN–HOUSE AND EXTERNAL CONSULTANTS

Should companies appoint PR practitioners in-house or use the services of an external PR consultant? This used to be an important debate in PR but is now gradually becoming redundant. It was argued that an external consultant was somehow 'better', the rationale being that as the PR consultancy worked for a number of different clients they were likely to possess not only more skills but also a wider range. In a way this line of thinking demonstrated the low status that in-house practitioners used to have. It is now common for in-house PR practitioners to work alongside external PR consultancies because they have specific areas of expertise that can complement and supplement their own skills. Larger companies may well employ several different consultancies for a range of jobs.

This growth in consultancies offering specialist services and the emergence of niche players is, according to Andy Green, founder of Green PR, one of the main trends in contemporary PR,

> *What you're witnessing is greater fragmentation and specialisation in terms of tactical uses. You are also seeing PR moving up the ladder and being of greater strategic brand communication, sitting alongside the MD advising on how to develop their business.* (Green, 2007)

Jane Howard, chair of the London-based PR Consultancy Mandate, agrees that the growth of the specialist service providers is one of the main drivers of change in the industry:

> *But this fragmentation of supply, into ever more expert providers, brings with it a related need to get informed, holistic views of an organisation's corporate health, and there's also a shortage of providers at this level of consulting.* (Howard, 2008)

David Massingham, director of public affairs consultancy Interel Consulting, says there are many factors for why companies will use external advisers:

> *I think clients have lots of different reasons, including gaining access to skills and expertise they don't have in house, gaining external validation of strategy – sometimes difficult messages come better from outsider's additional resource. Often though it is to do the dull, routine work. I think the main advantage they get is in having access to skills that can deliver their objectives in a cost-effective way, without having to take on an overhead.* (Massingham, 2009)

Des Wilson, director of public affairs for the British Airports Authority from 1994 to 2000, summarised the differences between in-house practitioners and a consultancy and gave examples of when an in-house team would use external consultants:

> *For a major company with multiple stakeholders, I don't think you can beat an in-house team that is as close as it can be to the company, loyal, highly-motivated, working as a unit, and with only one objective – the company's success. An agency has two objectives: one is to serve the client in order to keep the business; another is to profit from the client. Also it has to be attentive to a whole list of clients. It is difficult for it to get close or to apply*

the focus that's needed. As a director of corporate and public affairs for a FTSE 100 company I much preferred to do as much as possible in-house. But I don't deny what an agency can bring: I can make a powerful case for agencies. If you take where I was at BAA, I saw three particular values in agencies: one, to undertake a particular one-off project requiring an injection of resource and energy that the full-time could not spare (for example, we hired an agency to manage the launch of the Heathrow Express); two, to add particular expertise to help a particular part of the business (we hired an agency that specialised in property to help our property division); third, to supplement our own weaker areas for example in financial and City related matters. (*Public Affairs News*, March 2005)

In-house teams will use external consultants on specific campaigns, such as for example, product launches or to provide geographical coverage to supplement over-stretched departments. In-house PR teams will be busy with the day to day tasks of running a PR department and having to respond to immediate issues and demands. Jane Howard says such teams will use external consultancies to provide a strategic insight: 'It is difficult to combine the needs of being strategic/creative and managing tactical demands. Often organisations keep the tactical work – usually trade and regional media relations – in-house and outsource the strategic/creative remit' (Howard, 2008). When a company embarks on a campaign or a PR activity which might be out of the ordinary or where additional resources are needed this will often require more time than the in-house team can manage.

Small and medium-sized companies will generally use external PR consultancies rather than an in-house practitioner because they will not be large enough to justify establishing and running their own PR department. In such situations it is also common to find the external PR consultancy working, as Jane Howard explains, 'as the organisation's marketing department'. It can be expensive to create and run an in-house PR department: in addition to salaries and benefits like pensions there are specific PR costs such as establishing and maintaining a media database whether this is done in-house or bought from an external provider. Companies contemplating establishing a PR department have to weigh up this additional expenditure against the benefits of having an in-house PR person/department and how important this would be to the firm. In practice, however, in order to save costs many companies/organisations will combine the PR and marketing functions to provide the company with a generic communications function.

Internal communications

Internal communications has become one of the most important functions of the in-house team and the responsibility of a dedicated specialist team. In fact, it is now possible to make a career in this area alone and to not any have dealings with external PR. This could be seen as another example of the way the industry is fragmenting. Internal communications is the communication between a company's management and its employees and this has grown because companies and organisations now recognise that good communication between the two can contribute to improved performance and also help resolve any issues that might give rise to conflict. The reverse is also true here, that poor communication can create mistrust in a workforce as we saw when dissatisfied British Airways' employees publicly attacked their employer (see Box 4.2).

Good internal communications is a worthwhile end in itself but there are specific situations involving radical change or disruption at a company where effective internal communications can play a role in easing tensions and concerns. Changing practices in a workplace can produce uncertainty which can then lead to speculation, rumour and unnecessary anxiety. Changes such as takeovers, mergers and introducing new working practices will create change and cause anxiety because the workforce does not know what to expect. This needs explaining and the concerns of the workforce need addressing. The problems created by the credit crunch and the economic whirlwind that swept through every sector of the world economy have created uncertainty in a number of firms, and in such situations clear and honest communications must be quickly carried out: even if it is bad news, this can help ease, but not always resolve, difficult situations.

As we have seen before there is an element of trust in all communication and we can also find this playing a role in internal communications. A breakdown or a lack of trust in management creates problems for internal communications. A survey for London Underground, for example, showed that only 39% of staff believed what their bosses told them and this it was thought was a contributory factor to poor customer service which in turn was having an impact on the reputation of the Tube (*PR Week*, 1/6/06). The problem was becoming so serious that London Underground undertook a major internal communications programme to try and resolve it.

A great deal of the actual content of internal communications is communicating information to employees about a company's HR policies and issues.

Box 8.3   Getting the Structure Right

There are Do's and Don'ts for getting the internal communication agenda right.

At times of instability such as takeovers, mergers acquisitions, and downsizing, staff not only deserve to know what is going on in their organisation, but to hear it from the organisation's most senior management. A pro-active internal communications team will:

(Continued)

(Continued)

- Identify staff's main concerns and fears
- Find the quickest, easiest and most efficient way of getting the message out
- Pick a media mix that suits and plugs all the gaps
- Remember it is the message and not the medium that counts
- Keep the message simple and avoid jargon
- Make sure that the senior management is fully behind the strategy
- Employees should be segmented according to different characteristics, such as, age. Effective messages will take into account the audience they target and it is no longer workable to treat everyone in the organisation as the same.

It is no good pretending that internal communications can be some great panacea that will remove the causes of conflict or disputes. These are often over serious issues such as rates of pay, factory closures, job losses, and health and safety, and to describe some of these issues as 'simply' communication problems is to demean how serious they are. It also demonstrates a lack of understanding about and respect for people's concerns. Employees will have legitimate concerns when viewing matters from their own perspective; they will also have their own opinion which will not necessarily be the same as that of the company management or shareholders. This does not mean that they are either wrong or unimportant. What it does mean is that their views should be treated with respect and that is why companies that are serious about good communication will always try and take staff with them.

Internal communications should help employees understand the organisation's vision, values and culture and involve staff members in those issues that affect their working life, thereby keeping staff informed on important decisions taken by management. It should not however be seen as a management tool. Internal communications should operate using a clear code of conduct and be:

- transparent
- clear
- concise
- informative
- independent

Those who work in internal communications should also try and adhere to a clear way of conducting business and adopt to values such as openness and honesty when practising two-way communications. Ideally internal communications staff should appear to be independent of both staff and management and not seen to be arguing in favour of one side or the other. This can be difficult as clearly it is management who pay the wages. If the internal communications function is seen as objective and independent it can then play a significant role in helping to bridge any gaps between the two sides and reducing tensions.

Sally Sykes's formerly ran a 30-strong department at Astra Zeneca which was responsible for communicating to 30,000 employees throughout the world. She highlighted how internal communications helped to address the issue of change in the company:

> *The most important part of the job was the degree to which internal communications is required to support change in the company. There has also been a more formal application of project management to communications, becoming more process orientated and standardised and less of a "black art".*

In the same way that external communications has target audiences, she defined her 'customers' as,

> *Senior managers in other departments. I prioritised my target audience by the impact they have on business results, the level of change and amount of employee engagement required and also the degree of face to face interaction that's needed.* (Sykes, 2007)

The impact of the internet and social networking sites has increased the importance of internal communications. Company employees now have access to information about performance, activities, directors, shareholders and problems faced by companies all at the click of a button. The manner and speed in which a company responds can be a major factor for whether a complaint or difficult situation spirals out of control.

In the 21st century even the most authoritarian organisations are operating in a different environment and management can no longer exercise power through its control of the information flow. Nor can it simply make announcements and expect to be obeyed by a passive workforce. Good and motivated workforces are those that are not just properly informed, but also those that have participated properly in the decision-making. Technically complex production processes also require a better-educated workforce and one which will no longer simply be told to accept what is good for them. This makes the idea of 'control' of the information flow by communication professionals in an age of citizen journalists, blogs and wikis virtually impossible. Employees can and will get their information externally. If companies want employees to be their ambassadors, they need to empower them with information and communication skills.

Organisational culture: Who is 'the company'?

As internal communications interfaces between management and employees it raises the question of what or who is the company? On one level a company is the legal and financial entity that produces annual results, makes sales profits or losses, reports these results to the shareholders, and if making a profit pays them a dividend. The company owners are the shareholders. However, on another level it is also the company culture, and often this is indefinable and expressed in such statements as: 'I go to work because of the people and to enjoy the "craick".' These are based on the interpersonal relationships and exchanges between the employees and contribute to a company's organisational culture. Organisational culture can be defined as the: 'Core values of organisations that unify social dimensions of organisations' or 'the rules of the game for getting along in organisations'. According to L'Etang (2006: 192) organisational culture includes,

> *Values, relationships, power and politics, formal and informal behaviour and relationships. Culture is reproduced in organisational discourse, rituals and symbols. Communications is fundamental for the co-creations and reproduction of organisational culture and values. Culture operates at conscious and unconscious levels.*

The excellence research team that we came across in Chapter 3 also analysed this issue of organisational culture. Their research on 4,000 companies in the USA, Canada and Europe found it made an important contribution to communications excellence. The culture of an organisation affected the way employees communicated with each other:

> *If an organisation's culture favors communication as a one-way flow of commands from supervisors to subordinates, then communications is less than excellent. If senior management makes strategic decisions in a highly centralised manner, seeking input from only those with formal authority, then PR is less than excellent.* (Dozier et al., 1995: 136)

The study found two broad types of organisational culture, participative and authoritarian. Companies with highly participative organisational cultures generally had highly symmetrical internal communications:

> *When patterns of internal communications are symmetrical employees are comfortable talking to superiors about work performance and things that have gone wrong. Communication is seen as a way for supervisors to help subordinates with problems and is described as two-way.* (Dozier et al., 1995: 142)

Organisations with highly authoritarian cultures, however, had asymmetrical patterns of internal communications:

Asymmetrical patterns of internal communications show when employees say the purpose of communication in their organisation is to get employees to behave as management wants them to behave. Internal communications flows one-way, from managers to employees. (Dozier et al., 1995: 142)

That is, the management will tell the workforce what its position is.

L'Etang believes that internal communication or 'organisational communication' can play a major role in helping employees to properly experience the organisation they work for:

Organisational communication helps us to understand how people experience organisations. It is essential for PR work, bearing in mind that employees are potential ambassadors for their organisations and this diplomatic role cannot be taken for granted. Organisations are political bodies struggling for power and influence externally but also internally as policy is formed. (L'Etang, 2006: 188)

Channels of communication

The following are the main channels of communication used in internal communications:

- staff magazines – these were once the only way that management communicated with staff but now the staff magazine is one of many channels and no longer the most important
- email
- intranet
- face to face meetings – e.g. staff meetings
- conference calls
- internet TV
- videos
- radio
- message boards
- range of print materials in addition to the newsletter

Measuring the effect of communications

Just as external communication programmes should be assessed and measured, internal communications departments also have to address the effectiveness of their work. A major problem is finding a consistent measure that will be acceptable to everyone not only in the company but also across in-house PR practitioners. Hewlett Packard for example identified 148 different ways that its internal PR could be analysed.

A US study, conducted by the USC Annenberg Strategic Public Relations Center in 2006, asked in-house PR practitioners which measures they used to evaluate effectiveness. The four most important were:

- influence on corporate reputation
- content analysis of clips (cuttings)
- influence of employee attitudes
- influence on corporate culture
- influence in stakeholder awareness

Interestingly, as we shall see in Chapter 9, these measures are not too dissimilar to those used to measure external communication programmes. The need for measurement is driven from two largely internal sources; firstly, the financial management of the company so that PR expenditure can be justified, and secondly, the internal communications team itself who need evaluation to assess the success or otherwise of their communications activity in order that they can change and adapt any future strategy.

SUMMARY

In-house PR practitioners work for one company or organisation and their status inside the company has grown rapidly over the last ten years. From having a relatively modest role many senior in-house practitioners now occupy important positions, offering strategic advice to the senior management of the company. In many ways this mirrors the role outlined by PR theories which argued that it should occupy a central role in the management of a company. The activities of the in-house PR practitioner cover external and internal communications, and these are beginning to emerge as separate and different disciplines.

With an organisation's employees now able to find information about a company and its activities electronically and then able to communicate with other employees throughout the world instantly, internal communications has an important job within a company in allaying fears and preventing misunderstandings.

To do this effectively internal communication must be operated in a transparent, impartial and honest fashion and should not attempt to simply be a management mouthpiece.

PUBLIC RELATIONS CONSULTANCIES

By the end of this chapter you will:

* understand the difference between an agency and a consultancy
* appreciate what its like to work in a consultancy
* know who it is consultants work for and the services they provide
* understand how consultancies get new business and how they charge for their work

INTRODUCTION

A PR consultancy is a company that works for a number of clients often across different sectors, although one of the features of the modern PR consultancy is increasing specialisation in specific sectors. In the USA independent PR consultancies have existed since the beginning of the 20th century: the first PR consultancy, the Publicity Bureau, was established in Boston in 1900 (Cutlip,1999) and Ivy Lee started his influential consultancy, Parker and Lee, in 1904.

In Britain the PR consultancy only really emerged as separate and independent from advertising agencies in the 1950s (L'Etang, 2006). The big stimulus for their growth was the arrival in the mid-1960s of large US consultancies, such as Burson-Marsteller and Hill & Knowlton, who opened offices in London. The development of their international networks in Europe and the Middle East and Asia followed on from their expansion into multinational clients such as Proctor & Gamble and *Coca-Cola* who wanted PR and advertising advisers who could offer help and guidance in new markets.

PR consultancies will not only implement campaigns, they will also help plan and measure their success. They vary widely in size ranging from the offices of multinational practices down to individual practitioners who might work from home. While similarities exist between these differently sized operations, there are also major differences between practitioners working at either extreme. The similarities might suggest they share a similar universe in reality they exist in very different worlds. The purpose of this chapter is to explore the modern consultancy and how these operate, and to look at some of the problems and opportunities they face.

TYPES OF CONSULTANCY

Broadly speaking, PR consultancies fall into one of the following categories, the largest consultancies will offer all four services.

Consumer: The biggest category by far. Consultancies assist clients, design and implement campaigns to promote a brand, products or services to customers. Often companies will have links with other marketing activities such as advertising. Their main target is consumers – the people who buy the products or services – and PR activity is likely to be supporting marketing campaigns. The communications will be one-way in order to try and persuade consumers to take a course of action.

Financial: Financial PR consultancies manage a company's reputation among financial journalists, analysts and investors. They work with public companies (plcs) on announcing annual results and also in specific situations, such as stock market flotations, takeover battles, and mergers and acquisitions. Their communications are targeted at financial audiences.

Lobbying and Public Affairs: Companies, public bodies and charities will get advice from lobbying consultancies on how to put their case to governments, politicians and local councils. Lobbyists will alert their clients to political and regulatory issues that could affect and assist them in mapping out the political landscape.

Corporate Communications: Cuts across several disciplines and involves elements from all the above. Corporate communications is about protecting a company's overall reputation rather than promoting products or services.

Technology and healthcare are other fields of PR that are growing quickly with their own language and mores.

Public affairs and financial PR are highly specialised and there is a recurring debate about whether a client can be better served by a so-called 'one-stop' consultancy that offers all these services under one roof, or alternatively whether they are better going to a consultancy that specialises in a particular field. The answer depends on the client and their needs – there is no easy response here.

CATEGORIES OF CONSULTANCY

A PR consultancy will fall into one of the following categories.

Offices of multinational PR companies: The growth of large multinational PR firms has been similar to that of international accountants and law firms – responding to the growth and demands of clients operating in global markets. Multinational clients and brands such as McDonalds, Starbucks, and Gillette need advisers and services that can operate in the same international markets as they do and understand both the needs of the company or brand and also the specific local needs and situations.

PR consultancies with a regional network: Such consultancies will typically have a central head office function covering accounting, human resources, management, marketing and a series of regional offices. For large clients wanting to work with regional media such consultancies are attractive because they provide regional support and, crucially, contact with and a knowledge of the local media. The National Lottery operator Camelot, for example, has used consultancies offering such services. The head office will feed accounts to the regional office which will not only be expected to work on the national accounts but also to win their own share of local business.

Large companies but with no regional network: Many special financial and public affairs consultancies are in this category: they are amongst the largest in the UK and several are only based in London.

Small/medium-size companies: By far the largest number of PR companies are those with 1 to 10 employees. Being small does not mean however that the company cannot handle large, national or even international clients. Unfortunately, in reality 80% of all PR spend in the UK goes through the top 100 PR consultancies (by size), so although smaller consultancies might be able to handle large clients, most in practice do not: 'PR is a sector where big buys big,' according to Jane Howard, Mandate chairman. Most small PR companies are regionally based, providing a PR service to local firms.

'Lifestyle'/freelance PR practitioners: Over the years there has been a significant growth in 'lifestyle' practitioners, mainly working on their own from home. This is an area which has benefitted from the changes and developments in modern communications such as email, internet and Skype, which means that a fully functional office can operate from anywhere.

BOX 9.1   Sole practice in PR: Should you follow this route?

Nigel Keenlyside, FCIPR, became a sole practitioner in 1997 when, following a career in consultancies and in-house on London and Leeds, he established Keenlyside Associates.

'I became a sole PR practitioner 13 years ago, after a 25-year spell in consultancies and in-house. Although I have achieved the targets I set myself it has not all been plain sailing. Without the 25-year experience I had behind me I might easily have foundered.'

(Continued)

(Continued)

The sole practitioner is an important and fast growing sub-group within the PR profession.

As the name suggests, a sole practitioner is an individual who runs an operation entirely on his or her own. In this regard they are no different to a sole practitioner accountant, lawyer or a self-employed plumber or electrician. In some cases sole practitioners will even provide their own administrative support, although a family member or full- or part-time secretary may often be available for support.

A number of factors have contributed towards the growth of the sole practitioner, and it is difficult to determine which has had the greatest influence. When times are good PR consultancies and in-house employers tend to recruit large numbers of practitioners. Conversely, when the clouds begin to darken, they will be released. As the job market declines, many of these individuals will set up their own operations as sole practitioners – the attraction of being your own boss can be very tantalising.

Convenience is one attraction, particularly for practitioners with young families or other commitments. Sole practitioners can chose their own working patterns, and run their lives along more flexible lines. The availability of instant and fast broadband connections enables them to work early in the morning or on late evening shifts. As the majority of communication is now via email, and internet and social media form a growing part of PR work, a laptop and Blackberry can be transported anywhere in the world and a practitioner can still be on top of his or her work.

With these clear benefits can there possibly be a down side? There is, and any aspiring sole practitioner should consider this very carefully before embarking on a solo career.

Cashflow

As with any other business cashflow is king, and from day one you have to put the past security of a monthly pay cheque out of your mind and accept the vagaries of self-employment. Make sure that you employ a reliable accountant who can ensure that you meet all your statutory obligations, and that you have enough funds to pay your taxes and suppliers. Remember there is no financial controller to hassle slow (or non) payers. The same person who earlier in the day was discussing the finer points of PR strategy might later on have to don a debt collecting hat.

Highs and Lows

PR is traditionally a rollercoaster occupation, where elation one day can quickly turn to despair the next. The wise consultant tends to remain level headed, and does not get too carried away by demonstrable success or disappointment. This state of mind is particularly vital for sole practitioners. There is no shoulder to cry on, no colleague to bounce ideas off. You have to rely on your own powers of self-motivation and self-deprecation to maintain equilibrium.

Networking

To avoid working in your own bubble, make as much time as you can for networking. The obvious medium is the Chartered Institute of Public Relations, where you will find myriad opportunities to share views and ideas with like minded people. There is also Facebook and Twitter for those who prefer to remain at their desks. Networking is also the most valuable means of business development for the sole practitioner. Again, with no new business executive in the next room, it is all down to you!

Learn to say no

Time is the most precious ingredient for the sole practitioner. You will either have too much of it or too little. Rarely do things seem to reach a happy medium. That makes forward planning even more important, together with the elimination (where possible) of any time-consuming surprises. Unless you are fortunate enough to have just one client (i.e. boss) you will need to keep all the balls in the air yourself without the luxury of delegation. So be careful about accepting too many assignments, no matter how tempting they might appear. Better sometimes to refer to another sole practitioner who will, when you have some slack, hopefully be more inclined to reciprocate.

Other questions to ask yourself before you embark on a career as a sole practitioner include, do you have the discipline to get up in the morning? Can you resist the distractions of home working, or should you find a small office, particularly with secretarial support? What do you do when two (or more) clients demand your attention or presence at the same time? Do you take more than a few days leave at one time?

You will by now have recognised that you face some real challenges if you want a fulfilling and lucrative career as a sole practitioner. I chose this route because I was confident about my professional capabilities, my self-motivation, my contacts, and my commercial nous. I have had a few sleepless nights, but have not found myself at any time staring into the abyss. I have had at least as much job satisfaction doing this as during my long time in consultancy and in house.

I deliberately chose to remain a sole practitioner, and have not considered, even in the early days when the portfolio was growing, taking on more people or partnering with another sole practitioner. Others have taken a different route and used the initial expediency of sole practice to grow their own business. Follow your own path in this regard. The most successful entrepreneurs both past and present started out as sole practitioners with little idea beyond ambition and seeing where their journey might lead.

'AGENCY' OR 'CONSULTANCY': DOES IT MATTER?

Is it PR agency or PR consultancy? Does it matter and is attempting to look for a difference here anything more than a question of semantics?

In many books, magazines and conversations, it is common to find the term 'PR agency' used rather than 'PR consultancy'. In this book however, we consistently use PR consultancy and PR consultant. Why? Do we use 'consultant' because it sounds 'better', more 'posh' and authoritative? And does it matter? Yes, it does and it is not simply a word game, as the distinction between advertising and PR raises some fundamental issues about the nature of the work carried out.

Advertising agencies are agents of the media, and some of their income is derived from the commission on advertisements they place on behalf of their clients. The commission is an incentive from the media owners to attract advertisers and sometimes it is split between agents and clients.

Only recognised media agencies will have accreditation with media owners and receive a commission.

The key is that there is a *financial* relationship between the agency and media. A PR consultancy has no financial relationship with the media because it cannot control how what it sends to the media will be used or even if it will be used at all.

If there is a financial relationship between PR consultancy and media owner, that is, if the editorial is paid for, then it is a form of advertising known as advertorial and should be clearly marked as such.

PROFESSIONALISATION OF THE INDUSTRY

An enduring problem for the PR industry is ensuring that the services delivered by all these different types of consultancies are of consistent quality.

Anybody can set themselves up as PR practitioner and there is no requirement for people working in PR to become members of the Chartered Institute of Public Relations (CIPR) or the Public Relations Consultants Association (PRCA) or even to go through any form of training. When companies complain that PR was a 'waste of time' or they 'didn't get value for money' from a PR consultancy, closer investigation will usually reveal that their bad experience of PR came from using an inexperienced practitioner who had little or no understanding of strategic PR or how to implement a proper and structured programme. Practitioners such as this give the industry a bad name and contribute to PR's image problem as discussed in earlier chapters. Another factor that has had an impact on the quality of PR has been the growth in number of 'do it yourself' books. These are no substitute for professional qualifications and practical experience. As this book hopefully illustrates PR is much more than media relations and the 'technical' skill of writing a news release.

Degrees in PR and the work of professional organisations like the CIPR and PRCA all help to drive up standards in the industry. They have a role in creating PR practitioners who can offer a consistent and quality PR function whether in-house or as part of a consultancy. PR graduates will bring a wide range of account management skills and an understanding of why some campaigns work and others do not. The PRCA has produced a guide to selecting a PR consultancy, advising prospective clients what they should look for. Clients should think carefully about who they employ and make use of the advice offered by professional bodies, as if they don't those who choose consultancies with little or no experience might have only themselves to blame.

BOX 9.2   UK PR Consultancies

- An estimate of 'probable' revenue for consultancies in the UK is £1.3bn.
- Only 10% of Britain's estimated 2,400 consultancies choose to belong to the CIPR or PRCA.
- Four in five consultancies and agencies employ fewer than 25 people and over three-fifths have annual revenues below £1m.
- Over a third of consultancies and agencies, weighted by turnover, have clients primarily in the public, health and not for profit sectors. Over a quarter (27%) have clients in the finance and business services sectors.

More than half of PR employees in consultancies work in roles that include: communications strategy development, corporate PR, reputation management, branding and marketing, issue management, crisis management, event planning, media relations, and strategy planning. (CIPR Survey, 2005)

SERVICES OFFERED BY CONSULTANCIES

The range of services offered by either large or small consultancies is broadly similar and includes:

- media relations
- crisis and issues management
- internal/employee communications
- strategic communications advice/planning
- media training
- outsourced/external press office management
- reputation management
- event management

Media relations (the shorthand term for getting coverage in the media) is the traditional role of the consultancy and significantly remains top of the list, constituting the main activity for the vast majority of conventional PR consultancies even though the channels of communication are changing. Jane Howard, chairman at Mandate Communications, says:

> *Managing – creating, monitoring and measuring – a consistent, positive, external image is vital for all businesses, and it's a tough job, akin to an ongoing three-dimensional chess game. Media relations is a key part of this, but now only a part, as direct stakeholder channels of communication become increasingly important.* (Howard, 2008)

Many in the PR industry would agree that new channels of communication are creating fundamental structural changes with the potential to fundamentally alter the nature of PR. Andy Green, founder of the eponymous Green PR and author of some of the more original books on PR practice, is one of the PR industry's more innovative and forward looking practitioners. He argues that no PR firm, large or small, can afford to continue in the long-run with traditional media relations alone and that PR practitioners have a duty to take up the challenge presented by new electronic forms of communication. In his blunt assessment those that do not, and remain wedded to old practices, will not survive:

> *Back in 1993, when I started Green PR, you could earn a good crust being a decent wordsmith and doing press releases and I'm sure there are still people out there doing that. Now though PR is more of a process of managing a client's brand using every aspect of communication and opportunities, it is much more of a strategic brand management role.* (Green, 2008)

If the PR industry does not accept the opportunities that new technology is creating then, Green believes, other disciplines such as advertising/marketing will, to PR's long-term detriment.

> *The challenge to the industry will be take up the tremendous opportunities in terms of social media, brand management and networking, or we will lose out like we did with the internet where we let the graphic designers take control and missed out on the PR side.*

Not everyone agrees with this analysis, however, and Jane Howard states that, 'PR is currently thriving at the expense of other marketing disciplines. All serious consultancies are competent with electronic media, social media and brand management' (Howard, 2008). And as we saw in Chapter 3 there is some evidence to suggest that PR is well-placed to take advantage of these new developments.

Interview: The PR Account Manager

Liz Hirst started work in the PR and communications industry two and a half years ago when she joined GREEN Communications as a trainee account executive, following her degree in Creative Writing and a brief stint at a weekly newspaper, the *Wakefield Express*. She is now an account manager working across a range of clients from public sector to professional, including Warburtons, Yorkshire Housing Ltd, the Chartered Institute of Marketing (Northern region), and Leeds University Business School.

She describes here what her job involves and shares with us a couple of typical days from her busy week.

What do you like about your job?

I have a wide range of clients from different industries, which means I am always working on interesting and varied projects. Daily tasks can include advising on PR strategy plans, being involved with community consultation and communication, advising on crisis PR situations, and managing the editorial content for regular client newsletters. I am also a keen photographer and PR gives me the opportunity to use my skills for client photocalls and design work.

What are the most important skills?

Communication and organisational abilities are absolutely vital in PR. You need to be able to manage and organise your own time and workload as well as being mindful of the workload of those around you. As a manager, it is also important to be able to communicate instructions, plans and ideas clearly and concisely to team mates and clients.

Does PR meet your expectations in terms of a career?

I have always been passionate about writing and knew I wanted a career which incorporated this. Having trained to become a journalist, and after working in a number of newsrooms, I quickly realised that was not the path I wanted to take. PR provides me with a fantastic career where I can indulge my passion for writing on a daily basis. I thoroughly enjoy working with my clients – planning events, scheduling stories and activities, and creating new campaigns.

Where do you see yourself five years from now?

As PR is continually changing and developing, I hope to continue to learn new ideas and new methods from other PR professionals. I also look forward to being in a position where I can pass my knowledge and experience on to others entering the PR profession.

Diary: The PR Account Manager
Here is an extract from Liz's diary.

Monday

9:00 Arrive at the office and check through all post and emails. Catch up with colleagues on their weekends (it's important to keep a social/relaxed element in a work environment).

9:30 Start the numerous meetings with colleagues to discuss each client and go through what activity was completed in the previous week and what we have coming up in the next. Delegate tasks to members of the team. Following these meetings I update the schedules for each client and make a note of which team member is doing what.

11:00 Plan my schedule for the week ahead, ensuring I prioritise work, and make a note of urgent actions (e.g. media responses, time-sensitive press releases).

11:30 Draft a press release for Rollits solicitors regarding an event they have coming up. Send it to the client for approval.

12:30 Call media titles to follow up on a Yorkshire Housing press release issued on Friday. I need to check it has been received and find out if they are planning to run it.

13:00 Contact Yorkshire Housing regarding a media enquiry I have received from a local paper. Once I have the relevant information surrounding the issue I draft a response. The statement needs to be approved by the relevant department with the client. (Sometimes this process can take a while so I ensure the statement is drafted as soon as I receive the enquiry.)

14.00 Lunch with colleagues. Although it's not always possible, I try to get out of the office for my lunch. I think it's important to take a break in order to stay fresh and productive.

15:00 Check for any emails sent through while I've been out of the office. I respond to any immediate queries and add non-urgent actions to my schedule for the week. Media statement has been approved by Yorkshire Housing so I send it on to the journalist for inclusion in the article.

15.30 Meet with road safety team at the local council to discuss a potential activity Warburtons could get involved with.

16.30 Produce a contact report from the meeting, ready to share details with team mates and client.

17.00 Produce agenda for a client meeting tomorrow and check schedule is up to date. Make copies of any coverage received in the past month to give to the client.

18.00 Make sure my desk is tidy and ready for the following day. If there is a piece of work I want to start as soon as I get in the office, I'll leave it on top of my keyboard.

Tuesday

8.30 Check emails and respond to any urgent queries. Check I have all the documents required for this morning's meeting.

9.00 Check the newspaper (inc. online edition) for coverage of the Yorkshire Housing story I submitted a comment for yesterday. Send any coverage to the client via email for their review.

10.00 Meeting with Leeds University Business School. We go through activities completed over the last month (since the last meeting), then go through any coverage received and find out what news stories, events and activities are coming up.

12.00 Arrive back at the office. Check emails and phone messages. A number of emails are simple questions but require immediate responses.

12.30 Produce contact report from the meeting. This details all the topics discussed and activities for the next month. I detail who is doing what, and when it needs to be done by.

13.30 Update Yorkshire Housing client schedule following the activity which took place yesterday, so all team members know what has been completed.

14.00 Receive approval from client on Rollits press release. Distribute it to all regional media and trade press (including online publications). Ensure it is directed to the 'diary pages' of local newspapers.

14.30 Leave the office to attend a photo call for Warburtons, who have donated a cooker to a local school. It's important for us to attend, not only to direct the photographer on the style of photo, but also to provide support for the client representative.

16.00 Return to the office and draft an award entry for the UK Housing Awards on behalf of Yorkshire Housing. A scheme developed earlier in the year is being entered for the 'sustainable development' category and needs to be submitted by Friday. Send to client for approval.

18.00 Complete timesheet for Monday and today. (This helps us to see how much time we're all spending on each client). Tidy desk.

WINNING NEW BUSINESS

Small or large, regional or international – it makes no difference as new business is the lifeblood of every consultancy, so how do PR consultancies win this? Good marketing? Being in the right place at the right time? Luck? One thing is clear – no one method is better than another and there are no easy answers to the question of what brings in new business. If you ask a hundred PR practitioners what works and what doesn't, you'll get a hundred different answers.

As well as winning new business, companies may also lose existing clients. Clients leave consultancies for all sorts of reasons: they may want fresh ideas, they might want to bring in a company or people they have worked with before, they may disagree with the tactics a consultancy uses or be dissatisfied with their work, or they might simply have a reduced budget to spend on PR. When clients are lost, new business is needed not just to replace the lost business, but also in order to build and expand the company.

It can, however, sometimes be a mystery as to why one consultancy has been chosen rather than another and sometimes this may be for the most obscure and apparently trivial of reasons.

Companies can employ new business specialists but there is no guarantee that this approach works any better than any alternative, only that a new business campaign will be more organised. Occasionally, and this does happen, a PR company is found simply by a potential client looking through the telephone directory and making a call.

Box 9.3   Consultancies and the Public Sector

In the UK over a third of PR consultancies now have clients in the public, health and not for profit sectors. (CIPR 2005 Survey) They have benefitted from public sectors use of outside consultancies: in 2009/10, for example, the Central office of Information (COI), the body in charge of central government's communications, spent £19.5m on PR.

While this has undoubtedly provided business opportunities for many consultancies the process by which they have been chosen has not been without controversy. Andy Green for example said:

I do have strong views about the public sector using online tendering services, the technology and sophistication of the services is not matched by the sophistication in managing the process. A vast number of consultancies have wasted a lot of valuable management time chasing contracts which have not been managed to get a

---

professional valuation out of people. The public sector has a responsibility to not waste the private sector resources.

The COI agency evaluation criteria include; expertise, rates and charges, quality control systems, financial soundness and size of the company. When the COI recruits consultancies on behalf of government departments it invites a shortlist of consultancies to pitch: they claim that from the brief being issued to a consultancy being appointed can take as little as four to six weeks. However there is criticism that, when the COI is not involved in recruitment, the process takes too long and appointments tend to go to consultancies with a track-records in relevant areas. This means that only tried and tested consultancies are used and other consultancies are unable to make a break through.

The brief

When looking to appoint a PR consultancy a company will often produce a brief, explaining why they want to appoint a consultancy, what its role will be, and whether they will be, working on a specific campaign or providing more wide-ranging ongoing PR support around a number of issues. It is in the interests of both the company and the consultancy that the brief should be as detailed as possible. Crucially it should outline the campaign objectives so that the PR consultancy can create a cohesive strategy with appropriate tactics. If clear objectives are outlined at the start of the process as well then the success of the PR programme can be properly evaluated and measured. It is important that both the client and PR consultancy agree on the substance of the brief; if the PR company feels that the brief is not clear enough, it should request further clarification.

If a PR company receives a verbal instruction they should confirm their understanding of it in writing as soon as possible. Andy Green agrees that the clarity of the brief is crucial.

> *The best pitches are those where people produce a clear, specific brief, with a clearly articulated idea of what they want and also a clear transparent decision-making process and one that does not take up too much of people's time. I'm a great believer in a prelim screen. We've wasted a lot of time where people have said to us 'you haven't got it because too small'.* (Green, 2007)

When preparing for a pitch, consultancies have the opportunity to carry out their own assessment of where the potential client company is in communication terms and will often undertake research to identify any problems and issues that need addressing. Although they will not have the opportunity to undertake a full communications audit to analyse the views of all stakeholders, a common practice here is to undertake a limited media relations audit to identify what key journalists think of the potential client. The hope of course is that responding journalists will say they've never heard of the company or that they have a poor reputation, thereby enabling the PR consultancy to present a media relations focused campaign that will at least lead to an improved media profile.

The basic pre-account research the PR consultancy should undertake must include:

- a communications audit
- SWOT (Strengths, Weaknesses, Opportunities, Threats analysis) – for more details see Chapter 10
- a media relations audit.

The pitch

The pitch is the presentation of a PR plan to a new client. While larger consultancies can afford to have a dedicated new business team to prepare and carry out a pitch, executives at smaller companies may have to combine preparing and presenting a pitch with their existing workload. Managing the two can be quite a difficult balancing act – the danger is that a disproportionate amount of time is spent preparing for the presentation at the expense of their main role as a fee-earner. Getting the balance right between winning new business and doing the ongoing work is therefore absolutely critical.

The pitching process is far from perfect and both PR consultancies and potential clients criticise it; some potential new clients have been accused of using the process simply to trawl for new ideas without having any intention of appointing a consultancy. Consultancies can sometimes find that they have pitched their ideas to a client only to find out later that the same company has used those ideas for themselves. There have also been accusations that some client companies will pass on the best ideas from the other consultancies will involved in the pitch to the winning firm. Gordon Beattie, chief executive of Beattie Communications, says:

> We only work for clients that we like and would not go to the pitch stage if the client gave off unscrupulous or unprofessional vibes. Most clients are honest, but there are wide-boys out there who want to steal ideas from agencies. These people should be blacklisted with agencies knowing they deal with them at their peril. (PR Week, 1/12/05)

Some PR practitioners argue that consultancies should charge companies who invite them to pitch while others believe the PR consultancy should not present creative ideas about how they would handle the account, instead they should simply present a credentials brief about the work of the consultancy and its background, saying in effect 'This is who we are, this is who we have worked for in the past, we know we can do the work.' However, in a competitive environment it would be a brave consultancy indeed who took such a decision.

Cutlip et al. state that the pitch should cover the following:

- Research findings and a situation analysis of the problem or opportunity.
- Potential harm or gain to the organisation.
- Projected difficulties and opportunities given various courses of action or non-action.
- Overall programme goals as well as objectives for various publics.
- Immediate action and communication responses needed to meet a crisis.
- Long-range plans for achieving goals and objectives. (1999: 89)

Usually three or four consultancies will be invited along to the pitch which will follow a standard format. A presentation of the PR consultancy's plans for the campaign will usually last approximately 30 to 45 minutes and be followed by a question and answer session lasting about 15 minutes.

It is common practice to produce a presentation and then leave behind a longer written document that covers some of the issues in more detail.

One common client complaint is that often the team that pitches is not the team who actually works on the account. PR consultancies sometimes stand accused of putting their star performers forward to win new business and then using junior members of the company to carry out the work. According to Cutlip et al.

> To get the business (win the account), usually an "A-Team" of experienced professionals makes the presentation (new business pitch). The client is duly impressed by the talent and depth of experience they assume will be applied to their problems. In some instances, however, that is the last they see of many of these people. Instead the account gets assigned to staff members who do not have the range of experience represented by the new business development team. Critics justifiably refer to this practice as "bait and switch" tactics. The firm's senior executives show up just often enough to assure the client, but in fact the work has been done by the junior staff. (Cutlip et al., 1999: 95)

There has to be a balance here. Clients should recognise that the work will be handled by other staff in the consultancy and the PR consultancy should, for their part, make it clear from the outset if this is going to happen.

Sometimes the eventual decision about which consultancy to hire and the reasons behind it can, at least to the losing consultancy, appear inexplicable. The main reason usually given is that the losing consultancies have not demonstrated sufficient understanding of the new client and their business and have not translated the brief into a comprehensive PR programme. It is common and good practice for the losing consultancy to go back to the company and get feedback on why they did not win. This can be a useful experience as losing a pitch can be a depressing exercise for a consultancy, especially if a lot of time and effort went into preparing and rehearsing it.

For all their complaints about the process when invited to pitch, PR consultancies will rarely say no.

Case study: The Board Director

Denise Mullen is a former daily newspaper feature writer and news editor who has spent 20 years working in PR in London and the north west of England. She was a main board director responsible for business development at the UK's largest PR company, Harrison Cowley (Trimedia/Greyling), working across the whole of the UK before leaving to set up her own business which she recently sold, becoming a main board director and shareholder at Paver Smith & Co.

Little has changed in the fundamentals of new business. It's still all about chemistry and relationships. People won't employ people they don't warm to and trust, even if they made the better presentation on the day. At the end of the day they'll have to work with the team they choose. It's got to be a rewarding relationship going forward for both sides. What has changed is the amount of hoops an agency is required to go through. Any sector that appoints through a tender process asks for a lot of reassurance around accreditation and examples of almost 'replica' experience, but the tender process isn't built to handle a race on the grounds of transferable skills, reputation and a cannot-fail approach. It also pretty much excludes chemistry and relationship – except of course for the incumbent agency.

So there are still fault lines even in the fairest of approaches, especially when 20 hopeful agencies put their tenders in – with all the attached time and thought – to find that a straight re-appointment takes place. PR companies spend huge amounts of senior time on these tenders and proposals: they have a high value, but if it's a losing pitch, that cost isn't recouped. Most good agencies will have at least a one in four win rate for pitches where there's no prior relationship, with much higher odds of winning where there is. Do the maths. Networking, staying in touch, treating clients as though each meeting is a first date, making time for informal social catch ups – the best place to get an honest opinion or pick up any grumbles – and delivering good work consistently are the core of good business development. New business is all very well, but doesn't count for much if yesterday's new business falls off the end of the conveyor belt for a lack of love and attention, so listening is pretty important.

Honesty too can't be overrated. Honesty about what is and isn't working, or about promises used to secure business. Over promise to win and fail to deliver and it's all lose-lose. The brief is only as important as the client believes it to be. Most PR professionals will have had the experience of losing to an agency that 'went beyond the brief' or 'came up with something completely different'. Either of those routes, coupled with the third – sticking to the brief – carries a risk! Presentations to mute audiences (usually public sector) are just terrible. Dull for the panel and for the presenters, it's like having the enthusiasm sucked out of you by Harry Potter's Death Eaters.

Presentations should be a conversation, reaction, counter, question and balance. I have picked up in the middle of a presentation and told my team to 'pack, we're leaving'. I won't have rudeness, especially when the brief's been changed halfway up the stairs to the meeting room and then again during the course of the re-angled presentation. Those kind of bullying, 'show off' tactics aren't clever, but they are an indication that a hasty exit right now is a much better investment for the agency than a miserable six months of junior colleagues in tears. Nervous presenters are never good. I've even seen some pass out (not at any of my agencies). A PR consultant shaking like a leaf is never going to cut it in terms of giving client organisations the confidence to buy. Not everyone's good at everything, so train hard, practise, or leave it to someone who can!

Working the Account

The presentation went well, the questions answered brilliantly and they liked the look of the team who were going to work on the account. Congratulations all round – the account has been won. The hard work then starts of translating the fine-sounding proposals into reality.

Managing the account: Who does what?

In most medium to large PR consultancies the account management and handling structures will be broadly similar with four basic tiers of responsibility. At the top, the consultancy will be headed (as with most businesses) by a *managing director or chief executive*. The next tier down will be section *directors* who lead (where they are separate) the various strands of the *business* – such as financial communications, lobbying or consumer PR. Clearly, whether there are such sectors will depend on the size of the consultancy. Their role is a mixture of company management, HR, and hands-on PR management, and accounts are all handled by account teams structured in the same way. An *account director* will be in overall strategic charge of the account and responsible for ensuring that the team can meet their commitments and deadlines and resolve any major issues that might occur. Most accounts are worked on a month by month basis, with a programme of work for the month ahead being agreed by client and PR consultancy along with specific tactics such as media relations, to be used to meet the strategic objective during this period. A timeline will list who is responsible for which activity and what needs to be done during the time-frame. In small consultancies the account director role will often be fulfilled by the business principal.

The actual day to day work on the account will be carried out by an *account manager* while *account executives* will carry out the implementation of the

PR projects tactical programme and be responsible for all the day to day activities – drafting press releases and features, getting client approval for these, submitting the copy and organising any photography, as well as dealing with any media and organising events.

Depending on the size of the individual account there may be one, two or several account executives and managers working on specific aspects of the programme. The account director will usually be responsible for two or three different accounts again depending on the size of the individual accounts. Structures like this are flexible, based on the size of the PR company, the size of the account and its scope (i.e. whether national, international, etc.). A typical account executive would work for two or three clients.

BOX 9.4   Working in a PR Consultancy

Below is a list of roles within a typical PR consultancy and the task that each role performs. This list begins with the the most junior position and ends with the most senior.

Account Assistant:

• Duties: writing press releases, planning/organising events

Account Executive/Senior Account Executive:

• Duties: briefing photographers, liaising with journalists/media contacts, selling stories, writing a range of features/articles/press releases

Account Manager:

• Duties: managerial – supervising others, delegating tasks, negotiating, budgeting, creating and implementing strategy, assessing risk, carrying out SWOT analysis

Senior Account Manager/Account Director/Associate Director

• Duties: managerial – leading/motivating teams, managing PR and internal communication strategies, risk assessment, crisis/issues management, coaching, writing (e.g. speeches, proposals)

Client satisfaction

Clarity in the programme and PR objectives is important to the evaluation process. When there is a clearly defined PR programme agreed by both client and PR consultancy, it becomes easier to measure the effectiveness of what has been achieved. If, for example, the aim of the PR programme is to raise awareness amongst a key target audience, then by measuring and comparing awareness both before and after the PR campaign has started, it should be possible to gauge its success. However, difficulties can and do arise when PR is only one element of a communications programme which can also include advertising and marketing; under such circumstances is it possible to separate out the various elements and measure them individually? According to Jane Howard, such joint campaigns are common, 'and can be measured quite satisfactorily by setting the right objectives at the start of the campaign'. The key to getting it right is agreeing upon and setting the appropriate objectives.

A clear sign that a campaign has been successful is winning an award. Every year the industry's professional societies and media hold awards ceremonies celebrating examples of excellence within the industry. The PRCA and the CIPR both hold annual awards ceremonies and *PR Week* refers to its awards as the equivalent of the film industry's Oscars.

The relationship between a PR consultancy and its client can be volatile because their working relationship has to be closer than, say, that between an advertising agency and client. There can be a degree of objectivity between the advertising agency and client – ideas can be presented and looked at dispassionately for whether an advertising campaign meets the requirements. The PR consultancy though at times will have to become the client; absorbing and reflecting their ethos and culture. This is not easy and it is therefore little wonder that sometimes problems can occur. For example, a common problem is that the consultancy might not interpret the client's wishes correctly or a client might not like giving so much information and influence to their PR consultancy.

Over-servicing

Account teams can spend too much time on an account and this is known as over servicing an account.

How much time should an account team actually spend working on a client's account? Jane Howard believes that the answer is, 'However much time it is agreed with the client should be spent. This question of executive hours is central to most procurement negotiations and key to efficient operations'. If the client is being charged by the hour, then the answer would seem obvious – as many hours as possible in order to generate maximum income. If there is an agreed programme of work, the answer should also be clear – until the agreed work in the programme has been completed. However the answer is rarely that simple. Consultancies will over service clients for all sorts of reasons. In a competitive industry like PR it reflects well on a consultancy if they are seen to give their clients extra work and time for free. Consultancies may actively do this when they want to retain the business of a reputable client whose good name might bring other clients their way.

Over servicing can also occur when clients push consultancies to provide more than they had originally agreed upon. In a competitive market customers have the upper hand, making it hard for consultancies to refuse demands for extra time. Over servicing can also sometimes result from bad planning, for example, when the consultancy has underestimated the amount of resources needed or they have simply not calculated properly. Over servicing of clients affects the profitability of an account but in a competitive environment, when there might not be a great deal of difference between PR companies, consultancies will continue doing this.

Reducing the amount of time spent working on an account, or charging more per hour, are both solutions to the problem of the financial impact of over servicing. However, in a competitive environment clients can afford to be choosy and a constant worry is that if fees are increased client loyalty will not be deep enough to prevent them from looking elsewhere. In economically difficult times there are plenty of consultancies prepared to undercharge to win a new account.

Over servicing is not always a bad thing, as it can help to foster good relationships with clients – consultancies however should not confuse volume of work with quality and should also remember that too much over servicing will affect their profit margins.

Charging

A PR consultancy will receive its income mainly from the fees it charges clients; the ideal payment method for the consultancy is an agreed monthly retainer. There is no set pattern to charging or the rate charged: consultancies will charge differently depending on the nature of the work involved and the client. Some will, for example, charge certain clients a low retainer because they want to keep their name on the account list or because the account will have opportunities to raise additional income through re-charging clients for print work. For many smaller consultancies this can be an important additional revenue stream.

BOX 9.5   Main charging methods

- A monthly retainer covering a fixed number of hours and services or ensuring that the client has an exclusive call on the consultancy's services (i.e. they won't work for anyone else in the same sector/line of business).
- A minimum retainer plus monthly billing for actual staff time at hourly rates.
- Hourly charges, scaled to reflect the experience and background of staff.
- A project fee – a fee for a specific piece of work.

Where consultancies buy-in work from outside, say designers or photographers, they will often charge an additional 17.5% 'handling charge' on top to clients.

SUMMARY

The growing trend in PR consultancies is for them to specialise in specific sectors such as consumer, financial or public affairs. This chapter has described the function of a PR consultancy and the job roles of those who work in them. The structure of PR consultancies and the job titles (account director, manager, executive, etc.) follow the convention found in advertising agencies. This is understandable given that both deal with a process that involves handling an external client. However, there are signs that some of the job functions and titles are changing to suit the specific circumstances of a PR consultancy. This also ties in with some new consultancies where the distinctions between PR and advertising are breaking down and integrated consultancies are working on a range of solutions based on specific needs.

There is a wide variation in PR consultancies, reflecting the growth of the industry and also its increasing specialisation and fragmentation. Yet growth and good news cannot disguise some of the problems the industry faces – staff churn, especially among new entrants, and the consistent delivery of quality services to clients. PR degrees and professional qualifications will play an important part in the drive to improve quality in the industry.

STRATEGY, RESEARCH, MEASUREMENT AND EVALUATION

By the end of this chapter you will understand:

- why planning and strategy are important in PR
- when research should be carried out and why it matters to every successful PR campaign
- the relationship between strategy and tactics
- why and how PR campaigns are evaluated and why this evaluation is important

INTRODUCTION

Good, effective PR does not just happen. At the heart of any successful campaign is research, planning and strategy – these are the essentials of any PR campaign whether it is carried out in-house or by consultancy PR practitioners. This chapter looks at how strategy is applied to and used in PR. Every strategy has tactics which are implemented to achieve campaign objectives. Historically in PR the most important tactic has been media relations and although the range and variety of tactics available are growing, media relations still remains by far and away the most important tactical element in a large number of PR campaigns.

Electronic communication channels and direct communication with the audience have had a major impact on the distribution of information. As we have seen in previous chapters, for many PR practitioners responding to these new channels is one of the biggest challenges currently facing the PR industry. During the course of this chapter when analysing the strategic structures of a campaign no distinction will be made about whether it is run by a PR consultancy or an in-house practitioner. The media make no distinction between them – they are all PR practitioners and in practice there are little or no differences in the actual way the media are approached.

STRUCTURING A PR PROGRAMME

The ideal PR programme should be based on the following structure:

- R: Research
- A: Action
- C: Communication
- E: Evaluation

The PRCA recommends that every PR campaign should contain a brief (see above) followed by an audit which looks at where the company/organisation currently is. The purpose of this is to gather information and through research build the foundation for a PR campaign or programme of activity. Depending on the nature of the campaign and the organisation the audit will probably contain one or all of the following elements:

- Key audience perception + an audit of competitors and own company
- Media profile or audit
- SWOT analysis (see below)
- Issues and problems analysis

Research will also look at which messages worked and also those that were rejected in either earlier or similar campaigns. All campaigns need to determine from the outset which messages are going to be conveyed during the campaign. Campaigns that have mixed or unclear messages will be more likely to fail because target audiences will miss these or not understand them. Where appropriate there needs to be co-ordination between advertising and PR messages.

Research

While identifying the strategy to be followed companies need to understand and be aware of the environment they are operating in and this is why research before a campaign is started is so important. Research should not be carried out for its own sake but should attempt to answer specific questions such as:

- Who is the campaign aimed at?
- What are the characteristics of the target audience – their geo-demographics, behavioural patterns, etc?

- What are the best channels of communication to reach the target audience i.e. which media do they access? If none, what kind of events do they go to?
- What does the target audience (publics) think about an issue/organisation?
- Have attitudes/opinions towards a company/product/brand or service changed over a period of time?
- What are the likely outcomes of different scenarios for the organisation?
- Who are the opinion leaders in a community on an issue?

Research also has another important role in a campaign – that of helping to identify and establish measurable benchmarks by which the programme can be evaluated. There are different categories of research and the category used will be the one that is most appropriate to the campaign:

- *Descriptive Research:* helps identify and delineate a situation process or phenomenon.
- *Explanatory Research:* helps understand why events happen.
- *Predictive Research:* helps predict the likely outcomes of actions or the failure to act

Defining PR: problems and issues
PR has developed its own specific research methods which are designed to look at the role and place of the organisation and its setting in the world. These are:

- Communication Audits: These analyse what has already happened with a company's communications and how effective or otherwise earlier communication methods were.
- Social/Environmental Audits/scanning/monitoring: This type of research has grown in popularity as companies have become more aware and concerned about their place and role in society and how they interact with the world outside.
- Stakeholder Mapping: This is a process that identifies and categorises an organisation's stakeholders, which interests they represent, and the amount of power they hold in relation to the organisation. All stakeholders have some form of power, whether it is formal power such as being in a position of authority or the social power of being able to persuade others to support or oppose a course of action. Stakeholder mapping is usually followed by the production of a stakeholder map which will show a stakeholder's relationship with the organisation and who has to be kept close (and dealt with as a priority) and those who can be accorded lower priorities.

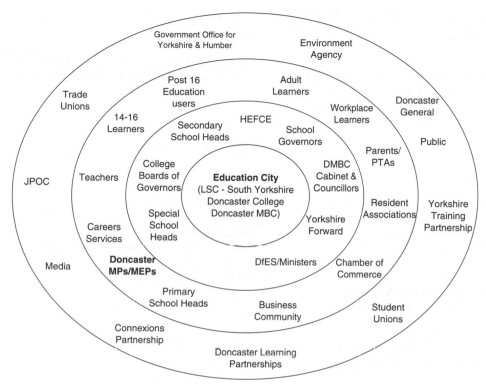

Figure 10.1   Stakeholder Wheel Key Stakeholders for Education City Project

A variation on this is the stakeholder wheel originally developed by Edward Bernays. This maps an organisation's stakeholders using a series of concentric circles, with those closest to the centre being the most important in communication terms. Figure 10.1 shows a stakeholder wheel submitted as part of a presentation to potential new clients.

SWOT and PEST analyses

Strengths Weaknesses Opportunities Threats (SWOT) and Political Economic Social and Technological (PEST) analyses are also common to other disciplines and have a role in communication research because they are not PR specific. They will generally only provide background information.

If it is not possible to carry out any research before the start of any campaign two basic questions NEED to be asked of the client:

- Why do you want to communicate?
- Who do you want to communicate to?

Table 10.1   Examples of SWOT and PEST analysis

SWOT analysis	PEST analysis
An analysis of the company's strengths, weaknesses,the opportunities open to it and any identifiable threats that might be posed. A SWOT analysis is applicable to many different situations and circumstances. Listed below are some questions a SWOT analysis might raise.	PEST research analyses the political and economic situations affecting a company. Listed below are some examples of such situations.

Strengths:
  What are the advantages?
  What does the company do well?
Weaknesses:
  What could be improved?
  What is done badly?
  What should be avoided?
Opportunities:
  Where are the possible opportunities?
  What are the interesting trends?
Threats:
  What are the obstacles faced?
  What is the competition doing?
  Is changing technology threatening the position?
  Are there bad debt or cash-flow problems?
	Political:
	  Environmental legislation
	  Employment legislation
	  Trade
	  Change/continuance of government
	Economic:
	  Interest rates
	  Inflation
	  Employment levels
	  Supplier costs – for example energy charges
	  Business cycle
	  External economic conditions
	Social:
	  Population shifts and growth
	  Lifestyles
	  Levels of education
	  Income/wealth distribution
	  Consumer spending trends
	  Social attitudes and concerns
	Technological:
	  New discoveries
	  Rate of change
	  Investment in technology
	  Spending on research and development
	  Impact of new technologies

At the very least, these questions will help focus client attention and should also help stimulate a discussion to clarify the basis of their communication.

Strategy

Based on the research, the campaign planners will then produce a strategy to guide and direct the campaign and from this the goals and structure of the campaign.

'Strategy' is derived from the Greek word '*stratego*s' and refers to an overall commanding role like a general commanding an army. In business, strategy determines the broad scope and directions of an organisation's development and how it can achieve a competitive strategy.

Every company whatever their size, should have a strategy. In a company strategies exist at several levels there will, for example, be an overall company corporate strategy while each operation or division such as marketing will also have its own strategy. The corporate strategy attempts to answer the big questions such as, 'what business shall we be in? Should we be in another?' While a competitive strategy asks specific questions such as: 'how shall we compete in each business?'

BOX 10.1   Levels of strategy

- Corporate-level strategy: This is concerned with the overall purpose and scope of an organisation and how value will be added to the different parts that are the business units of the organisation.
- Business-level strategy: This maps how to compete successfully in particular markets. A strategic business unit is a part of an organisation for which there is a distinct external market for goods or services.
- Operational strategies: These are concerned with how the component parts of an organisation can effectively deliver the corporate and business-level strategies in terms of resources, processes and people.
- Strategic management: This includes understanding the strategic position of an organisation, the strategic choices for the future, and turning strategy into action.

A PR strategy is the overall approach to a campaign or programme and the rationale behind the tactical programme and will be dictated to and determined by issues that arise from analysis and research. It is the foundation on which the tactical programme is built and moves the company from where it currently is to where it wants to be by the end of the programme.

Steps in strategic planning include determining the organization's mission, developing an organizational profile, assessing the external environment, matching the organizational profile with environmental opportunities, identifying best options consistent with the mission, choosing long-term goals, developing short-term objectives, implementing programs, and evaluating success or failure. Communication becomes a strategic management function when communication programs help manage relationships with key publics that affect organizational mission, goals and objectives. (Dozier et al., 1995: 85)

Box 10.2   Strategy/Tactics/Objectives

Below is an example of strategy/tactics/objectives in practice.

- OBJECTIVE: Publicise new products/services (must be realistic, achievable and measurable).
- STRATEGY: Media relations campaign (the methods used to achieve the objectives).
- TACTICS: Press conferences, press releases, interviews, competitions etc. (the specific actions that will be carried out in order to achieve the objectives).

If, as in the example above, the research shows that a media relations campaign is the best tactic to achieve the campaign objectives then this will be dovetailed into the wider communications strategy. The media relations campaign plan need not be complicated but should identify

- Key media – whether, for example, it should include any or all of the following: local, regional, national, ethnic minority media, the specialist or trade press, and professional organisations covering the issue.
- Key messages – ensuring the media work carries key messages relating to the overall objectives.
- Resources – whether budgets and staff are available.
- The communication methods required – including feature placement, photo opportunities, drafting news releases, briefing journalists, etc.
- Timescales and deadlines.
- How the campaign will be evaluated to measure its success.

In Chapter 11 we will look in detail at the specific tactics used in a PR campaign.

Measurement and evaluation

In 2005 the PRCA teamed up with other communication organisations, including the Institute of Practitioners in Advertising, the Marketing Agencies Association, and the Society of British Advertisers, to agree a joint industry framework for evaluation of effectiveness. *Evaluation: A best practice guide to evaluating the effects of your campaign* highlighted the importance of evaluation to each industry's respective clients. In PR's case the client feedback found that:

- Clients were fed-up with PR's apparent lack of commitment to measuring effectiveness.
- Fewer than 20% of agencies consistently evaluated their contribution to the profitability of their client.
- Only 36% of the agencies had had formal training in evaluation.

This lack of evaluation by PR companies makes them easy targets for budget cuts because in many cases they cannot demonstrate value for money. As budgets are scrutinised all too often cuts are made to the PR spend, and in many cases this is because PR is less able than other forms of marketing communications to evaluate its work and so justify the investment. This can and must change, because

- 84% of clients said evaluation was now as important to them as the creative product.
- 90% of clients believed that evaluation data should help determine how agencies should be paid.

Surveys like this highlight the problems that a lack of proper evaluation can cause and the difficulties this creates. All PR campaigns – whether carried out only for a specific period and related to a clearly defined set of objectives and goals, or as part of ongoing daily PR activity carried out by an in-house local authority department – should be evaluated for their effectiveness. The need for evaluation is simple: if there is no evaluation how does an organisation know whether its communication has been effective or not? Unfortunately assessment and evaluation have always been regarded as the least important elements of a PR campaign.

A distinction needs to be made between market research and media evaluation. Media evaluation is the measure of a PR campaign's physical results which is often the amount and type of coverage the company gained in the media. Market research measures the impact of a campaign on public opinion. Quite often the two will be linked and used as part of the same campaign, for example for the launch of a consumer campaign. The company behind the launch needs to understand how it is perceived in the media (media evaluation) and also with the target audience (market research). A more sophisticated evaluation will not only analyse media coverage, but also poll the 'influencers' such as journalists and analysts.

PR can be used in a number of different situations:

- To support the sales and marketing of a company.
- To increase a company's share price.
- To influence the legislative process for the company's interests.

- To improve employee relations.
- To generate community support for a course of action.
- For crisis damage limitation.

This is just a small sample of some of different types of campaigns and each requires their own separate methods for evaluating their effectiveness.

Although measuring and evaluating a PR campaign was once regarded as the industry's Achilles' heel, there have been improvements. Attempts by Cutlip et al. and Macnamara (1992) to produce formal evaluation models that could be used in a variety of situations are not used in practice because such models are too sophisticated, and if these were implemented would be too costly for the vast majority of PR campaigns. Cutlip devised a so-called 'step' model which offers levels of evaluation for differing demands and accepts that evaluation means different things to different PR practitioners (Cutlip et al., 1985) Mcnamara's Macro-Model of Evaluation identified the types of research methodologies that might be adopted at each level of the measurement and separated outputs and results.

Traditionally the industry has concentrated on relatively unsophisticated measures of evaluation, such as monitoring

- the number of messages sent
- the accuracy of the messages in the media
- the amount of media coverage generated, often referred to as 'column inches' or 'broadcast minutes'
- the number of people potentially exposed to the message

These however measure the *process* of communication and not the *impact* of the message either in the media or crucially and more importantly with key target audiences. Effective evaluation requires measurement not only of communication process and output but also of communication effects on the target publics, that is, what the impact is in terms of attitudinal and behavioural change.

Pseudo-measurement

In practice many PR practitioners have tended to rely on relatively unsophisticated measures such as the volume of media coverage generated by the media release, the type of media the release is featured in, and the frequency of mentions in the media. The rationale for using such methods includes the prohibitive costs of conducting pre- and post-testing of audiences, the lack of time to conduct research, and a lack of research skills amongst practitioners. However, as evaluation becomes a more widely established practice and clients expect to know what they are spending their money on, doing little or no evaluation is no longer an option.

Opportunities To See (OTS)

This is a simple way to measure outputs as a 'scorecard' is agreed with the client before the programme starts. Some consultancies, for example, will produce an A and B list of publications, so a press release appearing in the A list publications counts for more than appearing in a B list publication. Other pre-agreed measures with the client could include:

- How many key messages were delivered?
- Was the competition mentioned?
- Did the piece include a visual or logo?
- Was a company spokesperson quoted?
- What was the page position of the piece?
- How many readers did it reach?
- What was the quality of the readership? (the quality of the readership would be defined and determined by the nature of the campaign and who was being influenced)

Cuttings agencies that used to evaluate the number of cuttings and the size of articles in newspapers can now track coverage by the volume and tone of the coverage, looking at the impact in specific publications, journalists, external commentators. They will evaluate by deciding whether the content of the article/comment was favourable, what the message content was, and its tone (critical, favourable, supportive, unsupportive, etc.).

Advertising Value Equivalence (AVE)

AVE is one of the most popular evaluation measures and particularly among smaller PR consultancies, but it is also the least sophisticated and most criticised. AVE measures the amount of coverage gained, often by calculating the column inches in the publication, and calculates the cost of equivalent advertising space. Using the publication's advertising rates a 'cost' can be allocated to the story, so the PR company can then say to the client 'We have saved you £X in advertising.'

The UK Public Relations Consultants Association advises against the use of AVEs, arguing that:

> They are weak and imply public relations is a substitute for advertising when the two disciplines have different roles. AVEs take no account of positive or negative coverage, or the value (or damage) of editorial endorsement (or criticism). High quality editorial endorsement cannot be bought, so to put a value on it by using equivalent advertising space costs is misleading. (www.prca.co.uk, 2008)

Payment By Results (PBR)

PR consultancies are paid for the results of their work. Again, a number of measures can be used to determine this, such as, for example, the number of press cuttings generated or press releases issued. A financial measure might be the value of the additional business brought in as a result of the PR campaign. There could also be a combination of measures – for example, a base retainer fee with incentives to reach agreed targets. Alternatively, we have basic costs + AVE with more paid if coverage is achieved in key publications. Some financial PR companies use PBR that is related to the financial results of the client company. PBR was once a taboo subject in PR and a payment scheme to be avoided, however it has now started to appear more frequently.

There are clear advantages for clients here: it would for one thing ensure that the PR consultancy remained focused on the campaign as if there was no coverage then there would be no payment. There is, however, a clear risk to the PR consultancy as they have no control over what appears in the media, or even how a release might be used. A great deal of time and effort can be spent honestly trying to generate coverage and then at worst nothing appears or what does appear does not contain relevant or appropriate messages. PBR though does work in digital media where the coverage can be monitored more easily through hit measures or page impressions. In marketing communications the preferred evaluation appears to be econometrics – that is the measure of the financial effectiveness of the programme/campaign, and the first step to analysing the return on investment (ROI) would be to measure the effect on sales.

Professional organisations such as the PRCA do not believe that the evaluation of a PR campaign should be treated in isolation: they talk of the 'virtuous circle' of planning, research and evaluation which should be part of every campaign and also be a continuous process. Approximately 7 to 10% of the PR budget should be allocated to planning, research and evaluation (PRE).

Electronic evaluation

The process of electronic evaluation and online monitoring is expertly explained here by Michael Cooper, Online PR Business Manager of amaze public relations.

The first step in any project is to identify the current and pre-existing conversations taking place around the company, brand or particular issue stretching back over the previous 12–18 months. Within this audit, we will catalogue all references to the brand, in relation to specific keywords, across all news and social media outlets. These findings are then interrogated to recognise emerging themes, identify opportunities for engagement and highlight issues of concern or potential problems.

The audit will also identify the most influential online participants and could be journalists, bloggers, forum commentators or members of social networks such as Facebook or Twitter. Some will be the figureheads for the issues arising around the problem and so can be recognised as "advocates" who can assist in distributing positive news, or "badvocates" whose negative comments will need to be managed accordingly. (Cooper, 2008)

SUMMARY

Successful PR needs to be carefully researched and planned to ensure that the right target audiences are being reached. Research and establishing these audiences will also enable clear and effective benchmarks to be created which can then be used in the post-campaign evaluation process. The campaign strategy will determine the overall goals and also which tactics should be used to achieve the objectives. The issue of how effective PR campaigns are is an important one and is often driven by financial considerations. Whether it is a client spending money with a PR consultancy or an in-house department scrutinising the effectiveness of a communications department the issues are broadly the same – how do we know if what is being spent on PR represents value for money? Too much PR activity is front-loaded, that is, working on press releases and attempting to maximise the media coverage or organising an event. Far too little activity is actually spent on assessing how effective a campaign has been. There is a range of evaluation methods available, with some more effective than others, but the most effective campaigns are often those that have had clear campaign goals and objectives built into their strategy.

PUTTING EFFECTIVE PR CAMPAIGNS INTO PRACTICE

By the end of this chapter you will:

- understand how PR campaigns are structured
- understand the relationship between journalists and PR practitioners
- have seen how PR practitioners communicate with their target audiences and what works and what doesn't
- realise how electronic communication and social media are changing the nature of PR practice

INTRODUCTION

The specific tactics to be used in a PR campaign will be decided by the nature of the campaign and the target audience. A modern campaign has more tactical options available than ever before and the pre-campaign research discussed in the previous chapter will have established and identified the most appropriate channels of communication to be used. It would, for example, be no use to have a primarily media relations-based campaign if the target audience rarely read newspapers or magazines or listened to conventional electronic channels, such as TV or radio.

This is one of the challenges facing public health campaigns aimed at teenage girls warning them about the dangers of smoking. No number of worthy, well-written articles in newspapers will have any impact if the target audience never picks up the newspapers in which it appears. The channels of communication have to be appropriate to the target audience and sometimes this means thinking creatively.

TACTICS: THE BUILDING BLOCKS OF PR CAMPAIGNS
Journalists and PR – hacks and flacks

Although media relations remains one of PR's most important tactics, the relationship between journalism and PR still remains a difficult one and is arguably getting worse as the power and influence of PR in the media grows. The lowest point in the relationship was possibly reached after what become known as the 'Jo Moore Incident' (see Box 11.1) in 2001, which allowed many media commentators to vent their hostility towards PR.

For many journalists the PR practitioner has long been regarded as an unwelcome intruder, someone who prevents them from doing their job by restricting or controlling the flow of information in an attempt to manage and control a story. At best, the journalist will view a PR contact as the starting point for a story, a reliable source of information who responds positively and quickly to requests for information, who presents facts in a straightforward manner with no attempt at any form of 'spin' or interpretation on them.

For their part, PR practitioners can often be frustrated by what they regard as a wilful obstruction and a misinterpretation by some journalists, complaining about misquotes or information they have supplied being used out of context to produce a completely different story from the one originally submitted. However, there are issues here which are rather more serious than offended pride or the mutual distrust and suspicion of both parties towards each other. There is, or should be, concern about the increasing amount of PR-originated material that is appearing not only in trade and consumer magazines, but also in quality newspapers such as *The Guardian* and *The Times* as well as in TV and radio news. A study by researchers (Lewis et al., 2008) at Cardiff University analysed the news content of quality newspapers during a two-week period in 2006 and the results demonstrated how even in the quality broadsheets where the standard of critical journalism is thought to be more rigorous, the use of PR and news agency (especially the UK Press Association) sources was high. This 'Raises significant questions concerning claims to journalistic independence in UK news media' (Lewis et al., 2008).

Where does the fault for this lie? It should be easy to blame the PR industry for flooding news outlets with so much material. But this situation has been caused by cut-backs made by the media owners, a consequence of falls in circulation and advertising revenue. Faced with difficult economic circumstances newspaper proprietors are reducing staff numbers, which then makes it harder for the remaining journalists to critically check every press release. Press releases used to be regarded as the starting point for a story, to be checked and worked on, and not as the end material itself to be reproduced with no editing.

On the other hand the PR industry is huge – the majority of companies, charities and organisations now having their own PR adviser – and as a result the sheer amount of material produced and sent to the media is overwhelming, making it hard for journalists to be as critical as they would like to be.

Case Study: The Business Journalist

Terry Macalister is the energy editor of the *Guardian* and has been a business journalist for over twenty years working for, among others, the BBC and the *London Evening Standard*.

I have noticed during my 20 odd years in journalism a dramatic increase in the amount of PR generated material that business journalists have to deal with. One of the main reasons for this has been the growth of the Internet and the development of social media sites. I deal largely with public companies whose shares are traded in public through the Stock Exchange, but nowadays, investors, potential investors, employees can get access to company information from a number of different sources and companies have to respond to this by providing information and trying to control it.

For public companies (plcs) the demands of the regulatory authorities such as the Stock Exchange have also increased the volume of material they have to produce and business journalists have to deal with.

While most of this material might be seen as necessary or at least benign, I have also been subject to the 'darker side' of PR – the attempt by financial PR companies for example to correct what they regard as 'misapprehensions' on my part. It is incredibly easy to get sucked into the corporate mindset for seeing things from their point of view: they will criticise, flatter, use tempting corporate hospitality, interviews with chief executives – all sorts of means – all of which is intended to suck you into their point of view.

The current economic difficulties faced by newspapers also create their own pressures on journalists. There are more demands on us and we have less time for example to actually do the checking on stories. This is going to get far worse because of the economics of the media industry. The PR industry cannot be blamed for this situation. A chief executive of PR company said to me that this dilution of quality can actually be bad for business. If a video goes on a website unedited or a press release goes into a newspaper without any editing then people don't take it as seriously as if it were the subject of a critical piece of writing. Without the stamp of independence it doesn't have any credibility or effectiveness.

The PR industry argues that its growth is a response to the demands of the a 24 hour media which has to be fed with stories. The media's constant need for content has to be controlled and planned otherwise chaos would ensue. However, despite these difficult circumstances there is no reason why the relationship between the media and PR should always be adversarial. It is possible to have a creative relationship with PR contacts, using them as an extension of limited resources. This is the way that many trade journalists have to operate because they do not have the staff to undertake every job. But if they do engage with the PR industry in this way they must do so without compromising their editorial integrity.

The pressure for cost reduction affects TV and radio as well as printed media:

'Journalists just don't have the same resources available as they've had in the past. I worked in broadcast journalism for 15 years and when I started, a TV crew was made up of a cameraman, a soundman, a lights man and, a producer and a correspondent. These days, the journalist is sometimes doing the lot – then goes back to the newsroom to edit it. That doesn't leave much time for going out to find and investigate your own stories,' says Catherine Bayfiel, Director of Shout Communications. 'It (the TV industry) is consolidating, stripping out costs; already tight resources are being stretched even further, arguably creating the perfect environment for broadcast PR specialists to play the white knight and rescue editors and producers with offers of ready-made stories' (PR Week, 4/2/05)

BOX 11.1   THE JO MOORE INCIDENT

In the 1997 General Election Jo Moore was the Labour Party's chief press and broadcasting officer. After the election the new Labour Government appointed many party employees as special advisers to help get the party's political message across and Jo Moore was one of those who moved across from party to government.

In 2001 Moore was working as a special adviser to the then Secretary of State, Stephen Byers.

At 2.55pm on September 11 2001, after both World Trade Center towers and the Pentagon had been attacked by Al-Queda terrorists, Moore sent the following email to the press officers in her department: 'It's now a very good day to get out anything we want to bury. Councillors' expenses?'

The following day, the Department announced two minor changes to the system of local councillors allowances, a story which was, as Moore probably intended, virtually ignored

(Continued)

(Continued)

by the UK media, pre-occupied as it was with the events of 9/11. However, a month later Moore herself became the story when her email was leaked to the media, provoking a storm of criticism. In the subsequent stories that appeared in the media the text of the email was, incorrectly, reported as 'It's a good day to bury bad news ...' (Incidentally, this is an example of the type of misquoting referred to above that PR practitioners complain of.) While Moore had to make a personal apology on TV and survived in her job, the email was eagerly seized upon by a the press as a demonstration of everything they claimed was wrong with PR: 'There could be no starker wake-up call to spin doctors the world over than Labour adviser Jo Moore. Her tactics (have) fuelled the image of PR advisers as insensitive, manipulative charlatans,' said the *Guardian* newspaper in October that year (Echo, 2002). The incident damaged PR's already poor image. The media were vicious in their criticism as the incident appeared to confirm all their suspicions about PR. Research carried out by the trade publication *PR Week,* analysed how newspapers portrayed PR in 2001. 'Scumbags', 'Insensitive, manipulative charlatans' 'Sleazy ... disingenuous' – these were just some of the terms used to describe PR and its practitioners (Echo, 2002). The research showed that support for PR in the press had fallen since similar research in 1999, only 9% of articles in 2001 had a positive mention of PR compared with 22% in 1999.

A few voices in the media understood the nature of the relationship between journalists and PR was changing, *The Times* struck a lonely stance when it commented 'It is never edifying to watch the press explode with moral indignation against hands which have fed it so well'(Echo, 2002) and 'Honest recognition of the interdependence between PR and the media was in short supply.'

Moore eventually resigned her position the following year after accusations that she had suggested a similar course of action following the death of Princess Margaret.

In practice organisations will have varied and different relationships with the media. For a small regional PR consultancy working for a client company manufacturing products for use in industrial processes, the battle will be to get media coverage in publications read by potential purchasers of the products. However, if you are a PR practitioner working in-house for a large organisation such as the Treasury, and at the heart of the UK government's economic policy, there will be regular contact with both electronic and print media and constant requests for interviews and comments. Any press releases issued will be covered in the media and speeches by ministers or press conferences will be at the centre of the 24-hour rolling news agenda. The problem here is not getting media coverage but often the reverse. For such organisations there is too much media coverage and their concern is how to ensure that their core message i.e. what it wants to say, rather than the media's varied interpretation of the message, is covered.

While the Lewis study presents a critical view of the media's relationship with PR a more positive analysis was provided by the 2009 report, *What's Happening to Our News?*. Published by the Reuters Institute for the Study of Journalism at Oxford University, it recognises that PR is an 'Integral component of the media landscape' and argues that journalists should 'be more positive in their dealings with the industry.

Andrew Currah, the report's author, outlined the benefits of PR, supporting the argument made above that with journalists under an increasing amount of pressure PR can become an external source of newsgathering: 'Overall, we view the PR industry as an integral component of the media landscape, and as a pivotal agent in the gathering, packaging and dissemination of news to consumers. The symbiosis between journalism and PR can be argued to deliver economic efficiencies and social welfare gains'.

The report also highlighted how crucial PR was to informing the public about the activity of charities and NGOs: 'It is through PR that activities of charities and NGOs are disseminated to the public: for example, a significant amount of investigative journalism and undercover reporting ... now originates from this parallel universe of activism and campaigning, not from the mainstream media. To be sure, there are serious drawbacks to a PR-led media agenda, but there are also reasons for optimism'.

MEDIA RELATIONS IN THE PR CAMPAIGN

In order for it to be successfully used as a PR tactic media relations needs to be part of a structured programme and only used if applicable and appropriate (see above).

Media relations can be divided into two components:

- Authorship and distribution.
- Dealing with media enquiries.

Writing the news release

A basic requirement for a career in PR is strong writing skills and this is why ex-journalists are often employed in PR roles. The first job of any news release is to catch the attention of the person that the release is sent to. It is said that a news release only has 30 seconds in which to explain what it is about, and why it is of interest to the media. If the news release cannot attract attention in this window then it will be ignored.

That is why the structure of the news release has to reflect that of a news story. Journalists are told to structure their news stories like an inverted pyramid with the most important and significant parts of the story in the opening couple of paragraphs. A similar structure is used in a PR news release; the main point of the story must be contained in the opening paragraphs. It is no use burying the most important elements deep in the news release because these will be ignored. If the story cannot be expressed in the crucial opening paragraphs and attract attention, then it is likely to be rejected. There are many good books providing guidance on how to write a press release, one of which is John Foster's *Effective Writing Skills for Public Relations* (2008).

Distributing the news release

Targeting the right people

Many media outlets welcome and in many ways depend on news releases. However, if they are wrongly addressed or, even worse, are wholly inappropriate to the publication, then they are a complete waste of time, effort and money.

Identifying key media and the contacts relevant to a campaign's target audiences is central to a successful campaign; this means choosing from some or all of the following:

- Specialist/trade press.
- National press.
- Local press.
- Broadcast media (radio and TV).
- Electronic media.

Effective media relations starts with effective targeting (Bland et al., 2000). There is no point in sending a technical story to a general newspaper, or a photograph of a victorious works football team to a periodical which only carries product news. PR practitioners should target publications that are directly relevant to the product or person they are trying to promote, whether through trade magazines or specialist consumer publications. In many campaigns these will be the main focus of the company, so the PR contact should develop good relationships with the key journalists. Clare Newsome, editor of electronics magazine *What Hi-Fi*, says that

> The big problem is that PR people don't really read the magazine that they are sending releases to. To be in What Hi-Fi *is very different from two years ago with more coverage on developments such as MP3 players and downloading music for example. Today there is a new type of reader that we want to talk to. We have needed to alter our content subtly to appeal to these new readers.* (PR Week, 20/5/05)

Mark Westaby, founder and director of media evaluation COMPANY, believes that

PR agencies simply aren't doing enough to educate themselves about who reads publications and how their readers change. Advertisers go into great depth to find out who their targets are. PR agencies don't. If agencies pushed for the money (required for media planning) and made clients realise that they would benefit as a result, then the industry as a whole would benefit. (PR Week, 20/5/05)

Perhaps one of the reasons for this lack of planning and research is not only a resources issue, but that historically PR as a career has generally attracted ex-journalists where the main requirement was a working knowledge of the media because of the need to get media coverage for clients. Ex-journalists, however, would not have a background in media or campaign planning. The PR industry now demands more management and planning skills and this is a further reason why professional training and PR degrees are important as these can provide exactly the type of skills the industry needs.

Compiling an appropriate and accurate media list should be one of the most basic and important jobs undertaken by any PR team, whether in-house or consultancy based. The easiest way to do this is to buy a dedicated distribution list. There are many companies, such as PR Newswire and Vocus, producing such media lists. In the past these lists were in a folder that was updated on a quarterly basis, but now the information is available on disc and online.

Managing the data

When a list is bought it is important to ensure that it is relevant, appropriate, and up-to-date.

An alternative to buying a list, which can be expensive, is to produce your own and this is the option that many small and medium-sized firms will choose, creating and maintaining bespoke media lists that are relevant to and appropriate for their own needs. Developing a list can also be a useful exercise in defining the communication needs of the company and ideally should also be part of a communication audit (see above).

BOX 11.2   Media Roles and Responsibilities

It is important that media releases are sent to the correct contact. The list of media job titles below gives some examples of areas of responsibility:

(Continued)

(Continued)

- Editor – responsible for overall content and style of a programme or publication.
- News Editor – decides what areas will be covered.
- Letters Editor – takes letters for publication, usually covering stories that have already had some coverage in the paper.
- Features Editor/Programme Producer – responsible for longer feature articles.
- Forward Planning Desk – logs upcoming events.
- Correspondents – specialist writing (staff and freelance).
- Picture Editor – allocates photographers and selects pictures.

ENSURING MEDIA COVERAGE

There are some basic guidelines that need to be followed if a media release is to have a fighting chance of getting coverage. If the story is linked to a specific event or a launch it needs to be in the publication's news diary, as if it is not included then it is unlikely to be covered. A news diary is a publication's list of events that they know are happening. News diaries fill up quickly and limited staff numbers restrict a publication's ability to do ad hoc events. A publication's forward planning desk or journalist should be alerted in advance and not contacted on the day of an event. Most journalists are happy to have ideas floated past them and they should be asked directly whether they are interested in either the specific story or similar stories. This can save an awful lot of time and effort. Remember, if making a telephone call to any media contact care should be taken about when the call is made. Newspapers, for example, should not be contacted when they are at their busiest, such as press day on a weekly newspaper or in the morning if it's an evening daily newspaper. Conversations should be prefaced with: 'Is now a good time to talk?'. Journalists who are working on a story will usually be happy to give their opinion; it will, after all, help them if they are being offered material that is relevant to their story.

If the media release you are writing is part of a feature, make sure it covers all the necessary issues. In specialist publications especially, the relationship between the journalist and the PR source should be a creative and co-operative one where the journalist is complemented by the resources supplied by the PR contributor. Of course the PR contribution will have an angle as it is putting forward the views and opinions of a client paymaster, but providing everyone is clear and honest about this relationship it need not compromise the overall credibility of an article.

If a press release has been sent out as part of a general release and not as a contribution to a specific story or event, *never*, after sending it to a publication, telephone the recipient and ask them whether they've got the news release and if they are going to use it. A safer route to the dustbin or delete button can never be more guaranteed. The sheer volume of news releases, paper and emails that newspapers, magazines and broadcast media receive means that staff are often extremely busy, and going through it all is a headache, so it is little wonder that tempers will become frayed. When there is pressure on the PR practitioner from the client to know that the release has been followed up, it should be part of account management's responsibility to point out to the client that this practice is frowned upon and could be counter-productive to their interests.

Other important areas to keep in mind when writing media releases are to give as much information as possible, the more information provided the better, to keep the use of jargon and technical detail as minimal as possible, and to make sure the point of contact is available to speak to journalists for a few days after the press release has been issued.

DEALING WITH THE MEDIA

Effective media relations is not only a one-way process. There are many situations where the media will initiate contact with the PR practitioner, ranging from following-up a press release to a journalist needing information from the company for a story they are working on. If contacted by a journalist there are certain protocols that should be followed.

If the respondent does not know the answer to a question from a journalist details of the questions should be taken down along with the deadline. The answer should then be prepared and submitted to the journalist by the deadline, or if this is not possible a 'holding' comment must be issued such as: 'I do not have the information you need readily available, leave it with me and I'll get back to you with a detailed response. When is your deadline?' A PR practitioner should not try and make things up, waffle or evade the issue, or feel pressured into making a comment just for the sake of making a response. Careless words make headlines and the wrong response might indicate indifference while a negative attitude will send entirely the wrong message to the media.

It is important, however, to respond promptly to press enquiries as well as accurately and quickly. A press query should used as an opportunity to become a reliable source of comment and information and if this response is good and prompt the media will come back for more. It should be established whether the journalist will be quoting directly or if the information will form part of the background for a story. If the journalist or media is taking a hostile position against the company (for whatever reason) it is still important to maintain a good, professional relationship with them. The PR practitioner should continue to provide information and co-operate.

The PR industry has developed a range of additional services, all which can help either build effective relationships with the media or assist in the transmission of information.

The features list

Specialist and trade magazines produce forward feature lists which while aimed primarily at potential advertisers can also be a mine of useful information for PR practitioners. The most important section in a media pack is the forward features plan showing what the publication intends to run during the year. This enables the PR practitioner to produce a forward features list. If the list does not contain something that is relevant or appropriate to the client company, the publication should be contacted and a feature suggested. Journalists cannot know everything in their sector and will usually welcome the chance to discuss a new idea and approach, especially if there is the commercial potential for a story. Media packs can be supplemented by the information provided by the various editorial alert services. These are services which alert PR companies to forthcoming features. Websites such as Mediadisk (mediadisk.co.uk), Gorkana (www.gorkana.com), and FeaturesExec (www.featuresexec.com) allow PR consultancies to track hundreds of journalists and papers, electronically receiving details of job moves, new feature opportunities and publications. As with the media data it is important to check how often the information is updated and by what means.

Media training

Doing media interviews has become part of the job description for senior executives in many organisations and media training for the individual acting as a spokesperson is also now an essential requirement of the job. Audiences expect spokespeople appearing on TV and radio to be appropriately presentable and articulate.

Ironically, one of the problems with the increased media training even for middle ranking officials is that spokespeople are being trained to provide a standard response with little or none of their own personality being allowed to come through. One journalist said: 'You can tell when they've have been through media training because they've been taught how to speak to a journalist without saying anything very interesting.' In some cases, this will be to avoid answering the question all-together. Should it be the role of PR to try and inhibit what the company spokesperson says? A bland interview in which nothing is said or a contentious issue is avoided might be considered a good 'result' by the PR practitioner, but there is a risk that being seen to dodge answering questions might cause more damage to a company and its reputation in the long term.

Press conferences

Press conferences used to be the traditional means by which companies brought together a large number of journalists in order to make an announcement, launch a campaign, or disseminate information. Now, however, the situation has changed, with increased pressure on journalists due to declining resources and opportunities to spend time out of the office at press launches increasingly limited. At the very least press launches might be a chance to get a good picture and this is why celebrities are often used at a launch to try and generate more media interest. Tony Bradley, a former president of CIPR and a partner in the Newcastle-based consultancy Bradley O'Mahoney Public Relations, says journalists' needs have changed:

> *For generations the press conference in a swanky hotel followed by lunch was an efficient way of ensuring good media coverage, but things are different now. Unless there is a regulatory or legal reason why nothing can be said outside a set time and venue, it is easier to accept that everyone is looking for their own angle on a story and to work with them to meet aspirations and their deadlines.*

Electronic channels of communication

Electronic communication – emails, social networks, blogs – have fundamentally changed the way the PR industry operates and opened up the potential for direct communication with target audiences. As we have seen in previous chapters, it has also created vehicles through which critics of a company or organisation can vent their feelings, thereby making it harder for the organisation to control and monitor what is being said about them. One example of the way practice has changed is in how a journalist will gather a story; the traditional way used to be: 'Work your contacts, get leads, research material, interview people, ask questions, speak to a number of sources, check your facts, and then write your story.' However, email and the internet have changed this. Newspapers and magazines now email PR contacts, saying that they are writing a feature and inviting contributions. Once this is in, the journalist's job often becomes one of cutting and pasting the various contributions to make the article. This process can devalue the quality of the editorial and readers might not take as much notice of it if they realise how artificial the article is.

Online media

It is too early to say whether, as some believe, traditional newspapers and magazines will be replaced by online versions. An increasing number of people, particularly younger readers, are turning to and using online media and not print as their first choice of contact with the news media. Online media are becoming 24-hour a day operations that are updated regularly and dependent on a continuous flow of information.

Blogs: are they the future of PR?

The PR advocates of blogs believe they will change the face of the industry because they are a more direct means of communication with a target audience compared to traditional channels such as newspapers, TV and radio. Weblogs, or blogs, are written by 'bloggers' who record their thoughts on everyday incidents, such as news stories, products they have bought and companies they have been customers of. These are similar to the way a person might talk to their friends about good and bad experiences they have had with a product or company (Yang, 2006).

Large numbers of blogs are also used by bloggers to describe events that have occurred in their own lives, such as family news or social occasions, which might only be of interest to that person's friends and family. However, not all blogs are written by members of the public and many businesses have also started blogging as another way of communicating with their target audience. The content in these blogs differs greatly and often contains news related to the company and its goods and services, as well as analysing and reporting changes in the company's industry and assisting with recruitment (Yang, 2006).

Advocates of blogs believe they are important to PR because of their ability to convey messages easily and change consumers' minds either about products, businesses or brands. Research conducted by Ipsos MORI in 2006 into the effects of blogging in Europe found that 52% of Europeans were more willing to buy a product if they had seen it reviewed positively on a blog. Conversely a negative review on a blog would dissuade 34% from purchasing a product. This is not surprising considering blogs are the second most trusted source of information after newspapers which are trusted by 30% of Europeans compared to blogs – which are trusted by 24% – and television advertising – which is trusted by just 17% (HotwirePR.com, 2006).

In the UK, around 15% of the country's 26 million web users write a blog. Of these, nearly 20% are said to blog daily (the *Guardian*, 9 November 2007, p. 9). Yet the UK's blogs make up just a fraction of the blogosphere, which is said to contain more than 112 million blogs and to grow by around 120,000 new blogs daily. Of these blogs it is estimated that around 11% or 13 million blogs have been updated in the last 60 days (BusinessWeek.com, 2008). Estimates suggest that something like 75,000 new blogs are created every day, adding to the millions already in existence. It is fair to say that in the early days of blogging the PR community was slow to see the opportunities it offered: many corporate blogs tended to be critical of companies and produced by individuals and groups with complaints which had to be responded to. Now the cycle has changed and the PR industry is exploring how blogs can be used to good effect.

If they are to become an important part of the communication process how should they be evaluated? Some consultancies are now monitoring blogs in the same way as they would newspapers – attempting to read every blog relevant to the client and then sending them transcripts of what appeared. Traditional media monitoring companies are also developing blog-monitoring services.

Blogs are important because they have started to influence the way consumers and investors act, but are they of equal value and how should their value be measured? Do the numbers reading a blog translate into influence? James Davies, managing director of Impact Evaluation, believes high readership figures are not always important:

Blogs are about influence – and that is not just determined by volume of readers. It's about the migration of ideas. When you have individuals expressing their opinion about a brand, it's a form of qualitative research. There is no robustness in terms of the numbers, but it is always interesting to hear individuals talk about brands, because you can uncover things you didn't know. (PR Week, 2007)

BOX 11.3   Viral Language

- Seeding – the process of distributing branded content online by placing content on the most popular, influential, humorous, entertaining sites. A well-planned seeding campaign is capable of reaching tens of millions of people online and crucially is both affordable and measurable.
- Viral network – 100 top websites that are major players in terms of traffic and influence. *www.toolbar.netcraft.com* provides a listing of the most visited websites.
- Blog – an online journal run by an individual or group with regular entries about events, sometimes including graphics or video material.
- Podcast – audio or video content released episodically and downloaded to MP3 players via websites.
- Wiki – a document or collection of documents that anyone can contribute to or edit the content of (the most famous or infamous current example is Wikipedia).
- Folksonomy – an online community that organises content using one word tags.
- RSS Feeds – the lifeblood of social media, a way of publishing content to subscribers e.g. a blog or podcast.
- Web 2.0 – a phrase describing the wave of innovation in internet media business over the past couple of years, including blogging, podcasting and social media.

Diary: The Account Executive

Matthew Watson joined Speed Communications in 2008 after studying PR at the University of Huddersfield. Before graduating he became one of the first PR students in the country to be hired through the micro blogging service Twitter. The Managing Director of Rainer PR had been following Matthew on Twitter and contacted him when he learned through Matthew's posts that he was looking for a job in PR.

Matthew now works with several high profile business-to-business technology companies and uses social media to promote many of them. He has been a keen blogger since 2003 and has contributed to an eBook on ePR.

Diary

Monday
We had the heaviest snowfall in 18 years overnight, and with many commuters unable to travel to work I felt it was the perfect opportunity to draft a media alert offering companies advice on how to introduce flexible working practices, so that staff can work from home despite the weather. After getting approval from my client I began calling journalists and contacting a few key HR bloggers.

Once my outreach was complete, I opened up my RSS feed reader and reviewed a few blog posts by HR bloggers to see if they have written anything about the snow that my client could comment on. One of them had written a piece on how much the snow will cost in lost productivity, so I drafted a blog comment about flexible working technologies and sent it over to my client for approval before I uploaded it. Once I'd added the comment I kept monitoring the blog to see if the same blogger or any other readers had responded to it.

Tuesday
First thing, I take a look through a few national and regional newspapers to see if I can draft a letter to the editor in response to any of the articles about the snow. There's several articles about how much yesterday's snow cost in lost productivity and how companies could be affected by the snow forecast for later this week. So I draft several letters arguing my client's case and once I've had them approved I send them out to the newspaper editors.

As it's still snowing, one of the national newspapers has started to write a live blog about the weather, so I get in touch with the blogger and send over some information. A few of the journalists I spoke to yesterday haven't written about how the snow was affecting productivity, so I contact a few of them that I have good relationships with over Twitter to give them a gentle reminder.

Wednesday
We're issuing a press release today, so I upload it to the client's website and post a link to it on Twitter. I make several phone calls to journalists, and then pitch the story to a few more on Twitter. As I think the news

may interest bloggers, I put together a list of a few relevant bloggers, and approach them with the news. Later on I review their blogs to see if they've covered the story.

Thursday
I take a look at a few news sites and spot an interesting podcast. Once I've listened to it I flag it to my client as I think they'll find it interesting viewing. Afterwards I have a meeting with a potential new supplier to talk about search engine optimisation and how we could offer it as a service to clients. Once the meeting is over I take a look on Wikipedia to see if anyone has edited or vandalised the pages about my clients.

Friday
There's an interesting story on how businesses are beginning to use Twitter in the news today so I draft a blog post and upload it to one of our company blogs. I take a look at Google analytics to see how popular my client's website has been this week and check to see how many times the press release I uploaded earlier in the week has been downloaded. Afterwards I do a search online for coverage from my press release and add it to an end of week coverage report for my clients. Once I've put the report together I do a search of popular bloggers in another sector for a new business pitch I'm working on.

Events

The staging of events and their management has become a discipline in itself with clear ties to PR. The type of events typically associated with PR include:

- Drinks parties/social gatherings.
- Private lunches/dinners.
- Media lunches.
- Launches.
- Balls.
- Auction/raffles.
- Foreign trips.
- Company away days/weekends.
- Private shopping evenings.
- Press conferences.
- Seminars.
- Exhibition stands.
- Venue openings.
- Off-site meetings.
- Team building.

As can be seen from such a list, not all events are just about trying to generate publicity and can also be used for staff motivation and the improvement of morale which are internal communication functions.

SUMMARY

Effective PR programmes do not just happen but are the result of a combination of factors. They are all based on the fundamentals of planning and research about who to communicate with and finding the most effective channels of communication to reach target audiences. All PR programmes should have a strategy which outlines the objectives and the tactics that will be used. While an increasing number of PR programmes do contain strategic elements, too few undertake an effective evaluation of what has been done. This is particularly the case in the public sector. There are sophisticated electronic evaluation programmes available which monitor the way that press releases are used in the media and will analyse the quality of the readership, but too many of the evaluation programmes simply measure the process of communication and not the outcome. Electronic communication is a challenge that the PR industry is responding to with a range of new and innovative practices and how the industry responds to these new channels will be critical for its future.

CORPORATE COMMUNICATIONS & FINANCIAL PR

By the end of this chapter you will understand:

- why and how businesses communicate with important stakeholders
- what corporate and financial PR is and why companies have to carry it out
- the role that financial PR consultancy plays

INTRODUCTION

Corporate communications is the term used to describe the communication that takes place between a company and its external audiences. These communication programmes can include not only PR but also other forms of communication such as advertising and marketing. Corporate advertising is generic rather than product or sales based and occurs infrequently on television which is primarily the vehicle for sales and promotion-based advertising. Corporate advertising tends to appear in quality financial magazines and newspapers which are read by financial and political audiences. The *Economist* magazine, for example, regularly has adverts from Thomson, Reuters, Fedex and Skyteam. While such adverts might mention products or a company's brands their main purpose is to raise and reinforce the corporate identity. Corporate advertising does appear on TV during many major sporting events where sportswear companies such as Nike will use a range of footballers to advertise the brand but not specific products.

Financial PR is used only by those companies whose shares are listed on a public exchange such as the London Stock Exchange, the New York Dow Jones

Index, or the Paris Bourse. These are known as public limited companies (plcs) and include some of the largest and best known businesses. Financial PR consultancies work for public companies on a range of finance-related activity such as mergers and acquisitions (M&A), the buying and selling of companies, and communicating financial results during the annual financial calendar of a public company. Financial PR is an ideal example of a company using a specialist external consultancy to complement and supplement its in-house team.

WHAT IS CORPORATE COMMUNICATIONS?

Corporate communications is the communication activities that an organisation undertakes as a corporate entity and includes PR, the company website, the annual report, corporate identity programmes, the company logo, and any form of corporate advertising that the company carries out.

Van Riel (2005) states that corporate communications:

> Is an instrument of management by means of which all consciously used forms of internal and external communications are harmonised as effectively and efficiently as possible, so as to create a favourable basis for relationships with groups, upon which the organisation is dependent.

Corporate communications is not specifically aimed at supporting a company's sales function, rather it involves the whole company.

> External communication aims to ensure positive and supportive relationships now and in the future with those groups outside the organisation who influence access to required resources – this, of course, includes the sale of goods and services, new investment, changes to working practices, or in the provision of further financial support in the case of public sector and not-for-profit organisations. (Varey, in Kitchen, 1997: 112)

Customers and clients will form impressions of a company from its public activities, ranging from how quickly the telephones are answered to the way in which customers are treated by sales staff. Details such as these matter to many people and bad experiences can undo any amount of PR activity, especially if such experiences are then relayed to others through a social network. Of course, if neither the product or service produced by the company is right then no amount of sophisticated corporate communications, fancy logos and bright branding will make any difference.

Our impression of an organisation is not just based on a single image or perception, but on a whole series of interrelated experiences which when combined together help us to form our opinion of that organisation. As we have already seen the reputation of an organisation and its products/services is precious.

Increasingly consumers are concerned with how a company/organisation acts and produces – such as whether, for example, it engages in ethical or corporate social programmes. Corporate communication programmes will be managed by the company's in-house team who will be responsible for setting the overall strategic goals and for undertaking some of the communication activities, but where appropriate they will also use external specialist consultants to complement their own skills.

> *Corporate communications focuses responsibilities for narrowing the gap between the organisation's desired image and its actual image; establishing a consistent organisational profile; and, the organisation of communication by developing and implementing guidelines for co-ordinating all internal and external communications and controlling communications. Public relations complements marketing communication in achieving the aims of the organisation among external publics ... It translates an identity into an image.* (Varey, in Kitchen, 2007)

THE HISTORY OF FINANCIAL PR

Public companies have always communicated with their investors in one way or another. In the seventeenth century, for example, investors met in coffee shops around the Bank of England to buy and sell shares. Financial PR in its current form is a relatively recent innovation, really taking off after the privatisation boom that took place in the UK and USA in the 1980s. 'Privatisation' became a shorthand term for selling of state assets such as the utility companies – gas, electric and water – into the private sector. Selling shares to a public who were unfamiliar with the culture of share buying involved a huge communications programme on TV and in newspapers.

Financial communication became big business with financial PR companies taking the lead in selling not only the company shares but also the idea of privatisation, which the then Conservative government hoped would change the UK's working culture into a share-owning democracy. A further contributory factor to the growth of financial PR in the 1980s was the booming stock market of the time which led to many small entrepreneurial or family-owned companies changing from private to public companies. This then led to a large increase in Initial Public Offerings work. An IPO is the first sale by a private company of its shares to the public.

Those working in financial PR in the 1980s were primarily ex-financial and City journalists and at that time the most important job of financial PR was to get press coverage in the city and business pages. While former financial journalists still have a significant role to play, those working in financial PR today include people from a wider financial background such as merchant banking or accountancy, which shows the growing importance that investor relations now play in financial PR.

Financial PR is only used or undertaken by public companies (plcs) – i.e., companies whose shares are traded in public. These include some of the largest and best known firms such as, for example, Tesco plc, Barclays plc, M&S plc, and Vodaphone plc. Movements in their share price are watched carefully by investors such as pension funds and insurance companies. The dividends paid out by plcs then help to finance pension funds and insurance claims, amongst other things, and their activities can also have an impact on a country's economy.

Financial PR is the specialist PR activity concerned solely with communicating to financial audiences and especially those who can influence share prices. A public company has three main financial publics:

- Current shareholders – investors.
- Prospective shareholders – potential investors.
- The wider financial community – bankers, brokers, investment advisers (analysts), trustees, security analysts and the managers of insurance companies and pension funds – those who provide information to investors and potential investors.

In the UK, smaller companies can use the Alternative Investment Market (AIM) which enables smaller entrepreneurial companies to access finance to help them grow. Smaller companies will often only undertake minimal financial communication as it can be expensive, and sometimes companies in general will not see the necessity for engaging in it.

The importance of financial PR companies to quoted companies was highlighted by research carried out by stockbrokers Corporate Synergy who specialise in advising smaller companies. According to their study, public companies rated their financial PR advisers second only to their stockbrokers in importance, and more important than other corporate advisers such as lawyers, bankers, and accountants. This has not, however, always been the case as up until only relatively recently the main purpose of financial PR was seen as providing marketing assistance on Initial Public Offerings (IPOs) and financial PR was placed towards the bottom of the corporate advisory ladder. Luke Ahern, a director of Corporate Synergy, believes that the change has occurred because the PR industry has learnt what is of real value to their clients:

> It (the industry) learnt that quoted companies value consistency, honesty in terms of what can be realistically be achieved. The best PR agencies speak to their principal client contacts almost every day. Consequently, their clients appreciate and value this involvement and see the PR agency as very much an extension of their own company. (Synergy, 2006)

In economically difficult times, financial PR will play an important role in trying to explain any difficulties that a company might have been having.

Financial PR consultancies

Public companies will use Financial PR consultancies because of their specific background and experience in this sector.

The type of services that financial PR consultancies will offer includes many that are similar to conventional PR consultancies; the difference with financial consultancies is that they deal with specific financial audiences.

The three main activities of Financial PR are:

- financial calendar-related work
- PR/marketing activity surrounding flotation/Initial Public Offering (IPO) advice
- PR on major structural changes such as take-overs, mergers or acquisitions

Financial calendar work

The life of a public company will be driven during the course of the year by its financial calendar as it is a requirement of the Stock Exchange that quoted companies will produce and publish their financial results every six months. After six months of the financial year companies must produce their interim results, and at the financial year-end following a 12-month period they will have to publish their preliminary results to that year-end. The company has then to publish an Annual Report and hold an Annual General Meeting at which the final year end results are presented to the shareholders. For large, quoted companies this round of producing and explaining their results is important and time consuming but has to be done because it is the shareholders who own the company and it is to them that management are responsible. Finance directors will spend a large amount of their time on investor relations/financial calendar issues.

Companies must explain to shareholders why they have or have not made the level of profit they might have predicted in an earlier quarter. This is because shares in a public company are owned by outside shareholders, ranging from individual shareholders to large institutions such as pension funds. They will want to know how their money has been used and whether or not the companies are investing it well. Shareholders make their money from investments in the following ways:

- Receiving a dividend on every share they own. This is paid after the results are published at six monthly intervals.
- Selling their shares for more than they paid for them.
- Seeing the capital value of their shares grow.

The process for explaining the results to a financial audience will be carefully choreographed and involve presentations and meetings to analysts and shareholders – it can and does take up a lot of senior management time. The financial and business press are important here but are mainly a channel of communication to reach key financial audiences. It is the job of the financial PR consultancy to organise this communication. The key point is that information must reach everyone at the same time, as there must be no accusations that one group or individual has received this before anyone else. This is crucial because if information that has not been made public is acted upon then companies can be accused of insider trading. Deregulation of the Regulatory News Service (RNS) in 2002 by which the results used to be published meant UK traded companies had to choose what is known as a Primary Information Provider in order to release all price-sensitive information into the market. There are a number of FSA approved service providers whose role is to take an announcement and send it to the market through Secondary Information Providers (SIPs) such as Reuters and Bloomberg.

Prelim results for example will normally be announced to the market through the Primary Information Provider (PIP) at 7:00 am and then followed up with a range of meetings during the day. Although the reporting company chief executive and finance director will be closely involved in staging the meetings, inviting relevant audiences and crafting material for analysts, investors and journalists, financial PR practitioners will also be involved in fielding the follow-up calls that will be generated by results presentations. Small public companies have the same obligation to produce interims and prelims results as larger ones, but the degree of external scrutiny and reporting requirements is not quite as onerous as for the larger public companies. The opportunities to appear in the media are also more limited and the financial audience tends to be specialist investing institutions.

Profit warnings and the unexpected

The City hates the unexpected, especially if it is bad news and they need to be told in advance. Poor financial results, problems with a product, profits not being as high as expected – these represent the type of information that can affect a company's share price. Public companies then face the added pressure of having to announce whether or not they are going to meet the expected level of profits they made public in their previous results. Companies have an obligation to report any information or development that they feel might affect their share price. One of the most serious situations for a public company is if they are forced to issue what is known as a profit warning. This is when the public company has to make a statement saying that it does not believe that it will reach the level of profits that the City is expecting.

These can be quite difficult situations for companies and it is here that financial PR consultancy plays an important role in helping to present the results in a way that could prevent the share price from falling.

Case Study: The Vice-President

Caroline Harris is a Vice President at CJP Communications (CJP), a financial-services PR agency in New York. She started her career ten years ago in-house at HSBC, followed by a five-year stint as a Media Relations Manager at The Royal Bank of Scotland Group in London. Recognising the increasing need for a global understanding of the media she joined CJP in 2006, where she leads several global financial services accounts focused on private equity, insurance, sales and trading and real estate. She has a BA (Hons) in Event Management and an MA in Corporate Communications.

What do you like about your job?

I rarely have the same day twice. Being in financial services PR, particularly at the moment, is very exciting. The sector is changing so quickly, companies are changing or disappearing, and new companies are emerging all the time, meaning that I am constantly learning. In my current role I am responsible for ensuring that our clients get the best service possible and see quality results, like a story in the Wall Street Journal *or the* Financial Times *quickly. I also still get a buzz when I manage to secure a client a quality media placement!*

What are the most important skills?

Media relations is by far the most important skill in PR. Understanding each publication, which reporters cover which beats, what they have been writing about recently, and then having the drive and confidence to pick up the telephone and convince a reporter why they should write your story. Time management, organization and a strong work ethic are also vital.

Does PR meet your expectations in terms of a career?

Absolutely! I fell into financial PR and haven't looked back since. I am constantly challenged, surrounded by very smart people, and immersed in some of the biggest issues facing the world on a daily basis. How many people can say that they are able see the results of their day's work in the media?

Where do you see yourself in five years time?

PR is constantly evolving and the financial services sector has perhaps changed for good. I want to continue to grow my understanding of the sector and further develop my public relations skills in New York. An understanding of the global media landscape is going to be vital as time goes on and I see myself starting to develop a better understanding of the Asian media so that I can become a truly global PR professional.

Diary: The Vice President
An extract from Caroline's diary

Monday

7:00 Wake up and check the BlackBerry. Many of my clients are based in the UK, so by the time I wake up we are almost half way through their day. Deal with any urgent issues and then head off to the office.

8:00 Get the subway to work, respond to emails and scan the headlines in the Financial Times.

8:05 Press release for my insurance client crosses on PR Newswire meaning that it is now public information and available to the media.

8:30 Start work and check the Wall Street Journal *online. Reading the newspaper is a vital part of the job as it can help me identify new story angles for clients and keep me up to speed on the ever-changing financial services world. Scan Google alerts for any client news.*

8:45 Send out insurance press release by email to a targeted media list, personalizing each email to each reporter to ensure that they understand why the news is relevant to them. With reporters receiving so many emails each day it is important to make sure my pitch stands out.

9:30 Monday mornings tend to be dominated by client calls. Update my insurance client and one of my private equity clients on the last week's progress and the activity that we have planned for the remainder of the week. After each call, we will divide out the major tasks that need completing that week.

11:00 Follow up with reporters about the press release and see if they need any further information or would like to speak to my spokesperson for further colour.

11:30 Draft a press release announcing a new deal for one of my private equity clients and send this round my team for their input.

12:30 Grab a salad from the local deli and catch up with friends and colleagues. One of my favourite things about my job and company is the banter that we have with each other.

13:30 Head uptown to a client meeting to discuss a series of new hires they are making in their fixed income team. Discuss the best strategy to release this news to the media.

15:00 Continue to follow up on the insurance release that was issued this morning so that I can provide an update to my client at the end of the day.

15:30 Staff an interview that I set up last week for one of my clients to discuss trends in private equity with a reporter from one of the wire services. In the USA most interviews will have a PR representative present on the call.

16:00 Internal team meeting to identify angles for a client with no natural news. Look at areas that we can comment on in the media and decide on next steps to ensure a steady flow of media coverage for the client.

16:30 Media call from Private Equity Trade about a recent deal transaction. Speak with client and then respond to the call.

17:00 Start drafting a press release on new survey results commissioned by one of my clients.

18:00 Send over deal announcement to my private equity client and follow up with a phone call to catch up and make sure client is happy. I want my clients to see me as a partner rather than a vendor and having a great relationship with them helps me achieve this.

Tuesday
7:00 Wake up and check the BlackBerry. One of my UK clients has a brochure that needs writing urgently, so respond that I will have it to them in the next few hours.

8:00 Get the subway to work, respond to emails and scan the headlines in the Financial Times.

8:30 Start drafting brochure on a new line of insurance.

9:00 Send over agenda for client call at 15.00 – every meeting should have an agenda!

10:30 Client call to discuss upcoming philanthropy project they are working on. Discuss strategy to raise profile for the event.

12.00 Staff an interview with Reuters for a client of mine in the fixed income space. Follow up with the reporter to ensure he has everything and to check quotes.

13.30 Grab a bite to eat on the way to look at an event space in a hotel for an upcoming cocktail reception I am organising.

15.00 Weekly client catch up call – divide resulting actions between team members.

16.00 Speak with energy publications to try to garner some interest in a meeting with my energy clients.

17.00 Call with an executive at one of my clients to pick her brains on trends she is seeing in the public transportation space.

Wednesday
7:00 Leave home early to go to a breakfast meeting downtown with a hedge fund reporter and my prime brokerage client. Discuss trends in prime brokerage and the current financial environment.

9:30 Return to the office and catch up on emails.

10:00 Regular call with my insurance client to bring her up to speed on our activity over the last two weeks.

11:00 Check in with one of my team members who I share three accounts with, divide out the week's work to ensure we are delivering everything the clients expect.

12:00 Follow up with three business areas at my insurance client to determine their needs for marketing collateral.

Organize a media training session for six new hires made by my insurance client.

13.00 Meet with a client to discuss how to maximise a conference they are sponsoring.

14.00 Finalise a monthly activity report for my client.

15.30–17.30 New business pitch to a prospective professional services client to help with their private equity PR.

17.30 – Return to the office to deal with outstanding emails.

Investor relations

Investor relations is the activity that handles relationships with the shareholders – regardless of how large the shareholding. It is the communication of information between a company and the investment community. Such communication enables the investment community to understand and appreciate the company's business interests, thereby allowing the market to make an informed decision about many aspects of a company's business including – but not only – its financial performance and management. At some large companies this is done by in-house investor relations department, but specialist firms will be employed to maintain the share register recording who buys and sells shares and to look for any unusual activity that might for example provide evidence of possible take-over activity by an outside company. The in-house investor relations team can be a part either of the corporate affairs team or of the finance director's department.

Initial public offerings

An Initial Public Offering (IPO) is when a private company offers its shares to the public for the first time. This is also known as 'going public' or 'floating' a company. IPOs are usually carried out by young growing companies looking for new capital to expand their business. An IPO has many advantages over other forms of finance available to businesses but the main point from a communications perspective is that it radically alters the profile of the company. It literally becomes a 'public' company and open to media scrutiny. IPOs also tend to follow trends – when the economy is doing well and share prices are high IPOs will increase, when the economy is performing poorly, there will be fewer listings.

A financial PR company will handle all the communication activities of a company going through an IPO. On an IPO the financial PR company will be part of the advisory team which will usually include a stockbroker, a corporate lawyer, accountants, and sometimes depending on the size of the float, a merchant banker. The aim of an IPO is to market the shares to potential purchasers such as institutional investors and individual shareholders. The target audience for the IPO is potential investing institutions such as pension funds, unit trusts and their analysts who will recommend whether the shares should be bought or sold. Private individuals will be targeted through private client stockbrokers and the financial press. The only place shares can be traded in the UK is on the London Stock Exchange and companies have to follow a formal admission process based on set rules and procedures.

Financial audiences

Financial communication is aimed at two key financial audiences – analysts and the financial media.

Analysts
A key audience for quoted companies will be the analysts who work for various financial institutions. Their reports, analysis and recommendations to either buy or sell shares can influence a company's share price. Analysts follow various sectors and will usually concentrate on larger companies.

The financial media
The financial media are the distribution channel through which a company will communicate with key financial audiences. Financial media consist of the City pages of the main daily and Sunday newspapers, the *Financial Times*, and specialist financial and business magazines. Financial PR companies will place stories that are favourable to their clients such as brokers' tips and analysts'

reports. Smaller companies have always had problems communicating with their key financial audiences and for many companies, and these smaller ones especially, the internet has become important as a means of directly communicating with investors and potential investors.

SUMMARY

Corporate PR is one of the most important functions undertaken by in-house PR practitioners. It deals with an organisation's relationships with the external world and is not directly related to the sales function. It also deals with the whole company and not just one part of it and can often involve other areas of corporate identity programmes as well.

Financial PR is the specialist area of PR that handles communications on behalf of public companies. This communication is not just about communicating with the financial media but with the City audience in general and many financial PR companies will also use their City contacts to introduce companies to investors and potential investors.

GOVERNMENT AND THE PUBLIC SECTOR

By the end of this chapter you will understand:

- what the term 'spin' means and why it is associated with PR
- why governments need to communicate
- what lobbying is and who carries it out, as well as the ethical issues associated with political marketing and lobbying

INTRODUCTION

We saw in Chapter 1 how theorists Grunig and Hunt described the communication practised by both local and national government as a one-way form of communication which they called the Public Information Model. This suggests a useful form of communication and in practice many government campaigns are usually trying to persuade individuals from taking a course of action that might well harm them. Typical of these are 'Don't Drink and Drive', 'Give Blood', 'Test Smoke Alarms', etc.

This is a one-way communication process aimed at convincing the target audience to pursue a course of action. It also suggests a largely benign view of the type of communication that governments undertake. There will be many working in government communications who would wish that this was how everyone regarded their work, but as we saw with the Jo Moore incident (see Box 11.1) communication activity undertaken by government has become controversial for many different reasons.

This chapter will explore these issues and consider not just the PR practice of governments and political parties but also those who would attempt to influence and shape government policy. This analysis will also help us understand some fundamental questions of PR practice. Political parties, for example, no longer simply put forward their policies to an electorate who will then weigh up the various messages and choose the one they prefer. These days all political parties have become sophisticated communication organisations who know that they have to target key audiences in order to get their message across. Often their marketing and communication programmes will be at the very forefront of innovation in communication practice and the lessons learned there will often then translate in to the commercial field. One such example was the internet marketing and fundraising campaign of Barack Obama in the 2008 USA Presidential election. Mr Obama used the internet to organise his supporters and reached more of them than his opponents who tended to use conventional methods such as letter writing and telephone calls. His mobilised supporters then voted for him in the Democratic Party primaries, giving him the nomination. What this campaign demonstrated was that the internet could be used to communicate effectively to potential supporters and get them involved in political activity. The campaign also used YouTube effectively in place of traditional TV advertising. It was estimated that to buy the amount of coverage the campaign generated on YouTube would have cost $47m.

Mr Obama's internet campaign was run by political consultant Joe Trippi who had run an earlier presidential campaign for the Democratic senator Howard Dean (*New York Times*, 7/11/08).

Governments are also the objects of communication and persuasion and this chapter considers the work of political lobbyists – namely what they do and why they do it. This whole area has become controversial with numerous questions raised about whether it has any legitimacy or role at all. Lobbying is any action designed to influence the actions or institutions of government and this means government in its widest sense, not just the national government of Westminster or Washington but Brussels, the home of the European Union, the Scottish, Welsh and Northern Ireland Assemblies, and also the various levels of local government. It is not only business that undertakes lobbying, in fact some of the most successful lobbying campaigns have been undertaken by NGOs and pressure groups campaigning for special interest groups or sections of the community. The work that they do is important and will be analysed below in some detail.

SOCIAL MARKETING

The Public Information Model of communication (one-way communication) is the method of communication that public bodies use to communicate their programmes. Nowadays this process of communication might be called social marketing. This is a distinct type of communication, its purpose being to achieve and sustain behaviour goals on a range of social issues. According to the National Social Marketing Centre, social marketing is:

The systematic application of marketing, alongside other concepts and techniques to achieve specific behavioural goals, for a social good.' Health-related social marketing for example is*: 'The systematic application of marketing, alongside other concepts and techniques, to achieve specific behavioural goals, to improve health and reduce inequalities* (NSMC, 2006).

There are three key elements in social marketing programmes:

- The primary aim of achieving a particular 'social good' (rather than commercial benefit).
- A systematic process phased to address short-, medium- and long-term issues.
- The use of a range of marketing techniques and approaches to meet these aims.

Campaign examples include the regular anti-smoking or anti-drink driving campaigns that appear in the press and TV. Kotler (1982) offers the following definition of social marketing as the:

Use of marketing principles and techniques to advance a social cause, idea or behaviour. Social marketing is the design, implementation of programs to increase the acceptability of a social idea or cause in target groups. It utilises concepts of market segmentation, consumer research, concept development, communication, facilitation, incentives and exchange theory to maximise target response.

Product Marketing has its four Ps (Product, Price, Place, Promotion) and, according to Austin and Pinkleton (2006), social marketing has its six Ps:

- Public – who is the campaign targeted at? What are their needs, interests and perceptions?
- Product – for social marketing the product is the goal.
- Price – price in social marketing is, 'The cost of embracing the idea or behaviour from the public's point of view'.
- Promotion – the benefits of the campaign being promoted (e.g. if you do not drink and drive you won't kill anyone).
- Positioning – what makes the campaign/product special and unique: 'What will get yet another anti-drink driving campaign noticed among the crush of other messages about driving, drinking and safety?'
- Place – these are the distribution channels through which the public can access the campaign.

GOVERNMENT COMMUNICATIONS

For the purposes of this chapter, we shall divide government in two – central and local. In the UK both have been important to the growth and development of PR (L'Etang, 2006). PR practitioners working for central and local government will be in-house practitioners and share many characteristics with their counterparts in the private sector. Like private sector PR, it is only relatively recently that the job function has evolved from that of press officer to that of having a more strategic role. Other similarities between the private and public sector are that those responsible for strategic communication occupy senior positions and are helping to shape and influence policy. In addition to the external communications role there has also been growth in internal communications. Local authorities for example, even the small ones, will be large employers in their localities and sometimes the largest employers in a district: this provides an additional responsibility for good employee communications.

Box 13.1   Defining the Public Sector

The public sector according to the Office of National Statistics is defined as follows:

- The organs of state – such as Parliament, government departments like the Ministry of Defence, Defra, etc.
- Public sector corporations – the BBC and various regulators like the Financial Services Authority, Ofgen, etc.
- Nationalised industries/firms – nuclear power, the Post Office, and now nationalised financial institutions such as Northern Rock.
- Local government.
- The National Health Service.

LOCAL GOVERNMENT

Communication is seen as a really high priority now because the current agenda is about communications, consultation and community engagement and involving your staff. So it is vital in helping councils move forward ...

So says Sharon McKee, Head of Communications at Northumberland County Council (*Local Government Chronicle*, 23 February, 2006).

It has changed from years ago when it was just seen as a press office with a couple of people who dealt with media enquiries for local papers. It is now seen more strategically – the role is much wider than just media handling and PR. Its impact can be much greater. The challenge is: Finding effective ways to communicate with residents over a large geographical area, and improving internal communications to 13,000 staff dispersed across the county.

Sharon McKee likes the variety of roles that her job brings:

I like having to know lots of things about different parts of the council and feeling that I am really contributing something. I love the unexpected, the pressure of not knowing what is coming along next is one of those things that a lot of communications people thrive on. You have got to be flexible and enjoy and embrace change. You can get a lot of knock-backs in communications, but you have to keep bouncing and be very proactive. Be very assertive and do not take no for an answer.

The importance of local authority communication was boosted by the Local Government Act of 2000 which widened the range of activities that councils could spend their money on. It also required them to prepare community and communication strategies recognising that involving local communities was an important tool in getting community support for local actions. Communication was then no-longer an after thought, but an essential requirement. As a direct consequence of this local authorities began to recruit extensively.

Local government communication is, generally speaking, structured in two different ways. The first lies in a central communications unit that is based either in a corporate centre or the chief executive's department and works like a full service communications agency with responsibility for all marketing and communications functions. The department will lay down the rules and guidelines about the communications engagement and also monitor and oversee the ways they are implemented.

The second is based in a decentralised structure with no central unit but with a range of departmental officers providing marketing functions for a particular service.

There is no right or wrong way to organising communications: the structure chosen will reflect such variables as the resources available, the communication priorities, and the size of the authority.

RESTRICTING OR HELPING? PUBLIC SECTOR PR AS GATEKEEPER

We have already examined the idea of the in-house PR practitioner acting as a gatekeeper and this raises its head again in an interesting issue in the public sector. The police, fire service, and ambulance authorities all now have professional communication advisers. In addition to the press office function, communications departments in these organisations have responsibility for running and organising various preventative initiatives to help communities in such areas as health, crime and fire prevention schemes.

However, there has been criticism from some journalists that in the role of press officer they will act, whether they intend to or not, as 'gatekeepers' – a role which suggests that the flow of information is being controlled and that the public are therefore only receiving a partial view of the world.

The need for professional communicators who will exercise and control a situation can be justified on practical and operational criteria. Consider, for example, a major fire involving all three emergency services – they respond and the media, rightly and for legitimate reasons, want to know what happened. They start contacting the appropriate services to find out what has occurred and obtain quotes from those who were involved in managing the situation.

In such situations the communications function of each service helps to bring order to what could be an unmanageable situation. If the media have uncontrolled access, if there is no one responding to their questions other than the operational officers, then the following might happen:

- No-one would speak to the press because the priority is resolving the emergency.

Or

- Operational officers would speak to the press and possibly waste valuable time which might have been better spent dealing with the emergency.

The media need answers and work to tight deadlines, they require people who will provide them with information, so the role of the communications function in such situations can be seen as mutually advantageous, one that enables journalists to do their jobs while at the same time minimising the impact on operational staff. Most people would agree that in such situations there is a practical necessity for the communications function. However, the fact that access to the incident is controlled raises questions about whether the information that has been released can be wholly trusted if there is no external or independent verification of it.

Box 13.2   Northumbria Police and the release of crime figures

The negative and restrictive aspects of the gatekeeping role – where the communications function acts as a filter between the operational personal and the news gatherer and controls the flow of information – can be illustrated by the following accusation made by the journalist Nigel Green. He argued that Northumbria Police had deliberately not reported some crimes, accusing them of engaging in 'political spin' in their attempt to control the information flow (*Guardian*, 2008). According to Green, the police force played down certain violent crimes such as stabbings because it:

> Is all part of the force's attempt to convince the public that all is safe and well on the streets. The £700,000-a-year press office pumps out press releases on how crime is falling. Sadly, these stories are usually printed in place of the real crime stories we are no longer given. For the most disturbing aspect of all is the growing tendency for police not to release crimes to the media at all – or to release them many days, weeks or even months later. (*Guardian*, 2008)

He argued that the Northumbrian police force were doing this because they did not want to increase the fear of crime among the general population. Could this be a justifiable reason for not reporting facts?

According to another *Guardian* journalist, Duncan Campbell, this story is consistent with a growing trend across the UK – in-house police PR departments attempting to control the flow of information to journalists: 'Police forces across Britain have installed press bureaux, which have acted as a buffer-zone between most of the media and the officers themselves. While the individual reporters still have their own contacts, the majority of the information now comes from the various force media outfits, which often reflect the attitudes of the hierarchy in their particular force'.

Although Campbell suggests there is a deliberate policy, the accusation does not appear to be supported by research carried out by Rob Maunby (2006) showed that in 79% of UK forces (33 out of 42) the policy was to allow *all* officers to liaise with the media: 'This authorisation is often subject to logical criteria e.g. taking advice from the comms department, complying with legal and policy requirements, seeking clearance from a manager and speaking only about subjects within one's responsibility and knowledge. Just two forces mentioned that there were no restrictions only for those of the rank of sergeant and above; but even these mentioned that constables could communicate through the media when they were best qualified to do so.' The importance of this issue in the media is illustrated by a study from Lewis et al. (2006) which said that 21% of crime stories were sourced from news agency or PR sources.

While legislation has been one important driver in improving local authorities communication, another has undoubtedly been their collective desire to try and counter the widespread negative public perception that exists about local government. In some national newspapers, for example, local authorities are regarded as excellent targets for ridicule and hostility. Some of the red-top tabloids would have us believe that every local authority is staffed by nimby do-gooder, vegetarian pacifists intent on controlling every aspect of our lives through regulation. Only the European Union comes close as a tabloid object of ridicule and disdain. Headlines srceaming about councils wasting taxpayers money by hiring lifestyle coaches and the council chief who commutes 365 miles from Edinburgh to Bournemouth are typical of the way local authorities are regarded by many in the media.

In 2005, Ipsos MORI researched the press coverage of local authorities, exploring how this differed in regional and national newspapers and which type of stories received a good or bad press. Nationally, media coverage of local authorities is limited and, possibly because it is more general in its context, it is also more negative because bad headlines help sell newspapers. The survey showed that the national media were more likely, for instance, to pick up on local stories about crime or social services, especially when things go wrong, because such stories tended to be high impact and to have national policy implications. An example of this was the coverage that the national media gave to the case of Baby P, the tragic baby who died after suffering horrific injuries at the hands of his carers. The local authority, the London Borough of Haringey, who had placed Baby P on the child protection register, were deemed to have failed in certain functions, and the media furore surrounding the case lead to three national inquiries and a nationwide review of social service procedures.

Local newspapers, especially dailies that cover a specific authority, will have more local stories – in fact in some areas of the UK the local newspaper will depend on news coverage about the council to fill its pages.

> *Inefficiency, value for money and service quality are writ large across regional and national coverage, but it is the national press which again tends to be the most negative. Basically, for every positive article written about efficiency and value for money in the national press, eight negative articles appear.* (Ben Page, MD of IPSOS Mori, personal interview)

An example of a negative article is illustrated by a story from *Wales on Sunday* in July 2005. Under the headline 'SPUN-BELIEVABLE', the story said that the country's 22 councils were 'splashing out' (an implication that this money was being wasted) on 72 press officers 'to put spin on bad news' rather than on improving services. This type of unfair coverage does have an impact, especially on staff morale. Reacting to the *Wales on Sunday* story the Cardiff Council PR officer Rob Webb said: 'Self-esteem suffers when central government talks about staff cuts and when your job is described as a waste of money it leaves people feeling very jaded' (*PR Week*, 2005).

In such situations local authorities are faced with a problem. They need to communicate with the local population but how can they be certain that the local newspaper will a) use the story and b) use it in the way they want? Some local authorities now produce their own community newspapers which will go to all households in their area or additional resources will be put into electronic communication such as websites. The growth of local authority-sponsored newspapers is, according to some people, also contributing to the decline of the paid-for newspaper.

The Comprehensive Spending Review of October 2010 has changed the economic and financial landscape for the public sector and local authorities in particular. The money that had helped to finance the growth of communications departments was no longer there, and with local authorities having to concentrate on providing core services, that could mean communications had come under threat arguably at a time when this was most needed.

Changing situations however will present new opportunities and one creative solution was illustrated by the activities of two local authority comms departments who began selling their services to outside clients, thus operating in effect like a PR consultancy.

Essex Communications, part of Essex County Council, made over £50,000 in fees in 2009/10 from providing a range of services for, among others, Wandsworth Council and Thames Gateway South Essex. Westminster City Council's company, Westco, had 15 clients in 2009/10 carrying out a communications audit for Southampton City Council, and work for the Metropolitan Police Authority, and Capita Business Services (*PR Week*, 29/10/10). This could be the way forward for many authorities along with merging local authority and health department communications.

Careers in the public sector have been attractive to potential employees because they are seen to offer job security, regulated working hours, and a clear career development path. However, public sector jobs are no longer any safer than private sector job.

Case Study: The Head of Corporate Communications for a Local Borough

David Holdstock is currently Head of Corporate Communications for the London Borough of Hillingdon, and before that he was Head of Corporate Communications for Slough Borough Council from 2000 to 2005.

From 1987 to 2000 he was at the Metropolitan Police Service working in Internal Communications and parliamentary affairs, and also ran the North London Press Office Specialist Operations (Counter-Terrorism, Royalty and Diplomatic Protection, Fraud Squad).

Public relations is now a global phenomenon that knows no boundaries. Working in communications puts you at the heart of an organisation and gives you opportunities that sometimes only come along once in a lifetime. The unique nature of what we do also brings with it many challenges. That's what makes life in communications such a fascinating and exciting experience. So far, that journey has taken me to places such as Bulgaria, the East End of London and the Kray twins, and Buckingham Palace, and given me the chance to work on what time will judge as major episodes in history, such as Diana's funeral, the Docklands' bomb, and the Paddington Rail disaster. These are just some of the things that a life in PR can bring.

I started my career in the Parliamentary Briefing and Internal Communications Unit of the Metropolitan Police Service at New Scotland Yard. I then spent the next ten years or so working across the various and very different teams that make up the Directorate of Public Affairs. The scale and opportunities that came my way were like working for different organisations. My first really big role involved the implementation of a new internal communications strategy, following a wide ranging review of communications. Moving on to 'hard news' gave me a good grounding in the full spectrum of communications activities.

The public relations' landscape has changed significantly in the last few years. Technology has allowed access to information on a global scale. Anyone can get information about anything and they can get it immediately. News and access to information has changed considerably in that time. There's more of it, it's faster, and just about anyone can report on a breaking news story – and indeed they do. The public now create the story as well as being part of it. This makes managing reputations – both personal and organisational – more critical than ever. Global brands can win or lose reputations overnight and it requires communications professionals to be ahead of the curve, fleet footed, and able to deliver real outcomes that can be measured.

The public sector is also changing. Reputation is one of the key challenges for public sector communicators. Value for money is a key and continuing element that is crucial to managing reputation in the public sector. We have to demonstrate the value and worth of communications to improving reputation. The real challenge for us is to ensure we can influence the outcomes and not just deliver outputs. It is now about strategy and not channel management (i.e. newspapers, radio, TV, events, etc.) . Passion, commitment and enthusiasm are important but being strategically focussed with strong evaluation will always deliver the best outcomes. Communicators need to change behaviour, influence opinion, and shape the policy debate.

It is more important than ever that we get the basics right and, if done well, communications can play a vital role to boost effectiveness, deliver real benefits for communities, and improve reputation.

The thing about working in PR is that there's no such thing as a 'typical' day, although there will always be some absolutes: The Today programme to start the day, 'reading in' first thing in the morning to see what the news agenda is in the nationals, and then catching up on overnight emails. At the other end of the day, a final check of emails. What happens in-between can be hard to predict. That is the beauty of what we do. PR in practice is exciting, demanding, and ultimately delivers results that can influence and change behaviour.

For people starting out in PR enthusiasm is everything. If someone is hungry to learn and develop their skills, they will have a good career in the PR business. A naturally inquisitive nature and appetite for news will help keep your finger on the pulse and give you a good understanding of the political environment they operate in. Truth and honesty will ensure you are regarded as someone with integrity and a reputation as someone who can be trusted. Finally, energy and enthusiasm will help to see you through the occasionally difficult days.

CENTRAL GOVERNMENT COMMUNICATION

The communication activities of the Westminster-based national government have over the last ten years, been the focus for some of the most intense debates about the nature and ethics of communication practice.

Since the election of the Labour Government in 1997 there has been a huge growth in the amount of money spent by government departments on communication issues. In 1997 the government spent £111 million on PR, but by 2006 government spending on communication related-issues had increased threefold to £322 million every year (Robertson, 2007). According to its critics this growth showed a government that was more interested in *how* polices were presented rather than their substance. Overall some 3,200 people were employed by them to promote policies, however this figure included personnel involved in the design and production of websites and not just media relations. The Ministry of Defence had the most press officers with 229. The then government argued that the increase in the numbers of those working in communication was driven by technology and the way society has become a 24-hour news society – for example, BBC 24 hour news, rolling news channels such as Radio 5, and the websites of the newspapers meant there was an awful lot of space and time to fill.

Increased central government communication activity might also be justified as an example of more open government with a responsibility to communicate on issues that affected the national interest. They need to keep the public informed about matters such as health-related campaigns like anti-smoking or to inform specific target groups such as pensioners about changes to pensions and any special payments that might be due. Most people would accept that these are practical requirements. However, even these such apparently 'value-free' campaigns have a another dimension according to the critics, who argue that campaigns putting the government in a good light are political and support the government.

Spin

At the heart of this debate is the issue of spin which in many people's minds has become a shorthand way to describe PR and a term that arguably became at one point almost synonymous with the New Labour government (Jones, 2001).

'Spin' is a pejorative term in PR and is possibly one of the worst insults that can be thrown as it suggests deceitful PR practice, disingenuousness and the use of manipulative tactics. Although spin is a blanket phrase popularly and easily used to describe a range of activities and actions, it can sometimes be hard to be define what constitutes its actual practice. The most common technique associated with it is the selective presentation of facts to support a line or position. Safire's *New Political Dictionary* defines spin as the 'Deliberate shading of news perception, attempted control of political reactions', a combination then of propaganda and rhetoric.

Although the term is relatively recent, in PR the function it describes is not a new practice. Edward Bernays, for example, developed techniques similar to spin whilst working as a propagandist for the US Committee on Public Information during World War 1.

> *During the 1920s, Bernays tutored politicians on how to the use media and also the techniques of "engineering of consent". He believed that PR and spin were essential parts of modern politics because they were the only tools available to the politicians to convince people in a media-saturated mass society where the power lies with the media.* (Grunig & Hunt, 1984: 42)

However, when governments deliberately engage in such activities this has different consequences from when, say, a commercial PR company undertakes such activities. They, after all, might be expected to argue for a particular line, but if a government begins to obscure the truth through such actions they undermine the basis of a democratic society, which is that the electorate should all have access to the same information. In such situations the media are dominated by one side so much so that it effectively becomes propaganda.

Spin was first used in the context we now associate it with by Lee Atwater, a powerful political adviser to the Republican president Ronald Regan. Its first use in print occurred in the *New York Times* in 1984 during an article commenting on one of Regan's presidential debates with the Democratic candidate Walter Mondale. In an article, 'Spin Doctors', the author Jack Rosenthal, attributed the rise of spin to the conditions created by the rolling news found on CNN and news radio. Their 24-hour updates effectively made weekly comment obsolete and PRs were being forced to respond quickly, to offer not just facts but also their interpretation of them. With the news cycle shrinking Rosenthal argued that, 'You needed to get effects in to play instantly, you couldn't wait to go to your favourite columnists. It had to be instant, so you created your own columnist. Create your own opinion. Your own spin'. However, Lyn Nofziger, who served as Reagan's press secretary in 1981 and worked alongside Atwater on the 1984 campaign, remembers Atwater himself using the word after the first debate between the candidates two weeks earlier: 'Lee was telling us, "Now, we're going to want to go out there and spin this afterward,"' Nofziger remembers, 'Meaning making it look like Reagan had won the debate, which normally wouldn't have been hard to do, but that debate was kind of a disaster for Reagan'. Nevertheless, the president's campaign officials handed out quotes that worked in Reagan's favour, with Mondale's people right next to them working on behalf of their candidate (www.npr.org, 2009).

Perhaps the worst example of spin under the New Labour government centred around the dossier that was produced 'proving' that the Iraqi dictator Saddam Hussein had weapons of mass destruction. The dossier was subsequently found to be based on flawed and false information. Alistair Campbell, the government's director of communications, had played an important role in putting it together, and it was seen by his critics as another example of the way he tried to manipulate the media.

All governments, whatever their political colour, will try and present their policies in the most favourable light possible and this will inevitably mean a degree of 'spin'. The current Conservative/Liberal Democrat coalition government could for example be accused of spin when it blamed the economic crisis the UK faced in 2010 on the actions of the previous Labour government, thereby ignoring the actions of the banks who economists said were responsible for it.

How political parties are changing political communication

Political campaigning has changed: the arrival of the internet has, according to many observers, altered the nature of political campaigning.

Modern political campaigns still retain some identifiable traits of the traditional political campaign such as travelling around the country to carefully choreographed events, stage-managed to produce as much local publicity and as many photo opportunities as possible. However, political campaigns now use sophisticated research to identify the issues voters care about, and also to utilise the most up to date campaigning tactics such as the internet to speak directly to voters. Electronic communication will change the nature of political campaigning by opening up a direct communication with potential voters and allowing political parties to track the views and opinions of potential voters far quicker and in greater numbers than has previously been the case.

The Conservative Party was the first UK political party to hire an advertising agency (Colman, Prentis and Varley) to assist on presentational activities in the 1950s. However, it was in the 1979 General Election that political advertising really unleashed its power with the infamous Saatchi & Saatchi poster campaign – 'Labour Isn't Working'. The evocative poster of a long line of supposedly unemployed people queuing outside a job centre waiting for work played on a couple of crucial political themes of the day. First, it suggested that a vital resource – labour – was being wasted by the Labour government's economic policy, and second, that the Labour Government wasn't doing its job because people were unemployed. The poster was deliberately aimed at traditional Labour voters who the Conservatives needed to win over in order to take power. It clearly worked as they won a majority in the 1979 General Election – in fact the Conservative Chairman at the time even went so far as to state that the poster actually won the election for the Conservatives. Ironically, it was based on a deception – some people appear in it twice. Conservative Party opponents however did not spot this at the time and Saatchi & Saatchi went on to become one of the UK's most successful advertising agencies.

A darker side to this is that the success of such advertising campaigns helps to create a dangerous myth for a democracy, namely that politicians and political parties can be sold to an electorate in just the same way that soap powder is sold to consumers. All you need is to produce a glitzy enough campaign and through the power of advertising and marketing a gullible electorate will be swayed by the image rather than the reality of the political message. The danger then is that politics and political issues are reduced to 15 second sound bites.

An important consequence of the 1979 defeat for Labour was that a badly battered party was then determined to improve their election campaign, and in the 1987 General Election they ran a highly effective, media campaign with a series of novel tactics, such as ensuring policy announcements coincided with the day's main news broadcasts. A red rose logo was introduced to soften the party's image. In the 1987 general election campaign, boring party political broadcasts were elevated to a new level by film director Hugh Hudson who directed 'Kinnock the Movie'. Communications director Peter Mandelson worked with what become known as the Shadow Communications Agency and the Labour campaign leapt ahead of that of the Conservatives. However, despite the glitz Labour still lost the election which suggests that no matter how strong and attractive a media campaign might be, if the electorate still does not have faith or trust in a political party it will not win.

In the 1990s political campaigns became more centralised as well as more professional and longer. The election success of the Democrat candidate Bill Clinton in the USA in 1992 made a great impression on the Labour Party, with Labour strategists' forging close links with the Democrat campaigners to learn the lessons of Clinton's success. The result was the Labour Party operation working from Millbank Tower on the banks of the river Thames between 1995 and 1997 became the most professional and feared political campaigning unit in the world. Tactics such as the rapid rebuttal team, challenging wrong assertions made in the press, and bullying the media to force the Labour policy onto the agenda were characteristic of the operation. While such tactics contributed to the Labour Party's electoral success in 1997, it was the continuation of similar tactics when in government that brought the accusations of spin and media manipulation.

Political lobbying

Governments local – central, and European, – are also the objects of sophisticated communication campaigns. Activity which attempts to influence government is known as political lobbying and is a well-established part of the communications industry. In common with other sectors we have looked at it is also one where major growth has happened relatively quickly.

Diary: The Director of a Political Consultancy
Before joining Politics International in 1995 David Massingham worked as policy adviser to the Chief Executive of an inner London borough, where he was responsible for strategic regeneration issues. Subsequently, he was a senior civil servant in the Departments of Environment and Transport and the Cabinet Office. He now serves as the Director of Interel Consulting.

Monday
0830   *Arrive office*
          Catch up on weekend e-mails
          Go-through diary for week
0915   *Team meeting to discuss the week's new business development activity, major client events/issues and general 'housekeeping'*
1000   *Walk to parliament; call a couple of clients en-route*
1015   *Meet client about to give evidence to select committee; over coffee have last-minute run through key issues*
1045   *Sit in on select committee session as client gives evidence*
1130   *Session ends; quick debrief to agree follow-up actions as client finds cab*
          Walk back to office, making a couple more calls
          Run into a competitor on Victoria Street, compare notes on state of the market
1200   *Settle down to write detailed public policy and political risk assessment for a key client project. They want to know what probability I place on success to help in securing funding. Sandwich at desk as I write.*

1430   *E-mail paper to client*
Go through accumulated e-mails for the day
Phone calls to a couple of contacts inside government departments

1515   *Head to City for client meeting to discuss campaign plans for handling an issue relating to a piece of government legislation. Agree key messages for briefings and targets in both Commons and Lords to ensure no unhelpful amendments are accepted by government. Discuss possibility of raising the issue profile with some media work, but decide low-key is best.*

1745   *Use opportunity of being in City to meet friend in the venture capital field for quick drink to talk about a (long-term) initiative to develop a campaign on carbon-trading; also the prospects of Charlton Athletic.*

1930   *Get home; quick bite to eat*

2000   *Conference call with clients in USA to discuss paper written earlier in the day*

2145   *Call ends*
Just time to say 'good night' to kids before they go to bed …

Tuesday

0830   *Home: brew large pot of coffee and sip it while dealing with e-mails; make several calls to clients, colleagues and others*

0930   *Walk to meeting at local council offices to discuss a planning issue – interesting to have a client involved in something so close to home!*

1100   *Train to office – read latest government proposals for reform of renewable energy support mechanisms*

1230   *Write note of above for client, with recommendations for response*

1315   *Meet a senior contact in Transport for London for lunch at a local 'greasy spoon'. Some discussion of issues about Crossrail of interest to a couple of clients; progress of arrangements for the visit to London in July of Tour de France for personal interest; exchange snippets of gossip on the politics of London.*

1430   *Monthly management meeting*

1630   *Go though e-mails; call a couple of clients just to touch base; catch up with colleagues on a few client issues*

1730   *Attend London First networking event on planning and development; presentation and Q&A session on the Mayor of London's proposed new planning powers; wine and nibbles and chat to a variety of local government planners, private sector planners and developers.*

Companies carry out lobbying, not only because they want to influence government policy but also because government local and central are major purchaser of services. Companies need to know their way around how local and central government works, in order to know and understand where the decisions are made.

Lobbying companies

Professional lobbying firms fall into five categories:

- Political consultancies who specialise in dealing with government.
- Regulatory consultants, who specialise in issues such as pharmaceuticals and foodstuffs and technical aspects of utility regulation.
- Parliamentary agents, used to specialise in promoting Private Bills but who now increasingly provide broader monitoring and lobbying services.
- Public relations firms, some of whom will have dedicated lobbying divisions.
- Law and accountancy firms, who advise on issues such as budget or competition representations. A number will have specialist policy units.

They offer the following services:

- Monitoring parliamentary, Whitehall, political party, local government, public body, think tank, pressure group and EU institutional activity, debates, committee inquiries, statements, reports, legislation, and regulation and database management.
- Case assembly, involving advice on or handling research and the drafting of submissions.
- Strategic advice on whom to lobby, how and when.
- Campaign management, involving either administrative support for the client's own representations or handling briefing and debriefing.
- Media management and other PR support for lobbying programmes.
- Auditing the effectiveness of in-house resources and drafting programmes for implementation by clients.

David Massingham of Interel Consulting says the following services are in demand from clients: 'High-level strategic advice, legislative support and parliamentary relations; relationship management, especially with government and its agencies; intelligence gathering; message development and positioning' (2008). Howell James, a former Permanent Secretary for government communication, is well-placed to advise on the effectiveness of the lobbying and offers the following observation on its effectiveness: 'If lobbying is framed as a dialogue between interested parties, one that helps each party know and understand where the other is coming from and to be sympathetic and understanding about the pressures on both sides then yes, I think it does work. But I personally doubt whether lobbying can single-handedly deliver and industry or sector's interests over and above the wider public's interests' (*Public Affairs News*, June 2005).

Darren Murphy, a former special adviser to the Prime Minister and now a political lobbyist, argues that there are mutual advantages between government and client: 'Can lobbyists help through their connections and friendships? I think people see through that. If you tried to do your lobbying on a contacts–basis you would fail your client. What's valuable is the mindset, knowing how things work, not the address book' (*Public Affairs News*, June 2005).

The cash for questions affair was one of the UK's biggest political scandals of the 1990s. It started in 1994 when the *Guardian* newspaper alleged that the political lobbyist Ian Greer had paid Conservative MPs Neil Hamilton and Tim Smith to ask questions in Parliament on behalf of his client, Mohammed Al-Fayed.

David Hencke, the *Guardian* lobby correspondent, who broke the story about the cash for questions affair offered the following comments when asked 'does lobbying work':

> *I'm not sure whether it does, because it's very difficult to isolate a decision that's been taken exclusively because a lobbyist has said, "you must not do this". When government backs down it's because MPs and the public have an overwhelming objection, not because a lobbyist says it's a bad idea. In a way they're limited and it's quite right they are or society would be really bad. However, I think that lobbyists may be more influential on some of the smaller decisions that aren't seized on by the press.* (*Public Affairs News*, June 2005)

According to David Massingham:

> *Much of public affairs is "behind the scenes" and it is often hard to see a tangible connection between the work that we do and specific political or policy outcomes. It is easier to evaluate some kinds of activities than others. For example, a profile raising campaign can be measured through before and after benchmarking, which can be done in a variety of ways, including perceptions audits. Similarly, a campaign on a specific piece of proposed legislation can be measured directly by whether the desired outcomes (amendments, ministerial undertakings, etc.) are achieved. Other activities are much more difficult to evaluate, for example, it can be difficult to gauge how much influence a programme of public affairs activity has had on the outcome of a major procurement exercise, compared with say, the technical merits of the bid or the price.* (Massingham, 2008)

Is lobbying effective?

What makes an effective lobbyist? Both the corporate sector and NGOs engage in lobbying but which is the more effective of the two?

A 2007 survey carried out by the Hansard Society revealed the relative impact of lobbyists, showing that

- 91% of MPs believed that charities were effective at communicating with them.
- 88% of MPs believed that interest groups were effective at communicating with them.
- 57% of MPs believed that business was effective at communicating with them.

According to the Hansard Society: 'The survey suggests that lobbyists working in the corporate sector are not as good at communicating with MPs as they think they are – only 20% of MPs believe that "companies are generally more adept at lobbying than charities/pressure groups". Lobbyists taking part in the survey expressed an exasperation with MPs who, they feel, do not give businesses the "benefit of the doubt" in the way that they might to NGOs or charities working in the same policy area'.

The survey also showed that the two most important factors for MPs when dealing with lobbying organisations were the impact of the issue on their constituents and the accountability of the lobbying organisation.

An example of a charity that mounted an effective lobbying campaign is found in the Gambling Bill Campaign, run jointly by the Salvation Army and the Methodist Church. The award-winning campaign was a mixture of PR and lobbying: 'No major piece of legislation has changed so radically between White Paper and Royal Assent as the Gambling Act and this is due in no small part to this campaign' (judges' comments at the 'Third Sector' PR Strategy awards, quoted in *PR Week*, 14 October, 2005). Labour MP Rob Marris was concerned about the risks that gambling posed to small children: he said of the campaign: 'Lobbying of MPs and ministers had a significant effect on limiting the number of large-scale casinos that might (have been) introduced as a result of legislation'. The government had proposed increasing the number of casinos, including a number of so-called 'super-casinos'. The concern of those opposed to this was that it would lead to an increase in gambling. The Salvation Army and the Methodist church were among a number of organisations that campaigned against the proposals.

Examples of successful lobbying campaigns by the voluntary sector in the last few years include the RNID campaign that persuaded the government to commit £125 million to modernise audiology services in the UK, and the work of the Disabilities Charities Consortium (including Leonard Cheshire, Mencap, Mind, RNIB, RNID and Scope) in campaigning for and on the 2005 Disability Discrimination Act.

Is lobbying ethical?

The practice of lobbying is controversial but is it also unethical? There are examples of unethical practice which have had an impact on our perceptions of the industry. Perhaps the most notable case in the UK and one that had a major impact in that it led to investigations, resignations, and new regulations was the 'cash for questions' scandal where the lobbying firm Ian Greer Associates was alleged to have paid Conservative MPs to ask parliamentary questions. It was one of the biggest political scandals of the 1990s in the UK. In October 1994 *The Guardian* newspaper alleged that lobbyist Ian Greer had bribed two Conservative MPs, Tim Smith and Neil Hamilton, to ask questions about the takeover of Harrods on behalf of Mohammed Al-Fayed in order to stop a hostile campaign run by his opponent, the head of a company called Lohnro, Tiny Rowland. The scandal eventually led to resignations and reforms and the establishment of the Nolan committee which laid down new practices for everyone in elected positions, both MPs and councillors, and also those in contact with them, lobbyists.

In 1998 'Drapergate' saw Derek Draper, a former adviser to then minister Peter Mandelson, accused of boasting that lobbying clients could gain access to senior government figures. In Scotland, Beattie Media shut down its lobbying arm in 1999 after one its executives claimed that he could influence the diaries of MSPs (Members of the Scottish Parliament). There were echoes of the 1994 'cash for questions' scandal in 2009 when four Labour lords were accused of offering to amend legislation in return for payment, and then in 2010 former Labour Cabinet ministers were caught on record by undercover journalists posing as lobbyists from a fictional firm, Perry Anderson, offering to influence government ministers to amend legislation for money.

This might give the impression that this is a sector which has major ethical problems. David Massingham does not believe that in general there are any ethical issues involved in public affairs:

> The potential problems are by some who pursue public affairs activities in inappropriate ways – most obviously and controversially, peddling access, for example, cash for questions, etc. Most of the industry conducts itself in a highly ethical way and observes the clear rules that apply to engaging with politicians and public servants. A small minority do not and voluntary regulation is not I think, proving strong enough.

The case for lobbying is that it allows organisations, both commercial and non-commercial, that might be affected by potential legislation to have their say and attempt to change it. When legislation is proposed it can be useful for the government to be able to hear alternative views. This was recognised by John Grogan MP, a consistent critic of lobbying, when in 2007 he submitted an Early Day Motion (EDM) which called on MPs and peers to boycott any lobbying/public affairs company that did not support or comply with the Code of Conduct for the Association of Professional Political Consultants (APPC). Grogan's motion stated: 'That this House believes that public affairs firms have a key role to play in articulating the view of business, charities, trade unions and public bodies, to

Government and Parliament'. Public Affairs companies however, and the political lobbying process must always be open and transparent'. Grogan was calling on organisations who used public affairs companies to publish their client lists, which is a requirement of APPC membership. The problem here is that those who have the most money and resources might use them for their own sectional advantage at the expense of the wider community interest.

The House of Commons Public Administration Committee investigated the public affairs industry and made a number of recommendations that were intended to tighten up control and make the practice more transparent: eventually the committee recommended that the industry be given the opportunity to self-regulate and introduce its own register. Stung by the 'Perry Anderson' affair and the damage done to the industry, even though no lobbyist was actually involved, the PR industry reacted swiftly hoping to head off potential action.

The professional organisations representing PR, the CIPR, the Association of Professional Political Consultants (APPC), and the Public Relations Consultants Association (PRCA) established the UK Public Affairs Council (UKPAC). This is an independent body which sets the standards for behaviour expected of those who interact with the institutions of government or who advise on such interactions. One of UKPAC's main functions is overseeing a register of information on public affairs practitioners. This is precisely the register that the Public Administration Select Committee had demanded. It offers a voluntary rather than a formal legislation solution and ensures that all those involved in lobbying are governed by a clear set of principles which are underpinned by an enforceable Code of Conduct.

The register is important for transparency because it demonstrates who is lobbying and for whom. The agreed definition for lobbying suggested by UKPAC is:

Lobbying means, in a professional capacity, attempting to influence, the UK Government, Parliament, the devolved legislatures or administrations, regional or local government or other public bodies on any matter within their competence.

David Massingham believes that in the next ten years the industry will face a number of challenges:

The public affairs side of the industry will remain under close scrutiny and I suspect that we will move slowly into a more heavily regulated era. The problem then will be getting the balance right between an appropriate level of regulation and the ability actually to do our jobs. We have to respond to rapid technological development and the gradual breakdown of conventional forms of political activity. The rise of single interest groups, internet campaigning, etc. will change the way in which politics works and therefore the drivers for public policy changes. (Massingham, 2008)

191

SUMMARY

The practice of government communications on PR continues to exercise a major influence because of its size and the nature of the communication practised. Many argue it encompasses some of the worst aspects of communication, for example through social marketing programmes and the use of spin.

The rise in PR practice in the public sector as a whole has contributed to the growth of the industry. Now there is evidence that the use of direct channels of communication is making a major difference to the way that some local authorities communicate and also changing the way that elections might be fought in the future.

FROM CHARITIES TO CELEBRITIES: THE VARIETY AND DIVERSITY OF PR PRACTICE

By the end of this chapter you will understand:

- how diverse PR practice is
- how PR is practised in different sectors
- some of the ethical issues and implications involved
- how practice changes and adapts to different circumstances

INTRODUCTION

PR is a growing industry with a wider range of companies and organisations in different sectors now utilising professional communications. This diversity is probably best illustrated by contrasting the activity of PR practitioners working at different ends of the spectrum. At one end there are the publicists and PRs working for celebrities and sport stars who earn large fees, while at the other there is the work done by PRs in campaigning charities and some non-governmental organisations (NGOs). The contrast between the two could not be greater: celebrities, film and sports stars have apparently limitless funds available to promote and market themselves, while charities and NGOs have only limited funds for their work. Yet some of this is amongst the most effective and creative of all communication activity.

Diversity within the types of clients using PR was illustrated when the Girl Guides appointed a head of communications and publications. The organisation wanted to be seen as 'modern and relevant' and it was keen to move away from its image as an exclusively white, middle class, Christian organisation, looking to recruit more ethnic minorities and girls from deprived areas.

> *Communicating the message that guiding is for girls of all backgrounds, regardless of faith, race, or culture is vital. The biggest challenge is to change the perceptions of girl guiding UK. In the minds of so many, girl guides are frozen in time, but this is a modern, relevant organisation. Guides wear jeans, and uniform options range from a baseball cap to a hajib. (Sue Field, head of communications and publications.)*

Should we be surprised that in the twenty-first century churches of all denominations have media relations officers? They are after all engaged in communication with the wider community and are asked to respond by the media on a range of issues – from the events of the day to campaign issues. They therefore need to be able to respond in just the same way as any other organisation.

Football clubs have increased the volume of their communication and also outgrown the traditional programme that used to satisfy supporters. Interactive electronic media via websites now allow supporters to watch match highlights and interviews with managers and players and comment virtually in real-time. While this is welcome one negative impact here that these services provided by local sports clubs are contributing to the decline of local newspapers which once had a monopoly on sporting news.

CHARITIES AND CAMPAIGNING ORGANISATIONS

The third sector ('Not for Profit'/Voluntary) is very diverse, ranging from well-known campaigning organisations such as Greenpeace, Friends of the Earth and Age UK (formerly Help the Aged and Age Concern) to charities working for specialist interest groups that constantly struggle for funds and are dependent on donations for their existence. Charities campaign to:

- raise finance
- raise awareness of an issue

For many charities communication is an essential activity linked to fund-raising in addition to providing publicity for their campaigns or causes. This is why a number of charities have combined the roles of communication and fund-raising into the same post. Sight Savers, for example, has a director of fundraising and communications; Deafness Research UK, the UK's only national deafness research charity, appointed a head of communication with a direct brief to secure more donations. Charities also use communication to raise awareness about the nature of a problem; the Meningitis Trust for example launched a

UK-wide campaign to raise awareness of meningitis in the workplace and to highlight how it can affect adults. PR practitioners working for charities have fewer resources available to them than their counterparts in the commercial or public sector and consequently have to work harder in order to get media coverage. To attract attention they have to be more imaginative and it is in these campaigns that we can find some of the most innovative and creative PR efforts, illustrating its power and range.

Unfortunately, critics of the PR industry make no distinction between PR practitioners working for charities and those working for large corporations as to them these are all tarred with the same brush. The work undertaken in the charitable sector is central to raising the public profile of charities and thus characterising everything that PR does as bad is both simplistic and does a great disservice to everyone attempting to honestly pursue their careers.

As we saw in Chapter 13 some of the most effective lobbyists are NGOs and charities, with many MPs rating them better at lobbying than companies in the corporate sector. The voluntary sector often attracts people working in PR who would be uncomfortable doing a similar job in the private sector: 'There is a sense that you are making a contribution to making life better for society and that you are not part of some process that is attempting to convince people to buy things they don't want' (Litchfield, 2009). Although there are great differences in pay, the reward is more job satisfaction.

For many if not all charities, the PR work they undertake is not carried out for publicity's sake, but is necessary for their campaign goals. For example, PR is used to draw attention to major health issues such as the campaign on heart disease and the dangers of smoking. The Blood Pressure Association used PR to increase the number of public donations by keeping the charity's activities in the public domain, thereby reducing their reliance on grants. In this way numerous life saving and necessary campaigns have benefitted from PR activity.

PR activity also allows charities to monitor awareness of conditions and public attitudes towards them. The National Autistic Society (NAS) surveyed 28,000 people after its radio awareness campaign in September 2005. Similarly editorial and advertising slots across the UK's 270 commercial radio stations highlighted autism and encouraged people to respond to the survey: 'From these results we know that we must continue to raise awareness of the issues that affect people with autism and challenge misconceptions,' said Quentin Rappoport, director of communications and public affairs (*PR Week*, 2 December, 2005).

Charities will use a range of techniques and campaigns in order to continue to build new audiences – Help the Aged (now Age UK), for example, launched a campaign aimed at young people. Helping Unite Generations (HUG) was an attempt to attract younger fundraisers and highlight the prevalence of loneliness among older people. Consumer and specialist media such as publican, community, corporate and professional publications were targeted. One of the creative challenges facing charities is keeping public interest sustained; from a tactical perspective there is by and large little ongoing news that can be used to keep charities in the forefront of the media as the issues they campaign on are not necessarily newsworthy all of the time.

Another problem facing charities is that of 'charity overload', a phenomenon whereby consumers are bombarded with too many campaign messages and too many requests for donations and become confused or desensitised as a result. A favourite PR tactic to keep a charity in the headlines is a designated charity week. In the UK there is a Red Cross Week, an awareness week run by the Royal College of Midwives, a Big Eye Opener Awareness day for the Charity Sightsavers International, a Breast Awareness Week, an Alzheimer's Awareness Week, a Down's Syndrome Awareness Week, a Food Allergy and Intolerance Week, and even a National Poop Scoop Week! The British Heart Foundation used Valentine's Day to engage with a younger audience by staging a 'flirt walk' in conjunction with a dating agency to engage participants in 'speed-dating-style activity.' The charity hoped that as well as creating fundraising opportunities among a younger age group, the walk would also generate greater awareness of the work done by its nurses and boost its profile. All of these and the many other charity weeks are worthwhile and important, but they also raise questions about, firstly, what happens for the rest of the year, and secondly, the possibility that the general public may become fed up with them.

Diary: The Press Officer (The MS Society)

Jenna Litchfield is a Press Officer at the MS Society and started working there in 2009. Before that she worked at The Pasque Charity (now known as Keech Hospice Care) as a PR & Communications Officer. She graduated with a degree in PR & Media from Huddersfield University.

Monday
News is announced from two pharmaceutical companies that two new tablets to treat multiple sclerosis (MS) have finished clinical trials and have shown really positive results. This is significant for people with MS so I write a news story for our website and prepare a comment from our head of research on what these latest developments mean.

Several journalists from national newspapers and a major online news website call me to talk about the development; they want to know how significant it is and whether it's worth running something in the paper/online. I spend a considerable amount of time briefing each one – talking through the two different tablets, their similarities and differences, explaining when they might be available for people with MS and where people can go for more information on them. Some of the journalists ask for a case study, so I search through our case study database to find someone who has been on one of the clinical trials and can talk about their experiences – like whether they've noticed any improvements, or why they prefer swallowing a tablet compared to injecting medication. All the journalists ask for an official comment from the charity, which I provide.

With the national newspapers accounted for, I spend the rest of the day phoning round regional newspapers and radio stations – distributing our comments to reporters who may be thinking of running the story and lining up broadcast interviews with our head of research.

It's my responsibility to ensure staff and volunteers are well briefed for any radio interviews they participate in. For all interviews we provide agreed key messages and ask that they mention the MS Society's contact details for anyone wanting more information. Raising awareness of the condition and the work of the MS Society is vitally important if we are to increase donations and reach out to people who have been newly diagnosed – so we must secure a name check.

Wednesday
This year we have over 250 people running in aid of the MS Society in the London Marathon and many of them have a connection to MS and an inspiring story to tell about why they're running. Stories like this are great for local newspapers and so I spend a few hours interviewing the runners who've requested help with gaining media coverage, and prepare a press release for each of them. In the interviews I ask about their reasons for running – some have a parent or sibling living with MS, others actually have the condition themselves which is even more inspiring. Once the press release has been written I phone their local newspaper and speak to the journalist on the newsdesk. I briefly explain where I'm calling from and that we have a story about a local person who is running the marathon – I take the opportunity to mention anything quirky or unusual about their story that'll make them memorable. One runner is aiming to break a world record and the journalist is very keen to know more.

Out of the ten stories I sell in, eight receive coverage. You can't always guarantee a 100% success rate when it comes to media coverage, but by 'selling in' strong local case studies to local newspapers, you're half way there.

I spend the rest of the day working with the charity's policy & campaigns team to prepare a comment to send to journalists on a new proposal from the government about social care. We need to ensure the government's plans to reform the social care system consider the elements that people with MS have told us are important to them, so we prepare a comment that reflects this. It's a tough task condensing our thoughts into a few lines but that's where essential vocabulary and grammar skills come in – especially the ability to use choose a few words to convey a powerful message.

With the comment signed off, I send it out to several journalists whom I know are working on the story.

The workings of Whitehall and Westminster wasn't an area I knew too much about before working for a charity, but a solid understanding is essential – and I had to learn pretty quickly!

Friday
A major soap is planning to run a storyline involving a character with MS and so one of the show's researchers contacts the press office for background help and information; they also send through some scripts for our feedback.

I add some corrections to the scripts and provide further information on different scenarios that they might want to write in. The character is cared for by his on-screen son, who is a teenager, and so I seize the opportunity to secure some topical media coverage and search through the case study database to find any young carers who might want to take part in a interview; I find two willing volunteers.

With backing from the soap's press officer, I phone a national teenage magazine and talk to a journalist there about the upcoming storyline and how it involves a young carer – I add into my pitch the details of the two case studies I've found, along with the promise of exclusive quotes from a major celebrity who was also once a young carer. The journalist at the magazine is thrilled with the exclusive and, after running it by her editor, pledges to devote four pages of the magazine to it. She arranges to interview both of the young carer case studies and I pass on quotes from our celebrity supporter. As with all magazine interviews, I ask that the journalist includes a mention of the charity alongside our website and helpline number, and that they feature some details of the condition.

Case studies, and especially celebrity case studies or famous supporters, can be so powerful when it comes to media interviews. Some of the most influential pieces of press coverage I've secured have been as a result of a well briefed case study giving an inspiring interview to a journalist. I've found these can be the difference between a minor 'news in brief' or a page lead and such is their impact that more often than not a journalist won't run a story without one.

I started working in charity three years ago after finishing university, and now I wouldn't consider working in any other industry. I like it that we're accountable to our members, so at the heart of every decision made and action taken are the needs of people affected by MS.

Working in a busy communications team is both challenging and rewarding. The nature of cross-departmental working means my workload is extremely varied and it's exciting to be the first to hear about new announcements and projects.

Everyone I work with is compassionate and committed and many, like me, also volunteer and fundraise for the charity in their spare time too. I find I don't need much motivation to come into the office and work hard every day – I just need to talk to our volunteers and service users to realise how the work we're all contributing to can make such a difference to someone's life.

HOW CHARITIES CAMPAIGN

Charities will campaign for a number of reasons, ranging from generating publicity to raise funds to trying to change legislation on behalf of their members or challenge legislation that might impact on sufferers. The International Myeloma Foundation for example undertook a media relations campaign to address the problem of what it described as 'postcode prescriptions' for cancer drugs. The charity aimed to lobby government to boost the funding and resources of the National Institute for Clinical Excellence (NICE) which approves new drugs for prescription.

The importance of publicity to specialist pressure groups is illustrated by the pressure group Dignity in Dying. According to Mark Slattery, head of communications, 'Publicity is our oxygen. It's my job to keep it flowing'. He was speaking after the charity had managed to achieve ten front pages in two weeks, following publicity about its name change from the Voluntary Euthanasia Society.

Compassion fatigue is nothing but a myth: people generally do not run out of compassion, but the charity sector does run out of ideas. The enemies are marketing, fundraising and PR fatigue. The good news is that we can do something about this fatigue with the skills, ingenuity and creativity within the charity sector. (PR Week, 21/10/5)

An example of how charities have to be more creative in the way that they approach issues can be seen in the way that cancer charities have attempted to change the focus of what they do away from simply raising funds for cancer research to trying to encourage people to change their lifestyles and prevent cancer occurring in the first place. The World Cancer Research Fund had spent over 15 years studying the link between cancer and lifestyle but had trouble getting their message across to the public. The reason, according to Andrew Trehearnes, the head of education and communications at the charity, is that 'The press want triumph over tragedy stories. We can't say: "Look, here's someone who has not contracted cancer because he leads a healthy lifestyle." It doesn't work like that, so you have to be more creative' (*PR Week*, 6/1/06), a point confirmed by *The Guardian's* health editor Sarah Boseley: 'Prevention stories receive less coverage because the messages can be repetitive and not very exciting – don't smoke, don't drink too much, eat more fruit and vegetables. You can write that story occasionally, but not over and over again'.

Diary: The Press Officer (BRAKE)
Lauren Collins: a Press Officer for the Road Safety Charity BRAKE

Wednesday
9am–10.30am: Collect newspapers and go through all of them looking for anything road related; crashes, changes in legislation, court cases, etc. Then check online, particularly the BBC website, for more stories. I then write up what I'd found in a short, bullet point format, for the news section on the website and email the link out to all of the road safety professionals on Brake's databases.

10.30–1pm: Brake are issuing a press release, under embargo until 12.01am tomorrow, which is urging the government to take action on the 'confusing and dangerous' drink-drive limit, after research showed that women were closing the gender gap on drink-driving.

2pm–3.45pm: There was quite a lot of interest in the press release already, mainly from radio stations who wanted me to set up pre-recorded interviews for their breakfast shows tomorrow morning. I set up an interview schedule and arrange who could speak to which show at what time.

3.45pm–5.15pm: Once the phones had calmed down I could carry on with my task of marketing Road Safety Week to specialist industry magazines and emergency service publications. The aim of this was to gain as much media coverage as possible for the week to encourage fire, police and ambulance services to get involved and plan initiatives for it.

5.25pm: Home, after responding to any urgent emails.

Thursday
9am–1pm: Brake issued a press release, under embargo until 12.01am today, urging the Government to take action on the 'confusing and dangerous' drink-drive limit, after research showed that women were closing the gender gap on drink-driving. The release sparked huge media attention from the press, radio and TV who were ringing constantly for interviews and further comment.

1pm–1.30pm: Lunch could only be half an hour today because the phones were so hectic.

1.30–2.30pm: The phones in the press office had quietened down after lunch so I had chance to go through the newspapers and write the daily news e-bulletin for the website. Better late than never!

2.30pm–5.30pm: Once the interest from the morning's news topic had waned, I could carry on with the marketing of Road Safety Week to emergency service professionals' publications.

5.30pm: Home. Was out slightly later than usual because I had several emails I needed to respond to that I hadn't had chance to look at throughout the day.

Friday
9am–10.30am: Do the daily news bulletin and send out the e-cascade.

10.30am–1pm: Friday mornings consist of doing the press work for one of Brake's road safety initiatives, 'Beep Beep day', which is a safety day for children of nursery age. My task involves finding out which nurseries and playgroups are holding a 'Beep Beep day' in the following week and then writing a press release to sell-in to their local media. I have to ring up the nurseries to gain their permission for media coverage and the possibility of a newspaper photographer turning up at the event. I then get a quote off them to accompany Brake's quote, to give the press release a personal/ human interest angle. Once the release is written and approved by Cathy, my manager, I can sell the story of the nursery or playgroup to the local media in the hope of gaining coverage for the day.

2–3pm: I had lunch later today as there were a lot of 'Beep Beep day' press releases to 'roll out'.

3pm–5.15pm: My task for Friday afternoons is updating the Brake and Road Safety Week websites, and in particular the resource catalogue on the Road Safety Week website. This involves data-basing every resource the catalogue has listed and ensuring it is up-to-date and still available, also ensuring that links to other websites and services still work and looking for any new resources that could be listed. Once listed, I then make the actual changes. The updating of the website is an on-going task that I spend every Friday afternoon on.

5.15pm: Home on time!

Another example of how PR can be used to raise the profile of important issues is the NSPCC Full Stop campaign to raise awareness of child abuse. According to director of communications John Grounds: 'When we reviewed the Full Stop Campaign, we found it had raised awareness of child abuse to very high levels'.

Box 14.1 Three Days in the Press Office for the Campaign by War on Want

Student Sophie Rogers was on a work placement with the media team at the charity War on Want and observed how they launched controversial research which raised the issue of slave labour.

Background

War on Want is a campaigning charity that fights poverty in developing countries in partnership and solidarity with people affected by globalisation. It campaigns for workers' rights and against the root causes of global poverty, inequality and injustice.

In 2006 it launched a report called 'Fashion Victims' which linked sweatshop workers directly to the high street stores they supplied. In the past this link had been difficult to prove, but garment workers interviewed by War on Want (WoW) confirmed that they were sewing for Primark, Asda and Tesco.

The report was released on 6 December 2006 targeting the working conditions of factory workers in the Bangladeshi capital Dhaka who were making clothes for UK retail stores and was released to generate maximum publicity on the same day that the parent company of Primark, Associated British Foods, held their Annual General Meeting. This was a strategic decision by War on Want to focus on the issue: the charity's subscription to a news event service allowed it to time the report with the launch of Primark's parent company annual meeting.

This section follows the team, led by the media officer for War on Want Paul Collins, as they launched the report and attempted to generate substantial coverage for the cause.

Paul Collins worked for Action Aid for seven years and has a respected reputation in the field, staff at War on Want said that media coverage had increased dramatically since his arrival. The charity generally receives good coverage from newspapers such as the *Guardian* and *The Independent* and both newspapers have a tradition of supporting the campaigns of War on Want. *The Independent* wanted to have an exclusive on the report – but War on Want declined. Paul Collins explained: 'It is always a gamble to say no to an exclusive, but then if you agree to it, will the coverage be limited? Will anyone else cover it? Media coverage on campaigns is dumbing down, for example celebrities pose campaign exposure a tougher challenge.' Paul Collins believes they have to work twice as hard on developing world issues to make sure that they receive coverage. The key message to remember he says is: 'If you have a news story don't sit on it.' He points to another charity where he worked and a researcher found a story on the website – the charity delayed its release, then BBC Radio 4 broke the news – first on the *Today* programme and then in a 40-minute documentary.

Day One: Wednesday 6 December 2006

The War on Want Media Department – Paul Collins (Media Officer), Simon McRae (Senior Campaigns Officer, economic justice – retailers), senior campaigns officer (global justice – corporations and conflict), Ruth Tanner; Jackie Simpkins (Trade Unions Officer); campaigns officer (trade), Dave Tucker; campaigns assistant, Nadia Idle; campaigns assistant, Seb Klier; campaigns volunteer (trade), Graham Hobbs.

WoW release the Fashion Victims report on Friday 8th December, and embargo it until midnight Thursday. It has already been distributed before the release date and the following newspapers have already agreed to use it: the *Daily Mirror*, *Guardian*, and *Independent*. The BBC plans to cover it on its *Breakfast News* programme – the advantage of the early release was highlighted by Roland Buerk, then the BBC's Dhaka correspondent, who said that receiving the report even in draft form weeks before the launch enabled him to secure pieces in several programmes. During the day Paul Collins phones his media contacts to see who else will be reporting it. There is also a meeting with John Hilary to discuss how the report will be sold to the media: they discuss 'media messaging' and three points emerge in how the media will be briefed.

- Cheap clothes equal low pay in Bangladesh. Is this a lifestyle choice by the buying public? Are they willing to pay more for clothes and ensure better rights for workers?
- Effects: Factory workers in Bangladesh work 80 hour weeks for 5p an hour and this is below the living wage. On average a skilled worker receives £22 a month, with a sewing machine worker by comparison receiving just £16 a month.
- What are we calling for? The government needs to introduce legislation to deal with the exploitation of supplier workers right down the supply chain. War on Want blames the retailers for driving down factories' prices. There needs to be regular reporting on the supply chains and issues of redress on those that are affected outside the UK. What regulatory measures are the government taking? Companies should use their influence to make a difference and live up to their commitments not just in Bangladesh but also in developing countries such as China, Kenya and Honduras. There will be no 'consumer education' by the charity: it opposes boycotts, which threaten jobs, but the public can write to companies and state that they are unhappy with their practices. Not wanting to have a knock-on effect on prices, but consumers need to be aware when purchasing goods. Chancellor Gordon Brown and PM Tony Blair should be contacted. Non-government organisations should also be made aware of the report as well as the London fashion magazines. 3,000 copies of the report will be issues with 1000 copies for Trade Union stands, copies will be sent to the managers of the flagship stores of Tesco, Primark and Asda. The Irish media will also be sent copies due to the Irish link with Primark. A new Primark store is opening in Edinburgh so the *Scotsman* newspaper will also be contacted. During the meeting, staff are made aware that Tesco are considering legal action.

(Continued)

(Continued)

Day 2: Thursday 7 December, 2006

The eve of the report launch and the Primark and Asda press offices have made contact with War on Want with Asda wanting to sit down with the charity and discuss the findings. BBC Radio Kent has requested an interview after receiving information from the Press Association. The BBC's World News Service has shown an interest in covering the report. *The Independent* wants to do case studies on the factory workers mentioned in the report but WoW has told the newspaper that no details of the factories will be released in order to protect the workers' identities. The *Tonight with Trevor McDonald* programme plans to make reference to the issue on a piece on Bangladesh. Radio One has been in contact wanting to interview Simon McRae – this is seen as a positive development as the station reaches a young audience who shop in high street stores. *The Metro*, London's free paper, and *The Independent* both want direct quotes from the factory workers to include in their papers. Arrangements are made for a series of interviews with local and regional radio stations.

Day 3: Friday 8 December 2006

The 'Fashion Victims' report has been launched and a series of radio and television interviews carried out. Simon McRae and John Hilary have between them conducted interviews that started at 6:15am with the *Today* programme on Radio 4, followed by Radio Wales (7.00am), Radio Five Live (7.25am), Radio Scotland (7.30am), Radio Kent (7.40am), Radio Shropshire (7.45am), and Radio Essex (8.20am). The major BBC radio stations also covered the report with updates at lunchtime. Louise Richards, the Chief Executive of the charity, is interviewed on the BBC *Breakfast News* programme at 8.10am. This is regarded as a maximum prime time slot. Television interviews with Sky, Channel 4 News and Channel 5 News are scheduled for the day and more radio interviews with BBC Belfast and Three Counties radio. The British Red Cross has been in contact with WoW as it is concerned about its sponsorship with Tesco being affected by negative coverage of the company. This is an example of War on Want using different methods from other charities in terms of funding as it does not rely on corporate sponsorship but funds from different organisations.

Newspaper coverage of the report has included *The Daily Mail*, *The Telegraph*, *The Metro*, *The Independent* and *The Guardian*. *The Metro* ran a story on the report as its front page splash with the headline 'Tesco's shame'. *The Independent* followed with a spread on page 12 and page 4 of its earlier morning edition, and *The Guardian* covered it on page 28 with a full page and pictures. The report also received coverage throughout the night on BBC *World News*. Websites that have also given coverage includes: Brand Republic, *The Scotsman*, *The Telegraph*, 24 Dash, In the News, *Yorkshire Post* and Buzzle. *The Independent* states that it wants any future exclusives to itself, but Paul Collins asks whether a national paper would want to lead with a story if the *Metro* paper has it as its front cover. At 4.20pm Paul conducts a radio interview with Colourful Radio and discusses the issue of a living wage in Bangladesh.

CELEBRITIES

Celebrity promotion by dedicated specialist publicists takes us back to where we started. The means of communication might have changed, but the reasons for promoting the celebrities haven't. As we saw in Chapter 3, celebrities have been associated with PR from its earliest days and Grunig and Hunt (1984) used the practice of celebrity publicists as the basis for one of their models of PR. It should come as no surprise then, that in our celebrity obsessed culture entertainers and celebrities not only use PR but have moved some of its main practitioners into the spotlight, making individuals such as Max Clifford almost as famous as the celebrities they are promoting.

Sport stars, film and TV actors and actresses, authors and celebrities will all use PR to promote their latest film, TV programmes or books. The media are still an essential means for generating the publicity for a celebrity and they remain a one-way method of generating publicity. Practitioners of celebrity PR are regarded as being at the top of their profession. To the man and woman in the street, the one PR person they might be able to name is Max Clifford, who is routinely given the designation 'PR guru' by the media.

Max Clifford plays the game of not just generating news coverage, but of also trading stories to try and keep unflattering or destructive information about clients out of the media: this is a standard practice of the celebrity publicist. 'Inevitably, if the tabloids have a great story, then they will run it. But if you have excellent relationships with the editors and senior executives, then you can do deals to dilute some of the damage in some way,' says Neil Reading, managing director of Neil Reading PR.

We are now interested in the lives of celebrities probably to an obsessive and unhealthy degree and a whole industry is dedicated to feeding this obsession through magazines such as *OK, Hello* and *Heat*. The infamous paparazzi, photographers who provide these publications with an endless stream of photos, will show us film stars walking to the shops and starlets falling out of nightclubs. The paparazzi have come under a great deal of criticism for their role in hounding celebrities: this criticism was particularly virulent after the death of Diana, Princess of Wales, as some paparazzi photographers had been chasing her car the night she died. However, as long as there is a public appetite and big financial rewards for photos of celebrities putting their bins out the paparazzi will continue to flourish.

Case Study: Max Clifford, Publicist

'I'm not a celebrity publicist'. Max Clifford is one of the most famous names in PR, has been in the business for over 40 years, and is as instantly recognisable as the names he represents. Here he muses on the nature of celebrity, his relationship with the media, and how it has changed.

A modern-day celebrity is someone who is in the public eye and who you read about in the tabloids, someone like Katie Price, someone who is always in the news. The definition has changed. It used to be that you were famous because you had talent or because of something you had achieved or were good at – you were a football or pop star or a politician. But of course now you're famous just for being famous and clearly in many cases have no talent at all, just big egos and the desire to show off.

All my clients are different. My business is looking after companies and organisations as well as doing unpaid PR for a lot of charities. I'm patron of Children's Hospice UK and various other charities. It's looking at what the client needs, what's the best image for that client and most successful image, and what the most practical way is of achieving that. It's a combination of promotion and protection – keeping them out of the news. We haven't really used publicity stunts for a while – 'Freddie Star ate my hamster' was one of mine – but now it's more a gradual building up of an image. With Simon Cowell (another client) you know it was the 'Mr Nasty' thing, but it wasn't something we thought necessary to create. It just fitted and it worked, but generally speaking with publicity stunts sometimes it happens but in the industry they are very rare and usually generate a bit of 'quick fix' publicity. Most of the people we look after we work with for a long period of time and in such situations you need more than a publicity stunt.

I only take on people I like to work with. I'm very lucky we've never had to pitch for business. We're probably the only PR company in the country that's never had to pitch for business. So people come to you and if you don't like them you don't work with them. Life's too short. It matters to me and my team that we are working with people we like and want to work with.

I have a professional relationship with journalists. You understand their needs and so you try to work together as much as possible. I'm lucky because all the big stories that I've broken in the last 20–25 years give you a strong relationship with the editors because they desperately need their big stories. I think the media have become more hostile over the last 20 years because it's more competitive. Staff on newspapers are being cut, there are less people to do more. That puts greater pressure on the journalists because if they don't come up with the results they are out. It's more pressurised and far more ruthless than it used to be.

A publicist is someone who is on the phone all the time to the media giving them a story and giving them this and giving them that because generally speaking what they are offering is light relief with no substance.

I'm not a celebrity publicist. I'm a PR. Celebrity publicists have a lot of influ-
ence if they're good because journalists on the tabloids are craving this
stuff all the time. There's a lot of space for this type of coverage, it's not on
the decrease it's on the increase because it's a cheap and easy way to fill
the column inches.

Our implicit participation in this activity does raise some important ethical questions – we condemn the way that celebrity culture trivialises culture,
but still want to read more about the Beckhams. Within this febrile culture
the celebrity publicist would appear to have a relatively easy task – supply
the pictures and the stories. It is not that simple, but far more sophisticated in
its operation. What is important here is news management and news control;
ensuring the right and appropriate type of publicity gets out rather than just
publicity for its own sake. While much of the celebrity coverage is harmless
there is a harsher side to it, as can be seen in the 'red-top tabloids' of the
UK media. The UK tabloid press is known for its ferocity and obsession with
the minutiae of celebrity lives. Their coverage is a strange and heady brew,
obsessed with sexual activity but prurient in their comments on it – anything
that is outside the 'normal' definition or out of the ordinary is dismissed as
'perverted', 'sick', or 'disgusting'. In many ways it's a picture of Britain that's
caught in a time-warp from the 1950s. The existence of the red-tops and their
investigations into the personal lives of celebrities has lead to the existence of
PR agents/publicists who have to act in the role of protector in the interest of
their clients.

Case Study: Sam Delaney, Editor of *Heat* Magazine

Sam Delaney is a journalist and broadcaster and also editor of celebrity
magazine *Heat*. Here he considers the relationship between publicist and
editor.

You are more or less colleagues, you both know the kind of game you are
playing with each other. He will be one week asking me to give coverage to
one of his clients, then the next week we might get a story about the client
that he doesn't like. We put that on the front cover and then he'll ring up
and scream and shout his head off at me because he's trying to control the
press but he can't always control what we do. So it's difficult because on
the one hand you think that you're close and you're good friends but then
two days later you could be the fiercest of enemies.

But the good thing is that no matter how angry you get with each other
it sort of is like being in a relationship, because like a week later it is all
forgotten you know and you move on to the next problem. It's a mutual

understanding, but there is a tendency among publicists to print exactly what they want which is a very big misunderstanding of how the publicity machine works and how the media works, as well as an inflated view of their own importance and power.

Most of what passes for generating publicity for celebrities is largely pretty harmless stuff that plays its part and role in a game we all enjoy.

When celebrities are out to promote a new film or CD, we understand and accept the publicity process surrounding it. Film stars are interviewed, appearing on every chat show and breakfast TV programme. They have a round of ten minute interviews with journalists which are carefully controlled by their PR person. In fact the celebrity interview is now so carefully controlled and stage-managed with the attendant PR controlling what can and cannot be said that many journalists believe they are virtually useless.

Julian Henry worked as a music journalist before working in PR. After ten years with Lynne Franks he started his own company, Henry's House, which is now one of the most highly regarded communications agencies in the UK. He says:

People will sometimes ask if working as a publicist in the entertainment industry is a rewarding job. It's true that one of the perks is the fact that you get to develop subservient and one-sided relationships with people who are famous for one reason or another. And so when you are looking after a celebrity client at the peak of their power it can be very easy to lose sight of the truth. You might attend a glamorous party with a handful of film stars and pop talent. You find yourself having a great time. And who the heck wants to think about the truth at four in the morning when it suddenly seems that, for the first and probably only time in your life, you are actually a person of consequence and importance?

SPORT

Sport PR (Stoldt et al., 2006), like PR in other sectors functions as part of management and will specifically identify a sports organisation's key audiences and evaluate the organisation's relationships with them to develop favourable relationships.

PR in sport generally covers the following areas:

- Creating publicity for companies who through sponsorship have invested in sport and want to maximise their publicity.
- Internal – that is, acting for the sporting club/organisation in the role of press officer, which is similar in many ways to the in-house media relations officers working for companies/organisations.

Sponsorship

Sport is not only entertainment but also a multi-billion pound global industry in which vast sums are invested to pay wages and run clubs. The sponsors who invest in a sport at whatever level will want to see a return on their investment. Increasingly, the role of PR companies is to help the sponsors not only to generate publicity but also to try and control what is being said. Bell Pottinger Public Relations for example promoted the international airline Emirates' sponsorship of the FIFA and its World Cup in Germany in 2006, to ensure that they received international attention. Companies such as *Coca-Cola*, McDonald's and Nike are multinational sponsors who spend billions and it is understandable that they would want to try and ensure they are getting value for money from their investment. The issue is whether the sponsors' demands impact too much and change the nature of the sport they are investing in.

Ketchum, an international PR consultancy, works with clients to develop a strategic PR and event marketing plan with the aim of expanding the value of a sponsorship: 'KSN works with clients to develop a strategic PR and event marketing plan that expands the value of a sponsorship beyond the stadium' – they will, among other things, build a grassroots-outreach programme, tying the corporate sponsor to the community and providing long-term results, creating compelling media guides and collateral materials. On the media relations' side, 'KSN utilises the latest technology in providing advance, on-site and post-media support for our client's sponsorships, events and ongoing PR programs. Skills includes the following: Generating high-impact media attention – understanding that clients seek both no sports/lifestyles coverage in addition to traditional sports; facilitating credentials and press room operations at some of the world's largest sporting events such as the Olympics; coaching professional athletes, celebrities and corporate executives about how to respond to media with positive messages endorsing the sponsor'.

M&C Saatchi Sport & Entertainment worked for *Coca-Cola* GB before the 2006 World Cup. As a sponsor they had exclusive access to the Jules Rimet trophy for a week. The task of M&C Saatchi was to create a media event that maximised media coverage and to 'position *Coca-Cola* as the tournament's leading sponsor'. The need for an event that would produce maximum was heightened by the fact that other World Cup sponsors were also planning their own events. Adidas for example were planning to run the same event in London on the same day. *Coca-Cola* in turn recruited Wayne Rooney and Old Billingsgate Market in London was transformed into an 'interactive football zone' with a specially constructed 600-seat auditorium. As well as journalists 500 winners of a competition were invited; there was a photocall with Wayne Rooney and the trophy; and the highlight was a 45-minute 'chat show' hosted by *Grandstand's* Ray Stubbs in which he interviewed Rooney, Mark Lawrenson, and Peter Shilton. Press information was also distributed to various news and sports desks.

Media relations in sport

In the USA, media relations officers in sports clubs are well-established in the UK, however media relations in sport is still developing. For example, Arsenal only developed a press and PR office in 2002. Patrick Haverson (2002), the former communications director at Manchester United, said:

> *I think its fair to say that football at all levels clubs, leagues and national associations has been slow to embrace PR. For too long the sport took its customers – the fans – for granted. However, that has changed and many clubs and other organisations are now becoming increasingly sophisticated at dealing with the public the media and other stakeholders in the game.* (L'Etang, 2006)

Channels of communication

The main channels of communication by which sports clubs communicate with their fans are as follows:

- Programmes.
- Local newspapers.
- Websites.

PR in this area is not just about media relations, it encompasses the whole field of community/stakeholder relations. Professional sports clubs, whether cricket, football, rugby league or rugby union, now realise that they are in a competitive world and that their sport/club has to compete with many other different forms of entertainment. And while they might be able to rely on a loyal fan-base who will turn up no matter what those fans should be treated with respect. Poor communication can create problems for clubs – speculation about the sale of a favourite player, or the dismissal of the coach can create unnecessary resentment and problems.

Community relations in sport

> *Community relations may be defined as organisational activity designed to foster desirable relationships between sports organisations of the communities in which it is either located or has strategic interests.* (Stoldt, 2006)

Berkhouse and Gelbert (1999) believe that as a result of community relations programmes, sports organisations may realise such outcomes as demonstrating social responsibility, building public awareness, generating favour with customers, increasing employee morale, and contributing to their community's well-being. They may also be able to reach publics who are not targeted by the organisation's other PR and marketing activities or work with new and ethnic communities that are excluded from mainstream football.

Bolton Wanderers FC has a special section on its website explaining the work it carries out in the community: 'The most important aspect of any football club are the fans and the community. A PR team is responsible for the link between the club and the community and the overall reputation of the club' (BW, 2007).

SUMMARY

PR activity manifests itself in a wide variety of ways and not all of it is as negative as some of its critics would have us believe. PR practice allows charities and minority groups to have access to the media in a way that was once beyond their reach. This growth and diversity of PR practice is also good for those who are looking for a career in the industry – with so many different areas and type of practice, it should be possible for everyone to find a place. The question posed in the opening pages of this book was this: is it possible to still talk of a single PR industry with a definition that covers every type of practice, or has the industry become so big and so diverse that such a definition is now irrelevant? The answer will increasingly come from practice where the challenge of, say, electronic communication is opening up new areas for the industry and pushing conventional boundaries between PR and advertising for example. While there are no definite answers, what this does mean is that it is an industry with a challenging future for those who work in it.

WHERE PR (AND YOU) CAN GO NEXT

By the end of this chapter you will understand:

- the challenges and opportunities within the PR industry
- how to take the first steps in your PR career

INTRODUCTION

One of the reasons why many people enjoy working in PR is that it is fast-moving and intellectually stimulating and no two days are ever the same. It can also be a pressurised working environment, which might not be attractive to some but for others this will prove a key driver.

For students interested in a career in PR there has never been a more exciting time to join the profession. Graduates in PR and related degrees will have exactly the type of skills the industry requires. These include an understanding of strategy, a knowledge of account management skills, and an appreciation of the importance of evaluation and how to adapt programmes and change communication to target audiences.

THE CHANGING PR LANDSCAPE

In Chapter 2 we discussed the definition of PR and whether it was possible, or even desirable, to have one single definition that tried to cover every aspect of PR practice. As we are at the end of the book and have discussed both the strengths and weaknesses of the PR industry and how it has grown, where do we now stand on this definition? It should be clear after reading this far that while the PR industry is growing and expanding in to new sectors this growth is also paradoxically producing a more fragmented and diverse industry. It is dynamic and energetic and one that should always adapt and develop to new circumstances and demands. While that might be frustrating for those who want to tie it down with labels and definitions, for those working in it that same variety and dynamism provide a constant creative challenge. Definitions are simply short-hand phrases and it's important not to get too hung up on them. PR is a practice that is dependent on the delivery channels and as these change so will the industry – and as practice and delivery changes so will definitions. Perhaps the time is not far off when it will be no longer possible or appropriate to speak of one 'PR industry': on continental Europe, for example, it is more appropriate to speak of Communication Management.

What matters here is how the industry responds to the many and diverse challenges it faces. Business history shows industries and services that do not adapt and change do not survive. The indications are however promising, for with PR increasing its share of the marketing budget and many more senior PR practitioners employed at boardroom level offering strategic advice to organisations, it has remained largely unaffected by the economic recession of 2008/09. Growth rates in mature markets such as the UK and USA might be slowing down but within that some sectors will continue to expand. The UK public sector including local and central governments and the health sector will face more uncertain periods. Communication functions in them have grown quickly in the last five years but the concentration has been on building up the delivery of the services. Granted, in more economically difficult times the PR function will face more intense scrutiny also and the demand to demonstrate that it can and does provide not only value for money but also makes an impact.

In the UK and USA the structural changes the industry faces will have employment implications. It is likely for instance that the traditional skills, like a background in journalism, will no longer be as important. This will open up more opportunities for graduates from PR courses as they are being taught the practical and theoretical skills a maturing industry needs. PR practitioners will need a wider range of skills and must be able, for example, to plan and build a strategy to undertake research and introduce a proper evaluation of campaigns. This also includes a knowledge of PR history and theory, the relevance of which can sometimes appear obscure to some students.

A popular project for my final year PR students is to compare theory with practice on their work placements. The results are always interesting – many for example will return from work placements stating they have experienced little evidence of theory being used in practice. I often ask other fellow practitioners about their use and understanding of theory and again: apart from those who have been on PR courses, their understanding is limited. But theory is important to practice because it helps us understand and explain the nature of PR practice and also provide us with a credible intellectual base. I believe that even if theory does not influence any PR practitioner, then it is still important and valid. What will be interesting is to see whether, as PR develops internationally, alternative models to the current excellence theory will emerge from different cultural traditions. One key issue will be to see whether there will be the emergence of a critical PR practitioner, developing practice from the theoretical work done by L'Etang, Pieckzca, Motion and others. Such a critical PR practitioner would ask difficult questions of the established structures, however important these might appear.

INDUSTRY CHALLENGES AND OPPORTUNITIES

Of the many problems and challenges the PR industry faces one of the most uncomfortable that has to be confronted is that of its own reputation. There is evidence that the industry's poor reputation has an impact on those who work in it and it is cited as a reason why many young people leave. The industry, however, can only address its problems by recognising they exist but there are too many commentators on PR who will blithely skate over these issues and will pretend they do not.

PR has been demonised and blamed for everything from lowering journalism standards to contributing to the decline of democracy. The shortest definition of all: 'Public Relations = spin' is delivered with a dismissive sneer and has become a sort of shorthand for deceit and subterfuge. This however is unfair because such a dismissal includes everyone – from those working for asset stripping, resource depleting multinational companies to those working for charities attempting to change the world. Most PR activity is benign and largely involves the transmission of information that will be of interest to the people looking for it. PR techniques are however powerful, with the capacity to shape and influence people's perceptions and behaviour, and operating these in an ethically correct manner has never been more important. It is incumbent on PR practitioners to work in a responsible fashion and ethical considerations and what constitutes right practice should be at the heart of all PR work. This is another area where PR graduates possess advantages because they will have had the opportunity to explore these issues in depth.

There are many situations where there are no right or wrong answers. To some people it may seem unethical to be involved in promoting cigarette sales whilst others will regard it as perfectly justifiable and legitimate. PR practitioners have to weigh up the moral balance from their own perspective. In the UK the lobbying industry is being given a chance to introduce a series of regulations, at the heart of which is the necessity for transparency. If this self-regulation does not work then it is likely that government-inspired regulations will follow.

The greatest challenge facing the PR industry is how it collectively responds to the technological changes and the consequent structural challenges presented by new electronic distribution. Traditional print media are going through major structural changes and in 2009 there was a noteable decline in newspaper readership. In the USA, for example, the print newspaper industry faced decimination with titles closing that had been in existence for years. Since 1990 a quarter of all American newspaper jobs have disappeared and only 19% of Americans between the ages of 18 and 34 claim even to look at a daily newspaper. The average age of the American newspaper reader is 55 and rising. Philip Meyer, in his book the *Vanishing Newspaper* (2004), even predicted the final delivery date of the doorstep newspaper as 2043. The pattern is similar in the UK where young people are increasingly using online sources for news and information.

The decline in advertising revenue and the decimation of the traditional media business model have implications for the PR industry: not all of them though are bad and this is where opportunities are emerging for a totally new type of PR practice. The nature of journalism is changing as is the way news is collected – the key phrase describing the new process is convergence. As newspapers become multimedia news sources, with an online, print and video footage, journalists are having to learn a variety of multimedia skills. Journalism undergraduates will also have to learn these wider skills including the role and significance of PR.

Internet sites as a source of news and information are altering our consumption patterns, as consumers want immediate information with stories that interest them and that they comment on and share with other people. This might mean the creation of more specialist rather than general newspaper sites. There is likely to be an explosion in 'hyper local news sites' serving local areas in towns and cities. The opportunity here for the PR industry is not only in supplying these sites but also in making direct communication with target audiences that never seemed possible before.

How an industry responds to change will determine whether it will succeed or perish. No industry can get everything right at the first attempt, but nevertheless there are encouraging signs that the industry is responding positively. PR companies are now offering the capacity to manage the online reputation of firms/organisations whose reputation might be affected by comments made through social websites. New electronic sources of communication allow direct communication with target audiences. Readers/viewers/consumers will be able to choose what they are reading and watching and construct their own material according to their interests and prejudices.

The opportunities presented by direct communication and more distribution channels are exciting and in a small way we can see this in what is happening at a number of professional football clubs. Interactive websites, edited highlights of matches, interviews with the players, and online commentary while replacing the conventional news reporting of newspapers are also creating a whole new range of employment opportunities.

GETTING STARTED IN PR

These are exciting times to be starting a career in PR, especially if you can twitter, find your way around the internet, and know how to blog and use social networks. It is from these skill bases that PR will increasingly draw. Competition for advertised job places is and will continue to be fierce, but persistence does pay off: students on PR courses will have a head start not only because they are learning the practical and management skills that will be needed, but also because they are able to make industry contacts. Students in their third year PR courses at Huddersfield for example are encouraged to explore areas of the industry they are interested in and to develop contacts through a structured programme. Other PR courses offer similar programmes. The key to these is not to wait for employment opportunities to open up through career websites but try and create your own opportunities and use your initiative. It might not happen, but the experience of going through the process will be invaluable.

One of my students created his own blog and as a result of this got a job working with a large London PR consultancy.

Box 15.1   What Employers Want from New Recruits

Sally Sykes: 'Writing ability, people skills, project management, the creativity ability to manage competing deadlines under pressure, strategic thinking, and a sense of perspective.'

Andy Green: 'Main skills needed are a combination of attitudes – a desire to deliver a great service for clients and be responsive. They should be hungry to achieve goals and also have good technical and writing skills. Interpersonal and organisational skills are important too.'

Jane Howard: 'Media skills. They have to be able to write and also think. They have to have an understanding of business which generally takes young people a couple of years to get to grips with.'

Experience shows that most PR graduates who want a career in PR eventually do find a relevant and appropriate position. This is competitive and that's why students have to demonstrate a degree of flexibility and initiative to make them stand out. Match yourself to the organisation and show why you think you could do a job working for a particular company. Try to get some relevant work experience even if it's unpaid. Potential employers will be impressed with enthusiasm and determination and a willingness to work long hours as these are the characteristics that are needed if you are to succeed in PR. In addition to your degree and an interest in the area you are working in, the following qualities are often mentioned as being important:

- Ability to work with other people.
- Ability to communicate verbally and through writing.
- Organisation.
- Imagination.
- Ability to research and learn.
- Think for yourself and show some initiative.
- Patience and common sense.
- Enthusiasm and commitment.
- Ability to work under pressure.
- Capacity to adapt and learn to different circumstances.
- Be prepared to keep on learning new skills and abilities.

Employers are looking for people who can act on their own initiative and do not wait to be told what to do. This is an introductory PR textbook and if you are interested in a career in PR you need to start using the next two to three years of your university career to explore those areas you might be interested in. Whether, for example, that might be working in-house or for a consultancy, start looking at company websites, learn about what they do. Although the internship can be abused and needs to be looked at carefully, nevertheless using it to get a couple of weeks experience is to be recommended. Learn about the industry, contact people, look at the PR magazines and their websites.

If you are looking for an easy career PR is not for you: if you are looking for one that will be challenging, intellectually rewarding and stimulating, but can also be frustrating though rarely boring, then PR will be right for you.

SUMMARY

While many want to write the obituary for PR it is neither going to die or go away. Delivery channels are changing and this is opening up new opportunities to communicate directly with target audiences. Far from ushering in the decline of the PR industry, there are a number of exciting opportunities opening up and as a result this is changing the traditional recruitment patterns of the PR industry. Increasingly there will be openings for younger more technologically aware recruits who can find their way around the social networks and what we are finding now is that PR is not just reacting to new technology but actually attempting to dictate the course of events. For young people wanting a career in PR there has never been a better chance to make a mark in it: some sectors might in the short-term be relatively quiet, but other areas will open up.

It is an exciting and dynamic industry to work in, one full of intellectual challenges and stimulation. It is also demanding and can be pressurised, but its diversity and variety mean that there are many chances for those who are determined to pursue a career.

BIBLIOGRAPHY

Argenti, P.A. & Druckenmiller, B. (2004) 'Reputation and the Corporate Brand', *Corporate Reputation Review*, Vol 6. No. 4.

Austin, E. W. & Pinkleton, B. E. (2006) *Strategic Public Relations Management: Planning and Managing Effective Communication Programs* (2nd edn). London: Taylor & Francis.

Beard, M. (2002) *Running a Public Relations Department*. London: Kogan Page.

Bernays, E.L. (1923) *Crystallizing Public Opinion*. New York: LiveRight Publishing Company.

Bland, M., Theaker, A. & Wragg, D. (2000) *Effective Media Relations: How to get Results (PR in Practice)*. London: Kogan Page.

Boden, N. (1964) 'The Concept of the Marketing Mix', *Journal of Advertising Research*, (June): 2–7.

Botan, C. H. & Hazleton V. (eds) (2006) *Public Relations Theory II*. London: Routledge.

Brassington, F. & Pettitt, S. (2000) *Principles of Marketing*. (2nd edn). London: Financial Times/Prentice Hall.

Broom, G.M. & Smith G.D. (1979) 'Testing the Practitioners Impact on Clients', *Public Relations Review*, Vol 5.

Brooks, T. R. (1964) *Toil & Trouble, A History of American Labor*. New York: Delacorte.

Campbell, F.E., Herman, R.A., & Noble, D. (2006) 'Contradictions in "reputation Management"', *Journal of Communications Management,* Vol 10 (2).

Cannon, T. (1994) *Corporate Responsibility*. London: Pitman.

CEBR (2005) *The Economic Significance of Public Relations*. London: CEBR.

CIPR/DTI (2005) 'Unlocking the Potential of PR: Developing Good Practice'. London: CIPR.

Context Analytics (2009) *Media Prominence: A Leading Indicator of Brand Value*. San Francisco, CA: Jossey-Bass.

Context Analytics, (2009) 'Media Prominence Study', Los Angeles, USA.

Cooper, M. (2008) Personal interview with the author.

Currah, A. (2009) 'What's Happening to our News'. Reuters Institute for the Study of Journalism, Oxford.

Cutlip, S.M., Center, A.H., & Broom, G.M., (2000) *Effective Public Relations*. (8th edn). Englewood Cliffs, NJ: Prentice-Hall.

Davies, N. (2008) *Flat Earth News: An Award-winning Reporter Exposes Falsehood, Distortion and Propoganda in the Global Media*. London: Chatto & Windus.

Dewey, J. (1927) *The Pubic and its Problems*. New York: Holt.

Dinan, W. & Miller, D. (2007) *Thinker, Faker, Spinner, Spy: Corporate PR and the Assault on Democracy*. London: Pluto.

Dowling, G. (2000) *Creating Corporate Reputations: Identity, Image and Performance*. Oxford: OUP.

Dozier, D.M., Grunig, L.A., & Grunig, J.E. (1995) *Manager's Guide to Excellence in Public Relations and Communication Management*. Mawhah, NJ: Lawrence Erlbaum Associates.

European Commission Green Paper (2000) 'Promoting a European Framework for Corporate Social Responsibility'.

√Fauset, C. (2006) 'What's Wrong with a Corporate Social Responsibility'. *Corporate Watch,* CSR Report available to download at www.corporatewatch.org.uk

√Ferrell, O.C., Fraedrich, J., & Ferrell, L. (2005) *Business Ethics.* New York: Houghton Mifflin.

Fink, S. In Penrose, J.M. (2000) 'The role of perception in crisis planning', *Public Relations Review,* Vol 26 (2): 155–171.

Fiske, J. (1990) *Introduction to Communication Studies* (2nd edn). London: Routledge.

Fombrun, C.J. (1996) 'Reputation – realising value from corporate image', *Harvard Business Review.*

Foster, J. (2001) *Effective Writing Skills for Public Relations* (2nd edn). London: Kogan Page.

Gannon, Z. & Lawson, N. (2009) *The Advertising Effect.* London: Campass.

Gardberg, N.A. & Fombrun, C.J. (2002) 'For better or worse – the most visible American corporate reputations'. *Corporate Reputation Review,* Vol 4, No. 4.

Grad Facts: http://www.google.co.uk/search?sourceid=navclient&aq=0h&oq=&ie=UTF-8&rlz=1T4RNWN_enGB266GB268&q=the+guardian+grad+facts

Goldman, E.F. (1948) 'Two-Way Street: The Emergence of Public Relations Counsel', Boston Bellman, USA.

Green, A. (2008) Personal interview with author.

Grunig, J. (ed.) (1992) *Excellence in Public Relations and Communication Management.* Mahwah, NJ: Lawrence Erlbaum Associates.

Grunig, J. & Hunt, T. (1984) *Managing Public Relations.* London: Thomson Learning.

Harcup, T. (2003) *Journalism Principles and Practice.* London: Sage.

Harlow, R.F. (1976) 'Building a Public Relations Definition', *Public Relations Review,* 2, No. 4 (Winter) 36.

Harrison, S. & Maloney, K. (2004) 'Comparing two public relations pioneers: American Ivy Lee and British John Elliot', *Public Relations Review,* issue 30: 205–215.

Hiebert, R.E. (1966) *Courtier to the Crowd: The Story of Ivy Lee & The Development of Public Relations.* Ames, IA: Iowa State University Press.

Hobsbawm, J. (ed.) (2007) *Where the Truth Lies: Trust and Morality in PR and Journalism.* London: Atlantic.

Howard, J. (2008) Personal interview with the author.

Hutton, J.G. (1999) 'The definitions, dimensions and domain of Public Relations', *Public Relations Review,* 25 (2).

Hutton, J.G (2000) 'Reputation management: the new face of corporate public relations?', *Public Relations Review,* 27 (3).

IPSOS/Mori/IBE (2009) *Perceptions of Business Transparency.* London: IBE.

Johnson, G., Scholes, K., & Whittington, R. (2005) 'Exploring Corporate Strategy', (7th edition). London: FT/Prentice Hall.

Jones, N. (2001) *The Control Freaks.* London: Politicos.

Jones, N. (2002) *The Control Freaks.* London: Politicos.

Kitchen, P.J. (2002) *Public Relations Principles & Practice.* London: International Thomson Business Press.

Kitchen, P.J. & Laurence, A. (2003) 'Corporate Reputation: An eight country analysis', *Corporate Reputation Review,* 6 (2).

Kotler, P. (1982) *Marketing for Non-Profit Organisations* (2nd edn). Englewood Cliffs, NJ: Prentice-Hall.

L'Etang, J. (2004) *Public Relations in Britain*. Englewood Cliffs, NJ: Erlbaum.

L'Etang, J. (2008) *Public Relations Concepts, Practice and Critique*. Englewood Cliffs, NJ: Erlbaum.

L'Etang, J. & Pieczka, M. (eds) (2006) *Public Relations Critical Debates & Contemporary Practice*. New Jersey: Erlbaum.

Levinson, J.C. (1984) *Guerrilla Marketing: Secrets for Making Big Profits from your Small Business*. New York: Houghton Mifflin.

Lewis, J., Williams A., & Franklin, B. (2008) 'A Compromised Fourth Estate?', *Journalism Studies*, 9 (1): 1–20.

Litchfield, J. (2009) Personal interview with the author.

Littlejohn, S.W. (2002) *Theories of Human Communication*. (7th edn). Belmont, CA: Wadsworth Thomson.

Livesey, T. at http://www.wpp.com/NR/rdonlyres/20B82970-020F-466B-97DE-B7DE2D5DB39D/0/TheStore_newsletter_003_TanyaLivesy_YR_London.pdf

Local Government Chronicle (2006), 23rd February, www.lgcplus.com

Massingham, D. (2008) Personal interview with the author.

McQuail, D. & Windahl, S. (1993) *Communication Models*. (2nd edn). London: Longman.

Media Week, Haymarket Publishing Group 2007, 25th October.

Miller, D. & Dinan, W. (1996) *A Century of Spin*. London: Pluto.

Moss, D. & Green, R. (2001) 'Re-examining the manager's role in public relations: What management and public relations research teaches us', *Journal of Communication Management*, 6 (2).

Ogrizek, J.M. & Guillery, M. (1999) *Communicating in Crisis*. London: Aldine.

Oliver, S. (2001) *Public Relations Strategy*. London: Kogan Page.

Pearson in Toth, E. & Heath, R. (eds) (1992) *Rhetorical and Critical Approaches to Public Relations*. Mahwah, NJ: Lawrence Erlbaum.

Penrose, J.M. (2000) 'The role of perception in crisis planning', *Public Relations Review*, 26 (2).

Parsons, P. (2004) *Ethics in Public Relations*. London: Kogan Page.

Parvin, P. (2007) *Friend or Foe? Lobbying in British Democracy*. London: Hansard.

Piachaud, P (2007) 'Freedom to be a child: Commercial Pressures on children', CASE, LSE, London.

PR Week, Haymarket Publishing Group

2004, 31st December

2005, 4th February

2005, 14th January

2005, 20th May (Gray, Robert Evaluation Follow the Reader)

2005, 24th June (Issues Management. What Keeps You Awake?)

2006, 7th July (Hall, I Research 'proves' PR is more effective that ads)

2005, 1st December (Autism survey shows ignorance about disease)

2005, 1st December (R. Gray, Pitching End this Practice)

2006, 6th January (Cancer Groups in Message Rethink)

2006, 2nd June (Crush P. Strategies for Averting a Crisis)

2007, 2nd February (Robertson, S. Government PR spend rises amid ad decline)

2007, 9th November (Rogers, D. Staff 'churn' at consultancies reaches new high)

2007, 23rd November (Retailer ethics leaves shoppers cold)

2010, 29th October (Cartmell, M. Essex & Westminster Councils raise cash by Selling comms expertise)

Public Affairs News (March, 2005: Des Wilson Interview, Dod's Parliamentary Communications Ltd)

Regester, M. (2007) Personal interview with author.

Regester, M. & Larkin, J. (2005) *Risk Issues and Crisis Management: A Casebook of Best Practice* (3rd edn). London: Kogan Page.

Stoldt, G.C., Dittmore, S.W., & Branrold, S.E. (2006) *Sport Public Relations: Managing Organizational Communication.* Leeds: Human Kinetics.

Sykes, S. (2007) Personal interview with the author.

Tench, R. & Yeomans, L, (2006) *Exploring Public Relations.* London: Prentice Hall/FT.

Toth, E.L. & Heath, R. (1992) *Rhetorical & Critical Approaches to Public Relations.* New Jersey: Erlbaum.

Varey in Kitchen, P.J. (2002) *Public Relations Principles & Practice.* London: International Thomson.

Weber Shandwick in cooperation with the Economist Intelligence Unit (EIU) (2009) Risky Business: Reputations Online™ (www.online-reputations.com)

Whitehead, A. (2006) *Return on Reputation – Corporate Reputation Watch.* London: Hill & Knowlton.

Windahl, S., Signitzer, B., & Olson, J.T. (1992) *Using Communication Theory: An Introduction to Planned Communication.* London: Sage.

Zhao, D. (2008) PR in China, http://blogarchive.hill&knowlton.com/blogs/ampersand/articles/10492.asp

World Business on Council Development (2000) 'Corporate Social Responsibility: Making Good Business Sense'.

Yang, J. (2006) *The Rough Guide to Blogging.* London: Rough Guides.

Websites

www.businessweek.com	Bloomberg Businessweek
www.cipr.co.uk	Chartered Institute of Public Relations
www.csr.gov.uk and Skills	Archived content from Department of Business Innovation
www.ceogo.com/documents/RR_01_10_05.pdf	
www.hotwirepr.com	Hotwire PR
www.nsmcentre.org.uk/	National Social Marketing Centrewww.prca.org.uk Public Relations Consultants Association
www.sourcewatch.org	Source Watch
www.spinwatch.org	Spinwatch
www.webershandwick.co.uk	Weber Shandwick

INDEX

Research Methods Books from SAGE

Read sample chapters online now!

DISCOVERING STATISTICS USING SPSS **THIRD EDITION**

ANDY FIELD

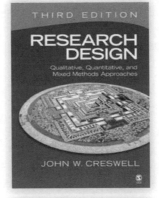

THIRD EDITION

RESEARCH DESIGN

Qualitative, Quantitative, and Mixed Methods Approaches

JOHN W. CRESWELL

Robert K. Yin

Case Study Research

Design and Methods

Fourth Edition

APPLIED SOCIAL RESEARCH METHODS SERIES

Second Edition

QUALITATIVE INQUIRY & RESEARCH DESIGN

Choosing Among Five Approaches

John W. Creswell

Doing a Literature Review

Chris Hart

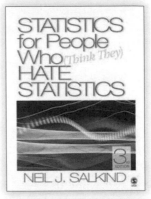

STATISTICS for People Who (Think They) HATE STATISTICS

NEIL J. SALKIND

SECOND EDITION

INTERVIEWS

Learning the Craft of Qualitative Research Interviewing

Steinar Kvale
Svend Brinkmann

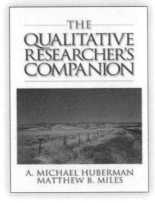

THE QUALITATIVE RESEARCHER'S COMPANION

A. MICHAEL HUBERMAN
MATTHEW B. MILES

Basics of QUALITATIVE RESEARCH 3e

Juliet Corbin
Anselm Strauss

www.sagepub.co.uk

SAGE

Research Methods Books from SAGE

Read sample chapters online now!

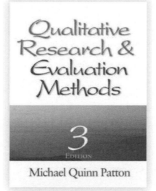

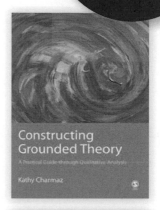

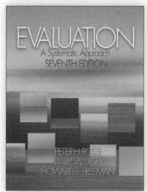

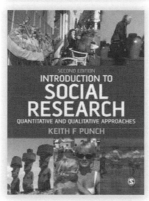

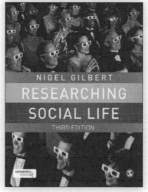

www.sagepub.co.uk